Adventures in Marxism

Adventures in Marxism

———————◆———————

MARSHALL BERMAN

VERSO

London · New York

First published by Verso 1999
© Marshall Berman 1999

All rights reserved

VERSO
UK: 6 Meard Street, London W1V 3 HR
US: 180 Varick Street, 10th Floor, New York, NY 10014-4606

VERSO is the imprint of New Left Books

ISBN 1 85984 734 X

British Library Cataloguing in Publication Data
A catalogue record for this book is available from the British Library
Library of Congress Cataloging-in-Publication Data
A catalog record for this book is available from the Library of Congress

Typeset in Dante by Steven Hiatt, San Francisco
Printed and bound in the USA by R. R. Donnelly & Sons

Contents

For Murray, my father,
and
For Eli and Danny, my sons

Preface

If Marx were alive today
He'd be rolling around in his grave.

– RANDY NEWMAN

When Colin Robinson of Verso first suggested this collection to me, I had my doubts. I knew I had done some good writing on Marx and Marxism, but I wasn't sure there was enough for a serious book. There were all these essays and reviews, accumulated over more than three decades, but at first it looked like a pile of fragments that just didn't add up. Why is this one short? Why is that one long? Why do I discuss Lukács and Benjamin, but not Adorno or Marcuse? Why Babel and not Brecht? Why nothing on mass culture? Why no analytical Marxism? Why no post-modernism? (And so on, and so on, and so on.)

Most of the time, the only answers I could think of were completely contingent. Nearly all these are *pieces*, I wrote them when editors asked me, and I wrote in roughly the size and shape they asked for (though I virtually always gave them *more* than they asked for). Those answers struck me as pretty pathetic. I grew up with the notion that a book should be an organic whole, and that it should spring from the depths of an author's soul. I actually managed to write one book like that, *All That Is Solid Melts into Air: The Experience of Modernity*. When I couldn't write another, I brought out no books at all.

It wasn't that I wasn't writing. I never stopped writing, but nothing seemed grand enough or profound enough to deserve the title "book." But as years went by, this idealism felt increasingly like a dumb attitude; I came to feel that I had painted myself into a corner. I had read enough to know that there are many different kinds of good books. A writer could say something, without saying *everything*. A book need not be whole in order to be good, and the attempt to make it whole can be a Procrustean catastrophe. I tried to learn from Marx, who spent half his life trying to make *Capital* whole, and only after fifteen years came to see this enterprise as a disaster. (And even then, he couldn't stop.)

As a writer on politics and culture, I knew how disastrous the hunger for wholeness has been in modern times; I could feel that hunger working in me, and I could see that it wasn't doing me any good. How could I overcome it? I told myself various things. I tried to think of a book as a form of dialogue and interaction. If something is missing, people will see that and say so, and then I can respond to them by writing *more* books; or else they will get it wrong, and then I will write more books trying to make it clearer, sharper, more vivid, so they will get it next time, and the metabolism between us will help make our collective life go on. I thought, only God can make it whole – and even the Ten Commandments are always in need of new commentaries. I thought of all the impressive modern art that is an art of fragments and multiple perspectives. I thought, "Enough, already."

In the fall of 1998, a sort of neon sign lit up in my head: the title, ADVENTURES IN MARXISM. Here was a way for me to bring things together. It evoked Marxism as a special kind of human experience, different from ordinary life, joyful, liberating, thrilling, but problematic, scary, dangerous. It was open-ended: it suggested a future that could offer *more* Marxist adventures. Maybe now I was ready to send my book out into the world and let it be.

Now I want to acknowledge some of the wonderful people who have helped me reach this point. At first I tried describing the relationships, but then I realized that if I really wanted to bring this book out now, I would have to settle for the names. I know there are many good names I've forgotten, and surely some I've repressed, but here are some I've remembered: Jacob Taubes, Meyer Schapiro, Isaiah Berlin, and Irving Howe; Georges Borchardt, Jerry Cohen, Todd Gitlin, Bob Christgau, Carola Dibbell; Elsa First, Lenny Kriegel, John Leonard, Steve Lukes, Bert Ollman, Jim Hoberman, Colin Robinson, Andrea Simon, Josh Wilner, Jeff Nichols; Michel Radomisli, Trude Pollock, Irene Javors, and Magdalena Berenyi; Michelle, David, and Steve Nathan. Then there are all my students and fellow teachers at the City University of New York; the Guggenheim and Rifkind Foundations and the NEH; all the folks, young and old, at Morningside Montessori; and all my friends at *Dissent* and the *Nation*. Finally, my dear family, Mom and Dad (I found a way to write about them at last), Didi and Jon, Eli and Danny, Idie and Mia, Marvin and Debbie, and, above all, Shellie, who not only is my partner in dialogue, but who fills and lights my sky.

New York City,
June 1999

Introduction

Caught Up in the Mix: Some Adventures in Marxism

Once a theatregoer buttonholed [Arthur] Miller and put the question
to him: "What's he selling? You never say what he's selling."
Miller quipped, "Well, himself. That's what's in the valise."
– JOHN LAHR, "Making Willy Loman"

Marxism has been part of me for all my life. Late in my fifties, I'm still learning and sorting out how. Until now, I think I've had only one real adventure in Marxism. Still, that one was formidable. It helped me grow up and figure out who I was going to be in the world. And it makes a good story. My father also had a Marxist adventure, one more tragic than mine. It's only by working through his life that I'll be in a position to take hold of my own. Life studies is one of the big things Marxism is for.

My father, Murray Berman, died of a heart attack in 1955, when he was just short of forty-eight, and when I wasn't quite fifteen. He grew up on New York's Lower East Side and in the Bronx, left school at twelve, and was thrown into "the business world" – that's what he and my mother called it – pushing a truck in the garment center to help support his parents and nine kids in one room. He called it "the rack," and often said he was still on it. But the garment center's friendly malevolence felt like home to him, and we would never leave that home.

Over the years, he graduated from outdoor *schlepper* to indoor *schlepper* (I guess it would be called stock clerk today) and then to various clerical and sales jobs. He was on the road a lot before I was born and when I was very young. For several years he worked, as both reporter and an advertising salesman, for *Women's Wear Daily*. All those years are vague to me. But I know that in 1948, he and a friend from the Bronx made a great leap: they founded a magazine. Its theme, announced on the masthead, was "The garment industry meets the world." My father and his friend Dave had little education and less capital but lots of foresight – the Yiddish word is *sachel*. Globalization in the garment center was an idea whose time was coming, and for two years the magazine thrived, selling ever more advertising space (my father's specialty), which, in capitalist economies is what keeps newspapers and magazines alive.

But then, suddenly, in the spring in 1950, there was no money to meet the payroll, and just as suddenly his friend Dave disappeared. My father took me to the Natural History Museum one Saturday morning; Saturday afternoon, we walked around the Upper East Side, searching for Dave. In his favorite Third Avenue bars, no one had seen him for two days. His doorman said the same but he directed us to Dave's floor and said we would hear his dog barking if he was around. We didn't, and he wasn't, and while my father cursed and worked on a note to slip under his door, I looked into a half-open door in the hall and saw an open elevator shaft. As I looked down, curious, my father grabbed me and threw me against the wall – it was one of the two times he ever touched me violently. We didn't talk much as we took the subway back to the Bronx. The magazine went bankrupt overnight. The next month my father had a heart attack that nearly killed him.

We never saw Dave again, but the police tracked him down. It turned out he had a mistress on Park Avenue, another in Miami, and a gambling addiction. He had emptied the magazine's account, but when they found him there was little left, and nothing for us. My father said the whole story was such a garment center cliché (that was how I learned the meaning of the word *cliché*), he just couldn't believe his friend could do it to him. Several years later, out of the blue, Dave called again, with a new name – another garment center cliché – and a new proposition. I answered the phone, then put my mother on. She said he had ruined my father's life once, and wasn't that enough? Dave urged her to be a good sport.

My father gradually got his strength back, and my parents were now the "Betmar Tag and Label Company." They lived in the garment center's interstices as brokers or jobbers, middlemen between garment manufacturers and label-makers. This company had no capital; its only assets were my father's aptitude for *schmoozing* and my mother's for figuring things out. They knew their position was precarious, but they performed a real function, and they thought they had enough local knowledge to stay afloat. For a few years, it was a living. But in September 1955 my father had another heart attack, and from this one he died.

Who killed him? This question haunted me for years. "It's the wrong question," my first shrink said fifteen years later. "He had a bad heart. His system wore out." That was true; the army saw it and rejected him for service during World War II. But I couldn't forget his last summer, when all at once he lost several big accounts. The managers and purchasing agents were all his old friends: they had played stickball on Suffolk Street, worked together and dealt with each other for years; these guys had drunk to his health at my *bar mitzvah*, just two years back. Now, all of a sudden, they wouldn't return his calls. He had said he could tell he'd been outbid by somebody; he just wanted a chance to make a bid and to be told what was what. All this was explained to us at the funeral (a big funeral; he was well liked) and during *shiva* week just after. Our accounts, and dozens of others, had been grabbed by a Japanese syndicate, which was doing business both on a scale and in a style new to Seventh Avenue. The syndicate had made spectacular payoffs to its American contacts. (Of course they didn't call them payoffs.) But it had imposed two conditions: it must not be identified, and there must be no counter-bidding. We pressed his friends: Why couldn't you tell Daddy – even tell him there was something you couldn't tell him? They all said they hadn't wanted to make him feel bad. Crocodile tears, I thought, yet I could see their tears were real. Much later, I thought that here was one of the first waves of the global market that Dad foresaw and understood. I think he could have lived with that better than he could live with his old friends not calling him back.

My mother carried the company on briefly, but her heart wasn't in it. She folded it and went to work as a bookkeeper. Together, one night in the summer of 1956, near the end of our year of mourning, my mother, my sister and I threw enormous reams of paper from the lost accounts down our incinerator in the Bronx. But my mother held on to the manila folders that they had used for those accounts. ("We can still get plenty of use out of *them*," she said.) Forty years later, I'm still using those folders, containers of long-vanished entities – Puritan Sportswear, Fountain Modes, Girl Talk, Youngland – where are they now? Does it mean that, in some way, I've stayed in my father's business? (Happy Loman, at the very end of *Death of a Salesman*: "I'm staying right in this city, and I'm gonna beat this racket!") What racket? What business? My wife defined the relationship in a way I like: I've gone into my father's *unfinished* business.

"The only thing you got in this world is what you can sell." Another line from *Death of a Salesman*.[1] It was my father's favorite play. My parents saw *Salesman* at least twice on stage, starring Lee J. Cobb, and again in film form starring Fredric March. It became a primary source of material in the endless affectionate and ironic repartee they carried on till he died. I didn't know that till I got to see the movie, just a few months before his death; then all at once the meaning of years of banter became clear. I joined in the crosstalk, tried it at the dinner table, and got all smiles, though the lines were tragic, and were about to become more tragic still. One hot day in the summer of 1955 he came home drained from the garment center and said, "They don't know me any more." I said, "Dad … Willy Loman?" He was happy that I knew he was quoting, but he also wanted me to know it was not only a quote but the truth. I got him a beer, which I knew he liked in the summer heat; he hugged me and said it gave him peace to know I was going to be freer than he was, I was going to have a life of my own.

Soon after he died, scholarships and good luck propelled me to Columbia. There I could talk and read and write all night and then walk to the Hudson to see the sun at dawn. I felt like a prospector who had made a strike, discovering sources of fresh energy I never knew I had. And some of my teachers had even told me that living for ideas could be a way for me to make a living! I was happier than I had ever been, steeped in a life that really felt like *my life*. Then I realized this was exactly what my father had wanted for me. For the first time since his death, I started thinking about him. I thought about how he had struggled and lost, and my grief turned to rage. *So they don't know you?* I thought. *Let me at those bastards, I'll get them for you. They don't remember? I'll remind them.* But which bastards? Who were "they"? How could I get them? Where would I start? I made a date with Jacob Taubes, my beloved professor of religion. I said I wanted to talk about my father and Karl Marx.

Jacob and I sat in his office in Butler Library and talked and talked. He said that he sympathized with all radical desire, but revenge was a sterile form of fulfillment. Didn't Nietzsche write the book on that? Hadn't I read it in his class? He said that in the part of Europe where he came from (b. Vienna 1927), the politics of revenge had succeeded far beyond anything Americans could imagine. He told me a joke: "Capitalism is the exploitation of man by man. *Communism is the opposite.*" I had heard that joke before, maybe even from my father; it had gone round many times, for good reasons. But it was a dark joke and it hurt to laugh at it, because what followed seemed to be a total human impasse: the system is intolerable, and so is the only alternative to the system. *Oy!* So what then, I asked, we all put ourselves to sleep? No, no, said Jacob, he didn't mean to immobilize me. In fact, there was this book he had meant to tell me about: Marx wrote it "when he was still a kid, before he became Karl Marx"; it was wild, and I would like it. The Columbia Bookstore ("those fools") didn't have it, but I could get it at Barnes & Noble downtown. The book had "been kept secret for a century" – that was Jacob's primal romance, the secret book, the *Kabbalah* – but now at last it had been released.[2] He said some people thought it offered "an alternative vision of how man should live." Wouldn't that be better than revenge? And I could get there on the subway.

So, one lovely Saturday in November, I took the #1 train downtown, turned south at the Flatiron Building, and headed down Fifth to Barnes & Noble. B&N then was far from its 1990s monopoly incarnation, "Barnes Ignoble," scourge of small bookshops; it was only one store, just off Union Square, and it traced itself back to Abe Lincoln and Walt Whitman and "The Battle Hymn of the Republic." But before I could get there, I passed another place that I had always walked on by: the Four Continents Book Store, official distributor for all Soviet publications. Would my Marx be there? If it really was "really wild," would the USSR be bringing it out? I remembered the Soviet tanks in Budapest, killing kids on the streets. Still, the USSR in 1959 was supposed to be opening up ("the Thaw, they called it), and there was a possibility. I had to see.

The Four Continents was like a rainforest inside, walls painted deep green, giant posters of bears, pines, icebergs and icebreakers, shelves stretching back toward a vast horizon, lighting that evoked a tree cover more than a modern room. My first thought was, How can anyone read in this light? (In retrospect, I realize it resembled the lighting in certain 1950s furniture stores and romantic comedies. It was the light scheme in the bachelor flat where the hero brought home Doris Day.) The staff knew just what book I wanted: *Marx's Economic and Philosophical Manuscripts of 1844,* translated by Martin Milligan, and published in 1956 by the Foreign Languages Publishing House in Moscow. It was a collection of three youthful notebooks, divided into short essays. The titles didn't seem to emanate from Marx himself; they appeared to be provided by twentieth-century editors in Moscow or Berlin. It was midnight blue, nice and compact, a perfect fit for a side pocket in a 1950s sports jacket. I opened it at random, here, there, somewhere else – and suddenly I was in a sweat, melting, shedding clothes and tears, flashing hot and cold. I rushed to the front: "I've got to have this book!" The white-haired clerk was calm. "Fifty cents, please." When I expressed amazement, he said, "We" – I guess he meant the USSR – "don't publish books for profit." He said the *Manuscripts* had become one of their bestsellers, though he himself couldn't see why, since Lenin was so much clearer.

Right there my adventure began. I realized I was carrying more than thirty dollars, mostly wages from the college library; it was probably as much as I'd ever carried in my life. I felt another flash. "Fifty cents? So for ten bucks I can get twenty?" The clerk said that, after sales taxes, twenty copies would cost about $11. I ran back to the rear, grabbed the books, and said, "You've just solved my Hanukkah problem." As I *schlepped* the books on the subway up to the Bronx (Four Continents tied them up in a nice parcel), I felt I was walking on air. For the next several days I walked around with a stack of books, thrilled to be giving them away to all the people in my life: my mother and sister, my girlfriend, her parents, several old and new friends, a couple of my teachers, the man from the stationery store, a union leader (the past summer, I'd worked for District 65), a doctor, a rabbi. I'd never given so many gifts before (and never did again). Nobody refused the book, but I got some weird looks from people when I breathlessly delivered my *spiel*. "Take this!" I said, shoving the book in their faces. "It'll knock you out. It's by Karl Marx, but before he became Karl Marx. It'll show you how our whole life's wrong, but it'll make you happy, too. If you don't get it, just call me anytime, and I'll explain it all. Soon everybody will be talking about it, and you'll be the first to know." And I was out the door, to face more puzzled people. I stopped at Jacob's office with my stack of books, told him the story, went through the *spiel*. We beamed at each other. "See, now," he said, "isn't this better than revenge?" I improvised a comeback: "No, it's the best revenge."

I try to imagine myself at that magic moment: *Too much, man! Was I for real?* (Those are things we used to say to each other in 1959.) How did I get to be so sure of myself? (Never again!) My intellectual impulse-buying; my neo-*potlatch* great giveaway of a book I hadn't even properly read; the exuberance with which I pressed myself on all those people; my certainty that I had something special, something that would both rip up their lives and make them happy; my promises of lifetime personal service; above all, my love for my great new product that would change the world: Willy Loman, meet Karl Marx. We entered the Sixties together.

What was it in Marx, all those years ago, that shot me up like a rocket? Not long ago, I went through that old midnight blue Four Continents book. It was a haunting experience, with the Soviet Union dead; but Marx himself moved and lived. The book was hard to read because I'd underlined, circled and asterisked virtually *everything*. But I know the ideas that caught me forty years ago are still part of me today, and it will help this book hold together if I can block out at least some of those ideas in a way that is brief but clear.[3]

The thing I found so striking in Marx's 1844 essays, and which I did not expect to find at all, was his feeling for the individual. Those early essays articulate the conflict between *Bildung* and alienated labor. *Bildung* is the core human value in liberal romanticism. It is a hard word to put in English, but it embraces a family of ideas like "subjectivity," "finding yourself," "growing up," "identity," "self-development," and "becoming who you are." Marx situates this ideal in modern history and gives it a social theory. He identifies with the Enlightenment and with the great revolutions that formed its climax when he asserts the universal right of man to be "freely active," to "affirm himself," to enjoy "spontaneous activity," to pursue "the free development of his physical and mental energy" (74–5). But he also denounces the market society nourished by those revolutions, because "Money is the overturning of all individualities" (105), and because "You must make all that is yours *For Sale* ..." (96; Marx's emphasis). He shows how modern capitalism arranges work in such a way that the worker is "alienated from his own activity," as well as from other workers and from nature. The worker "mortifies his body and ruins his mind"; he "feels himself only outside his work, and in his work ... feels outside himself"; he "is at home only when he is not working, and when he is working he is not at home. His labor therefore is not free, but coerced; it is forced labor" (74; Marx's emphasis). Marx salutes the labor unions that, in the 1840s, are just beginning to emerge. But even if the unions achieve their immediate aims – even if workers get widespread union recognition and raise wages by force of class struggle – it will still be "nothing but salary for a slave," unless modern society comes to recognize "the meaning and dignity of work and of the worker" (80). Capitalism is terrible because it promotes human energy, spontaneous feeling, human development, only to crush them, except in the few winners at the very top. From the very start of his career as an intellectual, Marx is a fighter for democracy. But he sees that democracy in itself won't cure the structural misery he sees. So long as work is organized in hierarchies and mechanical routines and oriented to the demands of the world market, most people, even in the freest societies, will still be enslaved – will still be, like my father, on the rack. Marx is part of a great cultural tradition, a comrade of modern masters like Keats, Dickens, George Eliot, Dostoevsky, James Joyce, Franz Kafka, D. H. Lawrence (readers are free to fill in their personal favorites) in his feeling for the suffering modern man on the rack. But Marx is unique in his grasp of what that rack is made of. It's there in all his work. But in the *Communist*

Manifesto and *Capital,* you have to look for it. In the *1844 Manuscripts,* it's in your face.

Marx wrote most of these essays in the midst of one of his great adventures, his honeymoon in Paris with Jenny von Westphalen. The year I had my Marxian adventure, I had just fallen in love, first love, and this made me very curious whether he would have anything to say about love and sex. The Marxists I had met through the years seemed to have a collective attitude that didn't exactly hate sex and love, but regarded them with impatience, as if these feelings were to be tolerated as necessary evils, but not one iota of extra time or energy should be wasted on them, and nothing could be more foolish than to think they had human meaning or value in themselves. After I had heard that for years, to hear young Marx in his own voice was a breath of fresh air. "From this relationship, one can judge man's whole level of development" (82). He was saying just what I felt: that sexual love was the most important thing there was.

Hanging around the Left Bank in Paris, Marx seems to have met radicals who promoted sexual promiscuity as an act of liberation from bourgeois constraints. Marx agreed with them that modern love could become a problem if it drove lovers to possess their loved ones as "exclusive private property" (82). And indeed, "Private property has made us so stupid that an object is only *ours* when we have it" (91; Marx's emphasis). But their only alternative to marriage seems to have been an arrangement that made everybody the sexual property of everybody else, and Marx disparaged this as nothing but "universal prostitution."

We don't know who these "crude, mindless communists" were, but Marx's critique of them is fascinating. He uses their sexual grossness as a symbol of everything that he thinks is wrong with the left. Their view of the world "negates the personality of man in every sphere." It entails "the abstract negation of the whole world of culture and civilization"; their idea of happiness is "leveling down proceeding from a preconceived minimum." Moreover, they embody "general *envy* constituting itself as a power" and "the disguise in which *avarice* re-establishes itself and satisfies itself, only in another way." They promote "regression to the unnatural simplicity of the undemanding man who has not only failed to go beyond private property, but has not even yet attained to it" (82–3). Marx is focusing on the human qualities of greed and crudity that makes some liberals despise and fear the left. He would say it is stupid prejudice to think that *all* leftists are like that, but it is right to think that *some* leftists are like that – though not him or anyone close to his heart. Here Marx is not only reaching out to the Tocqueville tradition but trying to envelop it.

When Marx calls the bad communists "thoughtless," he is suggesting not just that their ideas are stupid, but that they are unconscious of what their real motives are; they think they are performing noble actions, but they are really engaged in vindictive, neurotic acting out. Marx's analysis here is stretching toward Nietzsche and Freud. But it also highlights his roots in the Enlightenment: the communism he wants must include *self-awareness*. This nightmare vision of "crude, thoughtless communism" is one of the strongest things in early Marx. Were there real-life models in the Paris of the 1840s? No biographer has come up with convincing candidates; maybe he simply imagined them himself, the way novelists create their characters. But once we have read Marx, it is hard to forget them, these vivid nightmares of all the ways the Left could go wrong.

There is another striking way in which young Marx worries about sex and conceives it as a symbol of something bigger. When workers are alienated from their own activity in their work, their sexual lives become an obsessive form of compensation. They then try to realize themselves through desperate "eating, drinking, procreating," along with "dwelling and dressing up." But desperation makes carnal pleasures less joyful than they could be, because it places more psychic weight on them than they can bear (74).

The essay "Private Property and Communism" takes a longer view and strikes a more upbeat note: "The forming of the five senses is a labor of the whole history of the world, down to the present" (89). Maybe the joy of a honeymoon enables Marx to imagine new people coming over the horizon, people less possessive and greedy, more in tune with their sensuality and vitality, inwardly better equipped to make love a vital part of human development.

Who are these "new people" who would have the power at once to represent and to liberate humanity? The answer that made Marx both famous and infamous is proclaimed to the world in the *Manifesto*: "the proletariat, the modern working class" (479). But this answer itself raises overwhelming questions. We can divide them roughly in two, the first line of questions about the membership of the working class, the second about its mission. Who are these guys, heirs and heiresses of all the ages? And, given the extent and depth of their suffering, which Marx describes so well, where are they going to get the positive energy they will need not merely to gain power, but to change the whole world? Marx's *1844 Manuscripts* don't address the "membership" questions,[4] but he has some fascinating things to say about the mission. He says that even as modern society brutalizes and maims the self, it also brings forth, dialectically, "the rich human being [*der reiche Mensch*] and rich human need" (89).

"The rich human being": Where have we seen him before? Readers of Goethe and Schiller will recognize the imagery of classical German humanism here. But those humanists believed that only a very few men and women could be capable of the inner depth that they could imagine; the vast majority of people, as seen from Weimar and Jena, were consumed by trivialities and had no soul. Marx inherited Goethe's and Schiller's and Humboldt's values, but he fused them with a radical and democratic social philosophy inspired by Rousseau. Rousseau's 1755 *Discourse on the Origins of Inequality* laid out the paradox that even as modern civilization alienates people from themselves, it develops and deepens those alienated selves and gives them the capacity to form a social contract and create a radically new society.[5] A century later, after one great wave of revolutions and just before another, Marx sees modern society in a similarly dialectical way. His idea is that even as bourgeois society enervates and impoverishes its workers, it spiritually enriches and inspires them. "The rich human being" is a man or woman for whom "self-realization [*seine eigne Verwirklichung*] exists as an inner necessity, a need"; he or she is "a human being in need of a totality of human activities" (91). Marx sees bourgeois society as a system that, in an infinite number of ways, stretches workers out on a rack. Here his dialectical imagination starts to work: the very social system that tortures them also teaches and transforms them, so that while they suffer, they also begin to overflow with energy and ideas. Bourgeois society treats its workers as objects, yet develops their subjectivity. Marx has a brief passage on French workers who are just (of course illegally) starting to organize: they come together instrumentally, as a means to economic and political ends; but "as a result of this association, they acquire a new need – the need for society – and what [begins] as a means becomes an end" (99). Workers may not set out to be "rich human beings," and certainly no one else wants them to be, but their development is their fate, it turns their powers of desire into a world-historical force.

"Let me get this straight," my mother said, as she took her book. "It's Marx, but not communism, right? So what is it?" Marx in 1844 had imagined two very different communisms. One, which he wanted, was "a genuine resolution of the conflict between man and nature, and between man and man" (84); the other, which he dreaded, "has not only failed to go beyond private property, it hasn't yet attained to it" (83). Our twentieth century had produced a great surplus of the second model, but not much of the first. The problem, in short, has been that the second model, the one Marx dreaded, has had tanks, and the first, the one he dreamed of, has not. My mother and I had seen those tanks on TV, in Budapest, killing kids. We agreed, not Communism. But if not that, then what? I felt like a panelist on a TV quiz show, with time running out. I reached for a phrase I had seen in the *New York Times,* in a story about French existentialists – Sartre, de Beauvoir, Henri Lefebvre, André Gorz, and their friends – who were trying to merge their thought with Marxism and create a radical perspective that would transcend the dualisms of the Cold War. I said, "Call it *Marxist humanism.*" "Oh!" my mother said, "Marxist humanism, that sounds nice." *Zap*! My adventure in Marxism had crystallized; in an instant I had focused my identity for the next forty years.

And what happened then? I lived another forty years. I went to Oxford, then Harvard. Then I got a steady job in the public sector, as a teacher of political theory and urbanism at the ever-assailed City University of New York. I've worked mostly in Harlem, but Downtown as well. I've been lucky to grow old as a citizen of New York, and to bring up my kids in the fervid freedom of the city. I was part of the New Left thirty years ago, and I'm part of the Used Left today. (My generation shouldn't be embarrassed by the name. Anyone old enough to know the market's ups and downs knows that used goods often beat new models.) I don't think I've grown old yet, but I've been through plenty, and through it all I've worked to keep Marxist humanism alive.

As the twentieth century comes to an end, Marxist humanism is almost half a century old. It's never swept the country, not in any country, but it has found a place. One way to place it might be to see it as a synthesis of the culture of the Fifties with that of the Sixties: a feeling for complexity, irony and paradox, combined with a desire for breakthrough and ecstasy; a fusion of "Seven Types of Ambiguity" with "We Want the World and We Want It Now." It deserves a place of honor in more recent history, in 1989 and after, in the midst of the changes that their protagonists called the Velvet Revolution.

Mikhail Gorbachev hoped to give it a place in his part of the world. He imagined a Communism that could enlarge personal freedom, not crush it. But he came too late. To people who had lived their lives within the Soviet horizon, the vision didn't scan; they just couldn't see it. The Soviet people had been burned so badly for so long, they didn't know him; he called, and they didn't return his calls. But we can see Gorbachev as a Willy Loman of politics – a failure as a salesman, but a tragic hero.

Some people think Marxist humanism got its whole meaning as an alternative to Stalinism, and that it died with the crumbling of the USSR. My own view is that its real dynamic force is as an alternative to the nihilistic, market-driven capitalism that envelops the whole world today. That means it will have plenty of work to do for a long time to come.

There is a wonderful image that emerged early in the 1990s – at least that is when I first heard it, at my school, CCNY – from the street life of America's black ghettos, and particularly from today's hip-hop music scene, where music becomes itself not by being harmonized, but by being mixed. Here's the image: *caught up in the mix.* "She's all caught up in the mix"; "I got myself caught up in the mix." This image has caught on because it captures so much of so many people's lives. *My father was caught up in the mix. So were the friends who betrayed him.* I think Marx understood better than anybody else how modern life is a mix; how, although there are immense variations in it, deep down it's *one* mix – "the mix"; how we are all caught up in it; and how easy, how normal it is for the mix to go awry. He also showed how, once we grasped the way we were thrown together, we could fight for the power to remix.

Marxist humanism can help people feel at home in history, even a history that hurts them. It can show them how even those who are broken by power can have the power to fight the power; how even survivors of tragedy can make history. It can help people discover themselves as "rich human beings" with "rich human needs" (*MER*, 89–91), and can show them there is more to them than they thought. It can help new generations to imagine new adventures, and arouse their powers of desire to change the world, so that they not only will be part of the mix, they will get to do part of the mixing.

Notes

1. Arthur Miller, *Death of a Salesman*, first published and produced 1949; text and criticism edited by Gerald Weales (New York: Viking, 1977). The lament "The only thing you got," by Willie's neighbor Charlie is on page 97; Happy's graveside vow, 138–9. The story about Miller cited in the epigraph is drawn from John Lahr, "Making Willy Loman," *New Yorker*, January 25, 1999, 46–7.

2. In fact, these 1844 notebooks had been published in Berlin by the Marx-Engels Institute in 1932 as part of the projected (but never completed) *Marx-Engels Gesamtausgabe*. That edition was suppressed in Germany by the Nazis, but was continued for a time in Moscow, where Georg Lukács, by then a refugee, played some editorial role. Herbert Marcuse made creative use of the *1844 Manuscripts* in his *Reason*

and Revolution: Hegel and the Rise of Social Theory (New York: Oxford University Press, 1941). But there was no popular edition until the Khrushchev era, when Moscow sponsored translations into many languages and sold them by the millions dirt cheap.

3. I will refer to this volume as the *1844 Manuscripts*. Throughout this book, citations from Marx, unless I note otherwise, are drawn from the *Marx-Engels Reader*, 2nd edition, edited by Robert C. Tucker (New York: Norton 1978), which uses Milligan's translations of the 1844 material. The core of the *1844 Manuscripts* consists of five essays: "Alienated Labor," "Private Property and Communism," "The Meaning of Human Requirements," "The Power of Money in Bourgeois Society," and "Critique of the Hegelian Dialectic and Philosophy as a Whole."

4. Marx had offered a definition a few months earlier, in a "little magazine" called the *German-French Yearbooks*, published in Paris. That definition is mostly negative: you will know them by their multiple wounds and exclusions. They form "a class in civil society that is not a class of civil society," and "a total loss of humanity that can redeem itself only by a total redemption of humanity" ("Contribution to a Critique of Hegel's Philosophy of Right: Introduction," *MER*, 53–65). This is very different from the proletarians we will meet in the *Communist Manifesto* and *Capital*. There they are the primary source of power for the immense engine of modern production and industry. Here we come to know them by all they are *not;* they seem much more like the poor people portrayed by Dickens and Dostoevsky, or like the insulted and injured group that contemporary US social scientists have named "the underclass."

5. Engels, in his 1880 pamphlet *Socialism: Utopian and Scientific* (derived from his polemic *Anti-Dühring,* 1878) is perceptive in judging Rousseau's *Discourse on the Origins of Inequality* and Diderot's *Rameau's Nephew* as the "two great masterpieces of dialectics" produced by the Enlightenment (*MER,* 694). My first book, *The Politics of Authenticity* (New York: Atheneum, 1970, 1972), traces some of the roots of Marxism in the radical Enlightenment.

1

Marx: The Dancer and the Dance

An apparition floated by me on Upper Broadway not long ago: a girl in a red T-shirt that displayed, on and around her breasts, a group of Karl Marxes, four or five of them, in a semi-circle, arms linked, smiling broadly, kicking their legs high in a rousing dance. This delightful vision turned out to be real: after I'd backtracked a block and caught up with the girl, she told me that it was the emblem of URPE, the Union for Radical Political Economics. That shirt can tell us something about what has happened to Marx in the America of the 1970s. First of all, everybody seems to have accepted the existence of many Marxes: no party, movement or country has a monopoly on his thought. Second, these many Marxes seem to be coexisting rather well – a nice surprise, for weren't they only yesterday at one another's throats, each insisting that the others

Review of Jerrold Seigel, *Marx's Fate: The Shape of a Life* (Princeton, N. J.: Princeton University Press, 1978). This essay first in the *Nation*, January 27, 1979.

weren't really Karl Marx at all? Finally, they are coming together in an activity that's expressive, playful, even a little vulgar – an activity that would have been considered most un-Marxian not long ago. Today's Marxes have kept in touch with their youthful romantic visions of politics as dancing.

The cultural leap that made this dance possible was first assayed on a mass scale about twenty years ago, when Marx's unpublished essays and notes of 1844 were translated into all major European languages – they are generally known in English as the *Economic and Philosophical Manuscripts* – and published by Moscow in cheap editions for a large public. The central idea of these youthful essays was "alienation." The trouble with capitalism, they said, was that it alienated people from one another, from nature, and – here is where Marx was most original – from themselves: from their senses, their emotions, their imaginative powers, from "the free development of their physical and spiritual energies." Marx focused on work as a primary source of meaning, dignity and self-development for modern man; the bourgeois organization of labor was a crime against these human needs. But Marx also wrote lyrically about sexual love, and about its perversion by the power of money; about history as the unfolding education of the five senses, and the ways in which that education had gone awry; about the material roots of the widespread modern sense of spiritual rootlessness. These essays, coming out in the midst of the greatest capitalist boom in history (1959 in the United States), provided a searing indictment of capitalism even at its most triumphant. At the same time, Marx's critique cut just as deeply into Stalinist communism – there was even a model of a "crude, mindless communism" that Marx feared as a regression from capitalism – from the perspective of communism's own ultimate values.

The "young Marx" was condemned, of course, by the ideological commissars of the various CPs, and by their right-wing equivalents in the United States. But Marxism had gained, or regained, a sensual warmth and a spiritual depth that all the Sidney Hooks and all the Althussers (and Althusserians) could not take away. The spirit of the young Marx animated the radical initiatives of the 1960s, from Berkeley to Prague; and even when political energy was crushed, as in the East, or when it dissipated itself, as in the West, this spirit survived. Even after a barren decade, today's Marxes can dance. If Marx's early writings are no longer so central to his reputation as they were, say, a decade ago, this is mostly because their lessons have been learned, their themes and energies assimilated into our sense of his work as a whole. But there is one vital area in which our perspective on Marx has not deepened at all: the study of his life. Many studies have appeared over the years that have examined his life with increased political acuteness and philosophical sophistication. Almost without exception, however, these biographies have been emotionally flat, spiritually arid, psychologically remote. If we compare the current state of Marx studies with Edmund Wilson's magnificent *To the Finland Station* (1940) we will find that we have a far deeper understanding of Marx's ideas and yet, if anything, rather less of a feeling for the emotions at the heart of those ideas.

In this context, Jerrold Seigel's new book, *Marx's Fate: The Shape of a Life*, should be welcomed very warmly. Seigel brings us, in crucial ways, closer to Marx than we have ever been. He captures the desperate intensity and volatility of Marx's inner life, the exhausting anxieties that kept his mind inexhaustibly alive. I should say at once that the book has its problems. Seigel never makes up his mind whether he is writing a psychoanalytical "Young Man Marx" or a full-scale intellectual and political biography; hence he lurches uneasily between genres, changes gears at high speeds, frequently loses touch with his overall aims, gets lost in endless exposition and paraphrase, and writes a book that is twice too long. In other ways, though, the book is too short: it omits crucial aspects of Marx's life, even at the moments that concern Seigel most: it circles obsessively around a very limited number of themes, and wholly omits other motifs that are at least as urgent and fruitful; and it gives little sense of the expansiveness of Marx's mind. Nevertheless, *Marx's Fate* puts us in touch with much of Marx's deepest thought and feeling, and reveals the history of his ideas as a history of radical self-contradiction, as one of the great inner dramas of modern times.

Seigel thrashes around for the first couple of chapters, and it isn't clear for a while what the book's focus is going to be. He is frustrated in writing about Marx's childhood: neither he nor anyone else has found much solid material to build on here. Seigel takes off at the point where Marx himself begins to take off, in his late teens, when he is getting ready to leave home for the first time, to attend university and choose a vocation. Now, suddenly, Seigel and his readers find themselves flooded with material. Marx at this point was just beginning to overwhelm people with his volcanic intellectual power, and frightening himself and his loved ones as to what was going to become of that power.

Like many highly gifted adolescents whose brilliance at once amazes and frightens those around them (today we should have to include their therapists), Marx overflowed with endless fantasies and myths, models and conceptualizations about himself: Prometheus, of course; but also Faust, and his demonic pact; the philosopher Democritus, who supposedly put out his eyes so he could see ideas in their full clarity; Karl Moor, Schiller's robber-hero, who tears down half the world but yearns only for his father's blessing; Hölderlin's Hyperion, racked with inner darkness amid Greek sunlight; Rameau's nephew, with what Hegel called "the disintegrated consciousness"; spectres of suicide (on which Seigel has unearthed an early essay) and madness. Part of the problem for Seigel, as for any therapist working with gifted adolescents today, is to figure out which of the subject's marvelous imaginative constructs are essentially screens, and which are for real; the more brilliant the subject, the more ingenious the disguises are apt to be, and the harder and more elusive will be the analyst's work.

What Seigel considers real for Marx is, above all, his relationship with Hegel. This relationship is familiar enough as an organizing principle in Marx studies. But Seigel isn't really interested in Marx's criticism or transformation of Hegelian ideas. Instead, he wants to look at the history of social thought in much the same way that Harold Bloom, in *The Anxiety of Influence* (1973) and *A Map of Misreading* (1975). has approached the history of modern poetry: as an arena in which primal emotions, for the most part Oedipal ones, can be expressed, fought out, and sometimes worked through. Thus Seigel's Marx confronts Hegel more as a demon than a doctrine – a totemic figure that must be fought and overcome. This Marx strives incessantly to expel the demonic force, both from his own mind and from Western culture, only to find himself again and again in need of its sustenance or else to have it creep up on him unawares, like Freud's return of the repressed.

Marx's relation to Hegel is so complex and agonized, Seigel argues, because it is fraught with all the energy and agony of Marx's relationship with his father. The Marxes, like many an intellectual family then and now, seem to have mythicized their emotions, and fought out their deepest emotional conflicts in intellectual and ideological terms: then as now, the intellectual language may both reveal and conceal what is really going on. In any case, both Marx and his father, Heinrich, twisted Hegel into a mythical figure that had less to do with Hegel's works than with the Marx family's desires and fears. For both father and son, in the 1830s, Hegel seems to have symbolized a life of narcissistic ecstasy: the thinker's temptation to build up a self-subsistent world of inner life and activity, cut off from the material world, from people and human feeling, but radiant with joy and a sense of magical power that no human reality could give.

In fact, this temptation and danger, inherent in the activity of contemplation, are as old as the history of ideas. Plato's version – the visionary philosopher who dreads returning to the cave of normal human life – is already a relatively late one. Meditative and mystical circles, like the Jewish cabalists, have always sought to guard against the allure of unembodiment. The Romantics were especially tempted and endangered by it, as readers of Coleridge and Hölderlin know well. Seigel does little to put this strange longing in historical or psychological perspective – its full history has never even been attempted – but he does a lot to show how much it meant to Marx. For the adolescent Marx, Seigel argues (and illustrates abundantly), there was something intensely seductive about this vision of life: his reason and conscience condemned it as sterile and empty – if not, indeed, insane – but his desire to submerge himself in pure thought was too deep for mere reason or conscience or sanity to overcome.

This temptation, and the guilt it provoked, form the context for a fascinating and crucial exchange of letters between Marx and his father in 1837, when he was nineteen years old and studying in Berlin. Marx's father, who has always been warm and affectionate toward his son, suddenly turns on him with a torrent of hysterical fears. "Sometimes," Heinrich Marx writes, "my heart revels in thoughts of you and your future. And yet, I cannot rid myself of ideas that raise a presentiment of fear, when like lightning the thought closes in: does your heart correspond to your head? ... " He fears that his son's heart does not "beat in a purely human way," and that instead Karl is possessed by a "demonic spirit" that "estranges your heart from finer feelings." Should his son take the dark road that looms ahead of him, he would see "the finest aim of my life in ruins."

What was eating this loving and supportive father? What possessed this Voltairian rationalist to start raving about demonic possession? What did Marx do to deserve this? Nothing, so far as we can tell, and this may have been the trouble: he wasn't doing anything to choose a profession, to settle down, to work for family (he had just proclaimed his love for Jenny von Westphalen, the girl who would be his wife) and humanity – all he wanted to do at this point was to read, to speculate, to develop his mind as an end in itself. An innocent pursuit, most of us would think, for a youth of nineteen. In the terms of the family mythology, however, innocence equals temptation – indeed, in a sense, equals guilt: the young thinker enjoying his mind's powers is in fact being tempted by inner demons – the specter of Hegel first among them – that would spirit him forever away. Heinrich may have seen his curses as desperate attempts to drive them out.

This must have been very painful for Marx, not only because he loved his father and felt endlessly obligated to him but, also, as we will see, because he shared the mythology from which his father's fears sprang. We see this in a long letter of a few months later, in which, alternately proud and abject, lyrical, explosive and semi-delirious, Marx substantiates his father's worst fears: he has gone over to Hegel. This famous letter

(November 10, 1837) reads, in its central narrative, like a conventional account of religious conversion: dejection, melancholy, physical and mental wasting away; then, at the nadir of negativity, a great shot of light, a renewal of life and energy, a rededication of all the self's powers; finally, a plea for understanding and sympathy from the loved one, an affirmation of faith that everything can be made clear and the two of them can live in harmony once again. This drama, enacted by so many of us in our own adolescent years (or later), is deeply moving when we watch Marx go through it. And yet, interwoven with this archetypal experience of human growth, we find strands of stranger feeling, permeated with the Marx family's peculiar mystique. Karl's conversion took place, he says, in the midst of a lovely but anguished moonlit night. He had begun a dialogue on nature and God, and given himself up to the inner movements of his mind, when suddenly an unconscious current carried him away: "This darling child of mine [his mind? his dialogue?], nurtured in moonlight, bears me like a false-hearted siren into the clutches of the enemy." There are so many dimensions of meaning here: the language of sexual temptation and infidelity, seduction and betrayal, with Marx as a not wholly unwilling victim; the erotically charged radiance of ideas, intensely alluring but, like the sirens, lethal; the equivalence of woman (siren) and child, and the strong ambivalence toward them both, and toward their almost supernatural pull (the moon) on Marx's self; finally, Marx's way of placing himself in the same relationship to his father – beautiful but weird and dangerous child – that his uncontrollable thoughts bear to himself. In this remarkable sentence, Marx sees himself simultaneously as seducer and seduced, guilty and innocent, male and female, parent and child. He then pleads for his father's understanding – at a point where it is not at all clear that he understands himself – and guiltily affirms his undying love. He begs for a chance to come home – had his father forbidden him to come, or is he merely asking for carfare? – so that "I can clasp you in my arms and tell you all I feel"; then, maybe, "the clouds that hang over our family will lift." Finally, foreshadowing the most famous image of Marx's mature years, "I shall not be able to lay aside the spectre that haunts me until I am in your dear presence." Six months later, Heinrich Marx was dead.

Seigel's treatment of this crucial episode shows both his strength and his weakness. His strength lies in a feeling for the emotional intensity, conflict and agony that underlie Marx's ideas; his weakness, in an inability to keep these searing emotions in focus. Seigel surmises, plausibly enough, that Marx must have been deeply haunted by guilt when his father died, just as he was coming into his own powers. (I'm here to testify that this guilt doesn't go away, not even after twenty years of normal adult life.) But he tells us nothing about how Heinrich actually died, about where Karl was when he died, about what transpired between them in the interval between the letter and the death. Deathbed reconciliations were central to nineteenth-century sentimentality; when they didn't happen, survivors often carried the wound in the heart all their lives. Did Karl make it home, was there a kiss before dying? Or did the last embrace never take place? Did Karl repress the pain, or sublimate it, or just carry the weight for fifty years?

The answer, if we could find it, would tell us a lot about his life and work. It appears that here, as so often in Marx's life, we just don't know, and Seigel knows no more than you or I. But Seigel has given us the impression that we are going to find something out, so it is disheartening to find ourselves back at the same old square one.

Seigel remains entangled in Marx's many webs, but he is perceptive and often brilliant in penetrating their intricacies and depths. He argues that, emotionally (unconsciously), Marx equated the solid material world with his father, and with his own sense of filial obligation: his desire to immerse himself in a world of pure thought expressed a kind of Oedipal will-to-power, the power to create a world of ideal freedom beyond his father's reach. Thus, even though Marx would criticize German Idealism as a conservative ideology, Idealism remained his own mode and symbol of personal rebellion. Materialism, though he portrayed it as politically radical, was for him emotionally conservative, a way back to the father he had tried to overcome. The dialectical fusion of materialism and ideal-ism, which Marx first imagined in his "Theses on Feuerbach" (1845, when he was twenty-seven), was also a symbolic emotional reconcili-ation between father and son, between his adolescent desire for total freedom and his father's insistence on the ties that bind. Seigel argues that Marx achieved a psychological synthesis that enabled him to come into his own – in the language of Erik Erikson, it enabled him to resolve the problem of his identity. His genius enabled him to sublimate his personal dialectic into a world perspective, and so to become the world-historical man we know. That perspective, "Marxism," sheds brilliant light on the mixtures of autonomy and constraint that define all our lives, and drama-tizes our need for a world in which we can fulfill ourselves with and through one another.

One primary force in Marx's synthesis seems to have been sexual love. Biographers have noted, as even police agents noted, that Karl and Jenny Marx had, despite much turbulence and suffering, a passionate and joy-ous marriage, sustained for forty years, ending only in death. Indeed, Marx is one of the very few great thinkers in all history to have enjoyed a happy marriage and family life. Some biographers have worked hard to magnify all the cracks in that life: mainly, a brief affair with his house-keeper in the 1850s, a love-child, "Freddy," who was adopted by Engels and who became a British trade union activist. But even they have gener-ally conceded that they haven't much to work with. (So they concentrate on Marx's inability to manage the pathetic amount of money that he had, or to get a steady job.) Seigel shows how sexual love played a vital part in the formation of his identity, helping to liberate Marx from psychic isola-tion and center him in the real world. Marx thought and wrote a great deal about sexual love in the mid-1840s, just after his marriage, when he was trying to fulfill his father's ideal of a life with people. Note the basis on which, in 1845, he would reject German Idealism: he remarks deri-sively that this philosophy and "the study of actuality" have "the same relation to each other as masturbation and sexual love." This is the image of a man self-confident in his newly fulfilled adult sexuality. He passes the same cruel judgment on a rejected mode of thought as on a discarded mode of sexual life: both are masturbatory, outgrowths of a solitary, barren self-absorption. He has outgrown them both, he feels, and grown into a healthier and more mature mode of thought – "the study of actu-ality" – which, like sexual love, reaches out and embraces other people.

And yet, even here, spectres haunt him. We can faintly see the shadow in another remark about love from this period: it is love, Marx says, that "first teaches man to believe in the objective world outside himself." A lovely image: and yet, imagine how deep a man's inner isolation must be for him to need such a proof! It should be easy to understand why, under the pressures of this psychic undertow, Marx should need inner ballast to hold him to this world.

Sexual love could fulfill a vital part of this need. But materialist thought, which Marx also embraced in the mid-1840s, seems to have served the same purpose. Hence the sense of intense exhilaration and relief that animates Marx's first materialist manifestoes: "One has to leap out of philosophy, and devote oneself like an ordinary man to the study of actuality"; "as history moves forward [intellectuals] ... have only to take note of what is happening before their eyes, and to become its mouthpiece"; and, of course, "the philosophers have only interpreted the world, in various ways; the point, however, is to change it." It is as if a crushing burden had been lifted from Marx's soul, so that he might live in the real world "like an ordinary man" at last. But there is also something unsaid and disturbing beneath the surface. Marx's project sounds remarkably like Kierkegaard's "leap of faith," with which it is exactly contemporaneous. There is an aura of religious renunciation here: Marx seems to be hoping that he will never have to think another thought; the forward movement of history, he thinks, will do his thinking for him, and he will need only to speak for it.

Seigel argues that Marx's leap, rooted in his inner need for ballast, made a certain kind of sense in the Europe of the late 1840s. This was a time when everyone, regardless of philosophy or politics, believed that material forces were moving toward a final polarization and confrontation that, whatever the outcome, would decisively resolve everyone's fate. Not only the *Communist Manifesto,* but equally the 1848 writings of Tocqueville, Herzen, Baudelaire, and a hundred lesser figures – indeed, everyone who lived through these years – are full of the imagery of veils and masks being stripped away, and of social forces revealing themselves in their naked truth. What made the defeats so dreadful for Marx and his generation was not merely the repression and mass murder – this was to be expected from the Party of Order – but the mysterious, even bizarre character of the new social formations. The mystery seemed deepest in

France, where reality had once seemed so clear: the Second Empire, a strong centralist state that repressed bourgeois liberalism as much as proletarian socialism, that stood above all classes and exploited them all.

The defeats of 1848–51 shattered Marx's life, not only politically and economically but psychologically as well. In exile, unconnected, unemployed (except for intermittent journalism, often brilliant and original, but often underpaid or not paid at all), always hounded by the police, Marx was more than ever thrown back on himself and the dangerous dynamisms of his inner life. And yet, Seigel argues, in the depths of his solitude, Marx was saved by a return of the repressed. He rediscovered the power of pure thought: his conceptual and theoretical powers, which he had dreamed of putting to sleep, now came marvelously awake and brought him a new and fruitful life. He renewed his inner links with Hegel and his strengths as a philosophical thinker. He accepted the mysterious nature of post-1848 capitalism, and the mystery of his (and so many other people's) isolation in its midst, and he concentrated all his inner resources on penetrating beneath its surfaces and plumbing its depths. In searching out the hidden structures and dynamics of capitalism, Marx came into touch with buried sources of energy and dynamism within himself. Thus a traumatic isolation prepared the ground for a series of new syntheses and triumphs, from *The 18th Brumaire of Louis Bonaparte* to *Capital*. The Hegelian conceptual structure of *Capital* has been known since the 1920s, when it was unveiled by Georg Lukács and Karl Korsch. Seigel is original in showing that structure's psychological foundations – and in showing, too, its terrible human costs. First of all, just as Heinrich Marx had feared in the 1830s, the part of Karl's nature that pulled him toward Hegelian pure thought also pulled him away from the material world, from human feelings, from the people who loved and

needed him most. Thus, while Jenny and the children starved and suf-
fered dreadfully for fifteen years (circumstances eased up only in the late
1860s), Marx largely withdrew from responsibility for their material and
human needs, to wrestle in solitude with ultimate ideal truths. ("When
you, poor little devil, have to go through the bitter reality" – he writes this
to Jenny as she is fighting off landlords, grocers, bailiffs – "it is no less
than just that I live through the torture at least ideally." Thus he cordons
off his wife to deal with reality on her own while he floats freely, though
perhaps not happily, in the sphere of the ideal.)

Second, his flight from material reality led him cruelly and systematically to wreck his own health: as much damage as he did to his loved ones,
he probably did even more to himself. (Maybe, unconsciously, he was
punishing himself for punishing them.) Third, his immersion in thought
often alienated him from the human realities that his thought was meant
to grasp. Hence, Seigel argues, especially in the later parts of *Capital*,
Marx's thought turned increasingly in on itself, and became hopelessly
uncommunicative; the deeper he delved, the closer he came to drowning
in his own material. Fourth, especially in his last years, Marx drove himself and everyone around him crazy by his refusal to finish *Capital*. "I had
to use every moment in which I was capable of working in order to
complete my book, to which I have sacrificed my health, my happiness
and my family." Marx wrote this in 1867, just as *Capital* Volume 1 was
about to appear; but he would keep making these sacrifices for another
sixteen years, indeed till the moment he died. Engels, Jenny, their daugh-
ters, all Marx's friends, urged him to let the work go, accept its imperfec-
tions and incompleteness, let it take its chances and do its work in the
world; but he held on for dear life, plunging ever deeper into its dialectics,
refusing to give it up until, somehow, its ideas would realize them*selves*.

Seigel is inexhaustible in generating ideas about Marx's life and his work and the connections between them. Sometimes his conjectures seem arbitrary and forced, and occasionally – as in dealing with Marx's mother, the most elusive figure in the story – gratuitously bitchy. But the overall level of his intuitions and speculations is impressively high, and *Marx's Fate* is full of fruitful suggestions for future working through. Sometimes, however, even where Seigel is doing well, we wish he would stop. He tends to do what he shows Marx doing: drown in his material. It is a measure of the book's peculiar power that this reviewer, too, feels himself pulled under with them.

This is a pity, because *Marx's Fate* would have twice its impact if it were half its size. Instead of trying to cover everything and prove everything, Seigel should have presented his vision as clearly and vividly as possible, and let it run on its own power. It would have gone far, because as an intellectual vision it is very impressive. It reveals the isolation and anguish that were interfused with Marx's most radical creativity. It explains why Marx so often tried to represent his thought – and, indeed, thought in general – as a passive mouthpiece for material forces; but it also makes clear what a desperate and pathetic piece of wishful thinking this was. It shows Marx as one of the great tormented giants of the nineteenth century – alongside Beethoven, Goya, Tolstoy, Dostoevsky, Ibsen, Nietzsche, Van Gogh – who drive us crazy, as they drove themselves, but whose agony generated so much of the spiritual capital on which we all still live.

Seigel is brilliant in illuminating Marx's shadows. In at least one place, however, he sees more shadows than are really there. For Seigel the great tragedy of Marx's life was his inability to finish *Capital*. He likens Marx to the hero of a Balzac story that Marx loved, "The Unknown Masterpiece." Balzac's hero, recognized universally as one of the great painters of his age (the age of Poussin, who appears as a character in the story), buries himself in his studio for thirty years to create a work that will not only be surpassingly beautiful – that, for him, would be nothing new – but will revolutionize all art. Finally, his peers win admission to his studio and are horrified by what they see: the canvas has been so endlessly reworked, and overlaid with so many layers of paint, and so many different ideas, that it is utterly unintelligible. In one corner of the canvas a human foot is visible, a vestige of the original inspiration, radiantly beautiful, but enveloped and overwhelmed by chaos. This, Seigel seems to say, is Marx's own story. (He doesn't take us to the end of the story, in which the old painter, finding his vision meaningless to others, burns all his works and dies in the flames.)

But there is a whole other layer of meaning in "The Unknown Master-piece," ignored by Seigel, but profoundly relevant to Marx. Balzac's de-scription of the old man's great work is in fact a perfect description of a twentieth-century abstract painting. The fact that Balzac could not have known this only gives it a deeper resonance. The point is that, where one age sees only chaos and incoherence, a later or more modern age may discover meaning and beauty. Thus the very open-endedness of Marx's later work can make contact with our time in ways that more "finished" nineteenth-century work cannot; *Capital* reaches beyond the well-made works of Marx's century into the discontinuous modernism of our own.

It is worth noting that, in volume one of *Capital*, Marx plays with the idea of an ending, makes us think he's bringing us to an ending, only to shift and surprise us at the last moment. The would-be ending comes in Chapter 33, "The Historical Tendency of Capitalist Accumulation." Here we find, in its most compressed and dramatic form, a scenario for the developing inner contradictions of capitalism, leading to proletarian revolution and bourgeois collapse. Increasingly, "the monopoly of capital becomes a fetter" on the modern forces of production that capital has brought into being. "The centralization of production and the socialization of labor reach a point at which they become incompatible with their capitalist husk. The husk is burst asunder. The knell of capitalist property sounds. The expropriators are expropriated." A fine dramatic climax, and a perfect moment, we might think, at which to end the book. And yet, although the end is a mere ten pages off, Marx suddenly takes us off into a whole new metamorphosis of capital: Chapter 34, "The Modern Theory of Colonization," or how capitalism transplants itself into virgin soil, and envelops the whole undeveloped world. As we fade out, we see capital, having torn the American continent to pieces, girding itself to do the same to Australia. The dramatic impact is stunning: it brings us down from the apocalyptic heights of Chapter 33, back into the real world in which, while we were out fantasizing about its end, capital was busy accumulating more capital.

So wouldn't it have been absurd for Marx to finish his great work: How can *Capital* end while capital lives on? To stop simply and abruptly, rather than create an ending, preserves far more of the truth that *Capital* has to tell: circling, spiraling, plunging one way and another, turning in upon himself, seeking endlessly for new axes to turn on, Marx kept his thought and his work as open-ended, and hence as resilient and long-lived, as the capitalist system itself. This is why we are still only beginning to explore the depths of Marx's thought: why he speaks to us in a voice fresher than ever today; and why he will be dancing up Broadway when we are all dead.

Seigel does not see all this, but he sees so much that his work deserves our warmest admiration. *Marx's Fate* helps us understand how modern social thought, as much as modern poetry and art, is at once an expression of personal loneliness and an attempt to overcome that loneliness. Once we can feel the depths of Marx's solitude – and his need for connections with people and life – we will appreciate his achievement in creating real bonds between man and man. In the depths of Marx's spirit, we can nourish our own.

Notes

1. One striking exception is Yvonne Kapp, *Eleanor Marx* (New York: Pantheon, 1972). Kapp, more than any writer I have come across, has an intuitive and nonjudgmental feeling for the dynamics of the Marx family. The fact that Karl is not her center makes her less judgmental and emotionally freer than Marx biographers tend to be.

2. [1999] Even after *forty* years. In *Civilization and Its Discontents,* Freud argued that having a father who was supportive and nice was no help to the growing subject, because revolt against a saint (and Heinrich Marx was close to it) had no moral legitimacy in the world, whereas revolt against a rat might be excused.

3. "… a time when so many writers who once made their living by explicit or tacit borrowing from the great wealth of Marxian ideas and insights have decided to become professional anti-Marxists, in the process of which one of them has even discovered that Karl Marx himself was unable to make a living, forgetting for a moment the generations of authors whom he has 'supported,'" Hannah Arendt, *The Human Condition* (New York: Anchor, 1959), 71.

2

Freedom and Fetishism

There is a certain paradoxicality at the heart of Marx's whole enterprise. Sometimes he understands freedom not as a value but as a fact, not as something men ought to pursue but as something they cannot avoid – a synthetic a priori truth about human action, a *liberté* to which (in Sartre's phrase) man is *condemné*. At other times, however, he regards freedom as an *achievement*: a difficult feat that is possible only after such "labor of the negative"(Hegel) – a labor of liberating oneself from the illusions of the particular "illusory community" that surrounds one, of getting out (as Wittgenstein put it) of the fly-bottle one finds oneself inside. When he describes capitalist society, Marx is constantly making the point that everything in it is under "illusions of the epoch," is dominated by "fetishism," and hence is unfree – except, of course, for the "fully conscious"

This is a chapter from the B. Litt. thesis I wrote at Oxford in 1963 under the supervision of Isaiah Berlin: "Freedom and Individuality in the Thought of Karl Marx."

revolutionary group. "As in religion, man is governed by the products of his own brain, so in capitalist production, he is governed by the products of his own hand" (*Capital,* 681).[1] The freedom Marx has given with one hand he seems to be taking back with the other: everywhere he looks, everyone seems to be in chains. Yet if men are "free," how is it possible for them to have got into such a state of "unfreedom" in the first place? Or, alternately, if men are encased in a fly-bottle, how will it be possible for them to see things in any way but through a glass, darkly? If their whole outlook on life is "fetishistic," how will it be possible even to recognize that they are enslaved, let alone make the effort to set themselves free? The paradox here is the familiar paradox of self-deception. Who, exactly, is supposed to be doing the "deceiving"? If the subject himself, in what sense is it meaningful to say that he is actually "deceived"? If it is meaningful, how, once having succeeded, can he undo the job, and "undeceive" himself? These are perennial problems for a therapist, not to mention a philosopher; they are also central to Marx's analysis of capitalism as an "infantile disease," he might have said, of man, who with its passing was "coming into his own."

We can find many passages in which the tendency of the capitalist system to enslave everyone is mentioned. In *The Holy Family,*[2] for instance:

> The slavery of civil society [*bürgerlichen Gesellschaft*] is ostensibly the greatest freedom, because it appears to leave the individual perfectly independent. The individual considers as his own freedom the movement (no longer curbed or fettered by a common tie or by man) of his alienated life-elements, like property, industry, religion; in reality, this movement is the perfection of his slavery. ... (157)

Again, in *Capital*, the achievement of individual freedom in modern times is seen, dialectically, to have generated its antithesis:

> ... the same division of labor that turns [men] into independent produc-
> ers, also frees the social process of production, and the relation of individ-
> ual producers to each other within that process, from all dependence on
> the will of those producers; and so ... the seeming independence of
> individuals gives rise to a system of universal and mutual dependence
> through or by means of the products. (121)

The exchange of commodities "develops a whole network of social relations spontaneous in their growth and entirely beyond the control of the
actors" (126). Freedom is here only an "appearance" (*Erscheinung*), and
appearances, notoriously, deceive.

A Whig interpreter of history, however, in the Victorian England in
which *Capital* appeared, might take Marx up on this. "*Are* Englishmen in
chains?" he might ask. "Suffrage and education, after all, are virtually
universal; religious tests have been abolished; the feudal ties that bound
men to the land or town, class or trade, have vanished long ago; protec-
tion against arbitrary arrest, detention or hindrance is enshrined in the
English Constitution; it is hard to see how the institutions of *any* country
at *any* time could be less obstructive, or more conducive, to human freedom. True, the lives of the majority may not be economically *secure;* true
again, the distribution of wealth may not be *just* – we don't pretend that
our social order is perfect (just yet). But in what sense is it meaningful to
say that it isn't *free?*"

Now according to certain commentators, this sinks Marx. Men are
free, he is supposed to have thought, only when they are "rational";
communism alone, he is supposed to have thought, is a rational form of

life; hence, it is deduced neatly, all actions and men under non-communistic forms of life are unfree: Q.E.D. (This is a crude caricature of the reading which Isaiah Berlin cleverly and subtly elaborates in his *Karl Marx*.)[3] If Marx were indeed saying this, he would be guilty of what we today should call a "persuasive definition": he would be stealing the prestige and good will that people attach to the word *freedom*, which has a fairly clear and measurable sense in daily life, and annexing it to a notion of "rationality" that is far more shadowy, ambiguous and hard to cash – we might say, appropriating surplus value. Having once discovered his intentions, we would realize that in alleging an absence of "freedom" in bourgeois society Marx was not telling us anything new about it, but merely trying to inflame us against it in a devious way.

In fact, however, Marx uses the word *freedom* in a way that is both more conventional and more illuminating. In a highly compressed passage on the fetishism of commodities, Marx suggests what a non-fetishistic society would be like:

> The life-process of society, which is based on the process of production, … does not strip off its mystical veil until it is treated as production by *freely associated men,* and is *consciously* regulated by them *in accordance with a settled plan.* (*Capital,* 92; emphases are mine)

To act freely here is to "consciously regulate" one's life "in accordance with a settled plan." Marx does not claim that the plan must have any particular content – that it must be communistic – for the planner to be free. The concept of liberty he presupposes is basically similar to the "negative" one used in ordinary language: an absence of restraint. He insists, however, that *being* free necessarily entails the *consciousness* that one *is* free. We can cash this behaviorally as a "disposition" to assess possibilities, investigate alternatives, weigh considerations, choose what one will do. For an "average individual," someone whose thought is "fetishistic," however, no such "consciousness" exists, no such disposition will be found. Now the hypothetical Whig whom I introduced (he could be any liberal democrat of the nineteenth century, perhaps of the twentieth as well) has described all sorts of possibilities for life that supposedly exist in the England of his day, and brought these forward as evidence of an almost total freedom. Yet if Marx could show that a significant portion of people, perhaps even a majority, are simply *not aware* of such prospects for choice, then the paradox he has advanced that men who are born free, and whose freedom has been so stridently proclaimed since 1789, are as firmly in chains as ever, would acquire striking plausibility and power.

There is one especially striking observation Marx makes, which runs like a red thread through *Capital*, about the radical difference between capitalists and all previous accumulators of wealth. The ordinary "simple circulation of commodities," he writes, the act of "selling in order to buy," is "a means of carrying out a purpose unconnected with circulation, namely the appropriation of use-values, the satisfaction of wants. The circulation of money *as capital*, on the contrary, is *an end in itself*" (*Capital*, 169). This endless pursuit is the very touchstone of capitalist activity:

> It is only insofar as the appropriation of ever more and more wealth in the abstract becomes the sole motive of [a man's] operations, that he functions *as* a capitalist, that is, as capital personified and endowed with consciousness and a will. Use-values must never be looked on as the real aim of the capitalist; neither must profit on any single transaction. The *restless, never-ending pursuit of profitmaking* alone is what he aims at. (*Capital*, 170)

Similar formulations abound. "Use-values are produced by capitalists only because, and insofar as, they are ... depositaries of exchange-values" (207). "As capitalist," a man comes to have "one single life-impulse, the tendency to create value and surplus-value, to make ... the means of production absorb the greatest possible amount of surplus-value" (257). Marx compares the capital to "a conqueror who sees in every country annexed only a new boundary," and the activity of accumulation itself to the labor of Sisyphus (150). In his monomania to accumulate, the capitalist is like "an automaton ... endowed with intelligence and will, animated by the longing to reduce to a minimum the resistance offered by that repellent yet elastic natural barrier, man." The social system he runs is "an industrial *perpetuum mobile,* which would go on producing forever, did it not meet with certain natural obstructions in the weak bodies and the strong minds of its attendants" (440). His course, like that of the lawyer Tulkinghorn in Dickens's *Bleak House* – another spirit of the bourgeois age – is "straight on – over everything, neither to the right nor to the left, regardless of all considerations, treading everything underfoot" along the single track of his life.

These vivid metaphors bring out the single-minded, relentless character of capitalist accumulation: yet for all that, the activity is not necessarily *unfree*. Its fanaticism might well be *"moral* fanaticism," freely chosen and carried out; after all, the great "world-historical figures" of the past have been fanatics themselves. Indeed, in a sense *every* morality is "fanatic," in that it rests on an arbitrary, ultimately unjustifiable choice of *something* as an end in itself. The skeptical questioner who always asked "But *why* is it good? What is it good *for?*" could never get an answer that would satisfy him. There is thus no reason why capitalist accumulation should be any less suitable "as an end in itself" than anything else.

But Marx sees evidence that would disqualify capitalism from the status of a morality, and hence free action. Whatever else *free action* may mean, it certainly entails that the actor must be aware of alternative possibilities; and we should not consider an action legitimately moral if the actor could not even conceive what it might be like to be *im*moral, where his act involved no element of *choice*. If we examine the ordinary language of the capitalists, however, it is precisely this element of choice we find lacking. For example, when the Children's Employment Commission suggests that twelve hours during the daytime are about long enough for children to spend in a factory, one E. F. Sanderson, a steel manufacturer, indignantly protests: "But then there would be the loss from so much expensive machinery lying idle half the time. ..." What is most intriguing about the Sandersons is their naiveté. It isn't as if they shrugged off the suffering of children as something morally *unimportant*; rather, this suffering seems to be something they simply don't *notice*. Every minute idle *is* a minute "lost"; it does not occur to them that other points of view are possible, from which twelve hours' rest per day for growing boys and girls might be a "gain." Marx explains this insensitivity by explicating the peculiar game the capitalists are playing:

> Messrs. Sanderson have something to make besides steel. Steel-making *is simply a pretext for surplus-value-making*. The smelting-furnaces, the rolling-mills, the buildings, machinery, iron, coal, etc., have something more to do than transform themselves into steel. They are there to absorb surplus-labor, and naturally absorb more in twenty-four hours than in twelve. (289)

Given these aims, it is only natural that when a capitalist looks at a worker he should see only one thing:

What is a working-day?" ... Capital replies: the working-day includes *the full twenty-four hours*, with the deduction for the few hours of repose without which labor-power absolutely refuses its services again. Hence it is evident that the laborer is *nothing else, his whole life through, than labor-power,* that therefore all his disposable time is ... labor-time, to be devoted to the self-expansion of capital. (291; emphases mine)

"The world," says Wittgenstein, "is all that is the case." Labor-power, capital, commodities, surplus-value: these *Tatsachen* encase the world of the bourgeoisie. But there is something odd about this world: its "atomic facts" serve as its basic values as well. All possible *de*scriptions have *pre*-scriptions built in; words themselves define the "proper" attitude to be adopted toward all the things they describe – and thus save men the trouble of morally making up their minds. But if, as we said above, freedom is logically bound up with choice; and if the capitalist outlook on the world tends to evade choice; and if, as Marx wrote in 1842, "Morality rests on the autonomy, religion on the heteronomy of the spirit" – then it is clear that it is as a religion, and not as a morality, that capitalist fanaticism must be understood.

This is precisely the sort of explanation Marx is attempting in his discussion of the "fetishism of commodities":

> ... we must have recourse to the mist-enveloped regions of the religious world. In that world the productions of the human brain appear as independent beings endowed with life, and entering into relation both with one another and with the human race. So it is in the world of commodities with the products of men's hands ... (*Capital*, 83)

The function of fetishism, and of religion in general, is to relieve the believer of responsibility for his actions. It is not *he* who is acting, it is the

God (or daemon) who is acting in and through him; *he* cannot criticize, modify or change the world; he, like the world itself, is merely the vehicle of an alien Will. Similarly, the capitalist denies that it is in his power even to try to alter the ruinous processes of the market: it operates according to "eternal laws" to which he and all men are helplessly subjected. The fiction of Natural Law – which plays on all the ambiguities of both "nature" and "law," and through which descriptive and normative discourse are fused – is immensely powerful in keeping men riveted to their roles. "The laws of commerce," Marx quotes Burke as saying, "are the Laws of Nature, and therefore the laws of God." A profitable confusion indeed: "No wonder," Marx comments caustically, "that, true to the laws of God and Nature, he always sold himself in the best market" (834). But it is vital for the stability of the system that the workers too should be enthralled by this sort of myth, lest they get inflamed by rebellious discontent. "It's not enough that conditions of labor are concentrated in a mass, in the shape of capital, while at the other are grouped masses of men who have nothing to sell but their labor-power. Nor is it enough that they are compelled to sell it voluntarily." If the locomotive of capitalist production is to advance at full steam, the workers must be reconciled to consuming themselves as its fuel: it must develop "a working-class which, by education, tradition, habit, looks upon the conditions of this mode of production as self-evident laws of nature" (809). The fetishism of commodities is a deterministic myth, designed to conserve the existing order by convincing the people in it that they can do no other. By picturing themselves as unfree, men *make* themselves unfree: their prophecy of powerlessness is self-fulfilling.

How can this paralyzing picture be shattered, this confusion dispelled? Sometimes Marx places his hope in a sort of therapy-by-history. He tries to show that the relationships which the bourgeois "laws of the market" describe are far from being eternal and necessary, that in fact they are only recent innovations, the outcome of specific historical events. Now it is true that any system of definitions can be stretched to cover all possible situations. Still, it is empirically possible to point out counterexamples which would necessitate stretching the definitions so far that even their adherents will see the absurdity and give them up. In contrasting bourgeois with ancient and feudal economic relationships, this is what Marx is seeking to do. To sum up:

> One thing is clear – Nature does not produce on the one hand owners of money or commodities, and on the other hand men producing nothing but their labor-power. This relationship has no natural basis, neither is its social basis one common to all historical periods. It is clearly the result of a past historical development, the product of many economic revolutions, of the extinction of a whole series of older forms of social production. (188)

Relationships and values which seemed as inexorable as space and time are shown by historical analysis to be contingent, determinate: their "sacred" character, as pillars of a world-order, is profaned:

> The categories of bourgeois economics ... are forms of thought expressing ... the conditions of a definite, historically determinate [bestimmten] mode of production – the production of commodities. The whole mystery of commodities, all the magic and necromancy that surround the products of labor as long as they take this form, vanish as soon as we come to other modes of production. (87)

In examining these different modes of production, we discover the one thing that persists amidst them all: "living labor," human will and energy, "the force that creates value" (340). Thus,

> the existence of things *qua* commodities, and the value relation between the products of things that stamps them as commodities, have *absolutely no connection* with their physical properties and the material relationships arising therefrom. It is a specific *social* relation, between *men*, which takes on for them the fantastic form of a relation between *things* ... (83; emphases mine)

Standards of value have "absolutely no connection" – no *necessary* connection, Marx means to say – with the structure of the world, but are "social relations between *men*" and can be changed if men so desire. In pointing this out, Marx is continuing a program he outlined twenty years before, in his *Critique of Hegel's Philosophy of Right*:

> The basis of irreligious criticism is this: *man makes religion*, religion does not make man. ... It is the task of history, once the world beyond the truth has disappeared, to establish the truth of *this* world. The immediate task of philosophy, which is in the service of history, is to unmask human self-alienation in its *profane* form now that it has been unmasked in its *holy* form. Thus the criticism of heaven is transformed into a criticism of earth, the criticism of religion into a criticism of law and right, the criticism of theology into a criticism of politics. (*MER*, 53)

In *Capital*, Marx is pointing out simply that man makes economics too, that modes of production are by no means beyond the reach of human direction and control. This may seem obvious today. But if we consider how much thought and action were frozen into rigid forms by the many fatalistic myths of the nineteenth century, we might wish that Marx had expended even more labor-power in the attempt to jar men loose – and indeed, that he had not occasionally damaged the cause himself by falling into just the sort of "fetishism" he knew how to expose so well.

Conceptual analysis, Marx believed, might play an important part in shattering false, fetishistic pictures of human experience, and restoring to men the freedom they seem to want to escape. But while this sort of strategy may be quite effective in shaking an exploited class out of apathy and showing it that it really *can* change the world, it is not likely to go over very well with a class on top. A ruling class is "comfortable in its self-alienation"; it "finds in this self-alienation its confirmation and its good" (*Holy Family,* 151); it has a very powerful interest in remaining deceived by the myths it propagates. Humankind cannot bear very much reality, even in the best of times; when the reality is embarrassing or grim, it is all the more difficult to face. A social group under stress is just as apt as is an individual in therapy to construct mechanisms of defense: to exhibit the most elaborate strategies of "resistance" (Freud), to put on the thickest, most impermeable "character armor"– one can find (Reich), to avoid coming to grips with disconcerting facts. The patient may "not listen" when the most telling arguments are advanced, or may repeatedly, conveniently "forget," or may just shout out abuse very loud in an effort to drown out any upsetting thoughts that happen to bob up. In such a case, rational argument is unlikely to be of much avail.

But Marx felt that he had a more formidable ally in his campaign: time. The capitalist social system itself, he saw, was evolving toward a situation in which the drives and illusions that sustained it in its youth would somehow wither away, and the men in it would once again come to regard themselves as free – without, however, necessarily changing its capitalist base. In Chapter 24 of the first volume of *Capital,* Marx very suggestively sketches out a typology of stages in the life of capitalism: a "classical" phase, whose features *Capital* vividly (and luridly) describes, and a "modernized" phase, which Marx felt was just beginning to appear on the scene. These stages are embodied in two ideal personality types – archetypal men, "average individuals," who crystallize the changing aspirations of the bourgeois "illusory community," represent everything its members want to be. Without going into the very difficult problem – in part psychological, in part sociological, in part conceptual – of precisely what leads men to stop playing one role, and start playing another, to discard one stereotyped "average individuality" in favor of another, I want briefly to examine the two types Marx develops and make clear the contrasting forms of life which they are intended to bring out.

The keynote of the first, "classical" phase of capitalism is production and accumulation (here Marx conflates the two) as an end in itself: "Accumulation for accumulation's sake, production for production's sake! By this formula, political economy expressed the historic mission of the bourgeoisie." The bourgeoisie pursue it with a missionary zeal: "Accumulate! Accumulate! That is Moses and the prophets. ..." (*Capital*, 652) Marx's images and allusions should always be taken seriously: the typical capitalist in this phase is as fervid and relentless in producing and accumulating as the religious fanatic is in fulfilling God's Will on earth – and his mind is just as much of a closed circle, just as impervious to doubt and debate. Marx is suggesting here a deeper connection between religion and capitalism than even Weber conceived: the religious and the capitalistic zealot share the same "fetishistic" frame of mind, in which the distinction between fact and value is blurred, and in which they "can do no other" because their system of descriptions blinds them to even the possibility of choice. And it is no accident that both these types of fetishist should be ascetic. "So far as [a man's] actions are a mere function of capital," so long as he plays the capitalist role, "his own private consumption is a robbery. ... a sin against his *function*" (649–50). The fetishist feels that he exists only to fulfill a function; the slightest deviation from his role brings his very "being" into question, evokes a guilt that shakes him to his quick.

After a time, however, a new ideal type comes to grip men's minds. "But Original Sin is at work everywhere. As capitalist production, accumulation and wealth become developed, the capitalist ceases to be the mere incarnation of capital. He gets a fellow-feeling for his own Adam. ..." Once again Marx's use of Christian imagery is crucial here. The classical capitalist lives on only to fulfill a function, to incarnate an ideal type; all his intentions follow logically from a principle – "Accumulate!" – and can be rigorously deduced in advance; his role, we might say, plays him. This systematic, methodist perfection typifies a recurrent Christian ideal: to be free of the burden of spontaneity, of unpredictable impulse and uncontrollable desire. To be all principle and no passion: this is the status which Christian theology reserves for angels (and indeed for devils of the more dangerous sort), but from which men, immersed in weakness and imperfection, are inexorably debarred. In this sense, it is illuminating to speak of the post-classical capitalist as getting infected with "Original Sin" and developing "a feeling for his own Adam": his spontaneous impulses and the "irrational" play of his desires come to matter to him, he no longer sees his accumulating function as the only thing in life. After his prodigies of production, he begins to see the pursuit of pleasure, the consumer's life, as equally appealing. This new outlook, plus a certain degree of education (gained through "practical-critical activity," perhaps), "gradually enables him to" smile at this rage for asceticism, as a mere prejudice of the old-fashioned miser. While the capitalist of the classical type brands individual consumption as a sin against his function, as a distraction from accumulating, the modernized capitalist is capable of looking on accumulation as a distraction from pleasure. The anguish and anomie which the modern capitalist must undergo are well expressed in Faust's lines, which Marx quotes: "Two souls are living in my breast."

Marx goes on to say, "At the historical dawn of capitalist accumulation – and every capitalist upstart must go through this historical phase – avarice, and the desire to get rich, are the ruling passions." (Here Marx makes the curious nineteenth-century assumption, found in every great thinker from Hegel through Freud, that each individual must reenact in his own life the entire previous life of the species.) These passions never pass away. But later on, "when a certain stage of development has been reached, ... there is at the same time developed in his breast a Faustian conflict between the passion for accumulation and the desire for enjoyment" (650–51). In this "consumer" period the capitalist becomes like other men: he regards himself as a free agent, able to step back from his role as producer and accumulator, even to give it up entirely for the sake of pleasure or happiness; for the first time he sees his life as an open book, as something to be shaped according to his choice. Fetishism, then, infuses the youthful exuberance of capitalism with a religious zeal – and a religious naiveté; disenchantment comes with a fullness of years, and may slacken the pace, but leaves a new freedom in its wake. Men no longer feel compelled to fulfill the infinite demands of an alien Will; they are free at last to think of themselves.

As capitalists in an age of consumption become free, one would think, and pursue their own happiness instead of the aims of a relentless alien Power, they must inevitably become less fervid and blindly compulsive, more mellow, pliable and humane – more "humane" if only because more *human*, less like angels or machines. Now of course, Marx felt, this might well happen in *some* cases; but there were very good reasons not to be too optimistic. Fetishism, he saw, might prove so powerful as to make a fetish of the very desire that would dissolve it. The capitalist system then would simply devour and assimilate this nascent desire for happiness, and turn it to its own advantage. Thus "a conventional degree of prodigality, which is also an exhibition of wealth, and consequently a source of credit, becomes a business necessity. ... Luxury becomes part of capital's overhead." Marx is anticipating Veblen's analysis of "conspicuous consumption"; but he sees that conspicuous consumption need not retard accumulation, and indeed might even drive it more furiously on. "Therefore, the prodigality of the capitalist never possesses the bona fide character of the open-handed feudal lord's prodigality, but, on the contrary, has always lurking behind it the most sordid avarice and the most anxious calculation ..." (651). Where pleasure becomes a business, it must acquire up-to-date business methods – that is, must duplicate all the compulsive calculation, all the cutthroat competition, all the frenzied self-alienation it was meant to allay. David Riesman, William H. Whyte and others have shown (without acknowledgment – though probably without knowledge either) how far Marx's prediction has come true: how much leisure today has become a business affair, a realm of "antagonistic co-operation" (Riesman) in which all the obsessions of the bourgeois working-day rage on and get re-enacted beneath a facade of idyllic calm. Still, Marx said, despite all this, "the desire for enjoyment" in its pure form, once ignited, could never be stamped out; hence men would never let their freedom entirely go again, and the "Faustian conflict"– would persist and modify capitalism as long as it lasted.

Marx does not say how he thinks the transformation of capitalists into free men will affect the class struggle. But based on the interpretations I have made up to now, we might try an educated guess. Men who are animated by "fetishism," be it religious, political or economic, will charge blindly ahead like locomotives at full speed on a single track; if they collide and destroy each other they can't help it, there is nothing to be done. For free men, however, there is at least a *possibility* of averting disaster. To understand what freedom means – that I am not compelled to live according to any a priori rules, but may prescribe my own rules and shape my life as I choose – is to recognize that other men are free agents themselves. To affirm myself and recognize others as free, in this sense, is to realize that orientations other than my own, and no less "true," are possible, that many different moral points of view may be sincerely held. This does not mean hedging on my own ultimate values – if I am a capitalist, it does not entail that I should stop accumulating; but it psychologically *may* (not logically *must*) mean that when ultimate values collide I will be willing to compromise, to step slightly back, to give a bit of ground without destroying the ground of my self-respect.

I have tried to throw into clear relief Marx's picture of the individual in history: in particular, his conception of individual freedom. Now no one saw more vividly than Marx the powerful pull which "illusory communities" of class interest could exert on men: stereotyping their thought into clichés; freezing the flow of their emotions into rigid, inflexible human forms; transforming human action into "acting out," into stale replayings of prefabricated roles; in short, reducing men to "average individuals," reproductions of ideal types which embody all the traits and qualities the "illusory community" needs. But such a reduction, Marx felt, could never be complete: no matter how hard men tried to dissolve themselves in roles, there would always be something left-over; human freedom might constrict, but would never disappear. It would always be open to every individual to "assert himself *as* an individual" over against the "illusory community" that constricts and constrains him. Marx's formula for free action is "practical-critical activity": the activity of forming projects and plans for one's life, modifying them in the light of experience, and striving to put them into effect. In a society that would dissolve all individual identity and press all men into molds – such as the bourgeois society of Marx's day – "practical-critical activity" must take the form of *"revolutionary* activity," for only through conscious resistance to such a society can individuality survive. But it was vital for the community of revolutionaries to avoid degenerating into just another "illusory community" themselves; and Marx felt that personal independence could be protected only in a *moral* community, in which individuals act not primarily for their own benefit, or for that of the group as such, but for the sake of all mankind. Only a "world-historical class," one whose interests and ideals are fused, is capable of decisively enlarging the scope of freedom for all. Marx saw the proletariat as the only group in his society that had any chance of becoming "world-historical," and he did all he could to guide it in that direction. In his historical works, he made it his own vocation to keep the revolutionary vision sharp and clear: to stress the distinction between ideal and real, to protect the proletariat from deterministic myths, and to emphasize that the revolutionary project was voluntary and free. With the advent of communist society, however, men will no longer have to revolt in order to be free: they will be able to work out their projects and designs, to develop themselves, in the everyday round of life, during their working-day, through the medium of labor. In a society of abundance and planned production, work can be made interesting and related to individual inclinations, so that the presently accepted dualism of "material" necessity and "spiritual" freedom, of maintaining one's life and enjoying it, will wither away. Such, then, is Marx's vision of individual freedom and his program for extending its scope – one quite different from that which is usually ascribed to him.

Notes

1. *Capital: A Critique of Political Economy,* trans. Samuel Moore and Edward Aveling (New York: Modern Library, n.d.). This edition was originally published by Charles H. Kerr in 1906.

2. *The Holy Family: Critique of Critical Critique,* trans. B. Dixon (Moscow: Foreign Languages Publishers, 1956).

3. Isaiah Berlin, *Karl Marx: His Life and Environment,* 3d edn. (Oxford: Oxford University Press, 1963 [1939].

3

Still Waiting at the Station

None of the eulogies for Edmund Wilson has mentioned what seems to me his most splendid achievement: to have written the last great nineteenth-century novel. *To the Finland Station* originally appeared in 1940, and it was hailed generally as a sensitive, exciting history of the modern radical movement that reached its climax (or, at least, one of its climaxes) in the Bolshevik Revolution. Now, a generation after, we have a new edition, and an occasion to reappraise the book in the context of a new age, and I want to argue that it is far more original and more powerful than its first generation of readers could have known. Its virtues are so striking now because they are virtues that are not merely absent, but virtually forgotten, in both the fiction and the nonfiction writing of today.

The first thing that strikes us about *To the Finland Station* today, as soon

Review of Edmund Wilson, *To the Finland Station: A Study in the Writing and Acting of History* (New York: Farrar, Straus & Giroux, 1972). This essay first appeared in the *New York Times Book Review*, August 20, 1972.

as we are a little way into the book, is the breathtaking vastness of its scope. It takes in the whole of Europe and America, over the course of a century and a half. It cuts back and forth, effortlessly, from Vico's Naples to Babeuf's Paris to Brook Farm to Marx's London to Trotsky's Petersburg. It is easily, equally at home in the philosopher's study, in the prisoner's cell, on the steppes, in the streets, melancholy in great country houses, choking in the fetid industrial slums – and it brings all these worlds vividly home to us. It interweaves philosophy, sociology, psychobiography, literary criticism, economic analysis, political history and theory, always in complex and sophisticated ways – and yet, for all this, the human narrative hardly ever flags, but sweeps us breathlessly along.

And the characters! An inexhaustible cast of brilliant, exciting, driven, beautiful, heroic, demonic people – Marx and Engels, Babeuf, Michelet, Proudhon, Bakunin, Saint-Simon, Fourier, Robert Owen, Lassalle, Lenin and Trotsky, and many more – at first they seem larger than life, but by and by we learn to live on their scale. And not only the great figures, but minor characters as well – dozens of them, wives and children, friends, enemies, lovers, rivals – nearly every one a real individual, drawn with exquisite sensitivity and care. As Wilson leads us, dizzily, on extended wings, we realize that we are back in the world of the great international novels, a world at once more concretely real and more marvelously romantic than any world we know. And we recognize in *To the Finland Station* a legitimate child of *War and Peace*.

The idea that binds all these people in all these times and places together, that animates this book and gives it an organic unity, is the great romantic dream of Revolution. Since 1789, Wilson makes clear, this dream has been absolutely central to Western imagination (increasingly, of course, to non-Western imagination as well, but that is another story);

what we understand today as the main traditions of modern culture could never have taken shape without it. It is a dream of people taking their lives into their own hands, coming together to forge a common destiny, to create a wholly new kind of society: a community based on liberty and equality, in which men and women can express themselves as individuals more freely, and love one another more intensely and deeply, than human beings have ever done before. It is "humanity creating itself."

Wilson starts his story in the reactionary torpor of the 1820s – the bleak years when Stendhal's Julien Sorel was coming of age. He explores the life and work of Jules Michelet, the Revolution's first great historian, to show us how the revolutionary dream could light up the lives of lonely men in dark times. In the pages of Michelet's *History of France,* Wilson writes, "The centuries leading up to the Revolution are like a long and solitary youth, waiting year after year for self-expression, release, the assertion of unacknowledged rights, free association with others." At last, in the great days of 1789–91, the release comes, the vision lives. "At no other times, I believe," wrote Michelet, "has the heart of man been more spacious." Poor and alone, Wilson says, Michelet "derived from the Revolution just behind him a sense of solidarity with others engaged in a great human undertaking, and through history he succeeded in making himself part of the human world. ..." He brought the vision beautifully to life and made its power available for generations to come.

The tragic hero of Wilson's story, filling the center of the stage, looming over all the rest even long after he is gone, is Karl Marx. For Marx grasped the vision more forcefully and thoroughly than anyone; he struggled unremittingly with its deepest contradictions in all his work and acted out, as Wilson shows, some of its darkest ambiguities in the course of his life. For Marx understood, better than any bourgeois thinker, the

revolutionary potential inherent in bourgeois society: its infinite produc-
tivity; its ability to break through the ice of entrenched prejudice, stupid-
ity and inertia; its largeness of vision, embracing the whole world, ap-
praising every human relationship and form of life; its will to grow and
develop, its openness to the future. At the same time, he saw – and
explained definitely in *Capital* – the human horror that all this progress
brings in its wake: the bourgeoisie can liberate human energy only by
destroying human beings, using them as raw materials, resources to exploit, throwing them on the slag-heap when they are used up, grinding
them to pieces when they get in the way.

Marx's life, as Wilson interprets it, incarnates the conflicting forces at
the heart of the society he understood so well. We see him in London,
desperately poor, helpless as his children sicken and die, withering with
rage against countless enemies, capitalist and socialist, visible and invisible, unable to work cooperatively with anyone – Wilson brings out the
darker sides of his "partnership" with Engels – exploiting cruelly the
people he loved most (his wife and children above all) in order to produce
his great work and help end exploitation forever, wracked with guilt for
the way he lived but powerless to stop the inner engine or demon that
drove him insatiably on. Wilson's characterization of Marx is brilliant and
probably unsurpassable, almost Shakespearean in its tragic grandeur and
anguish. Forced to wound in order to create, Marx, the supreme enemy
of the bourgeoisie, stands forth as one of the authentic heroes of the
bourgeois age.

The last section of the book traces the rise of the revolutionary movement in Russia, starting in the middle of the nineteenth century, and
leading up to Lenin at the Finland Station in April 1917, returning trium-
phantly from exile abroad to lead the Revolution and bring the Bolshe-

viks to power. The book ends with Lenin borne from the train on the
shoulders of the masses, carried through Petersburg in the middle of the
night, waving to the crowds under the spotlights – a new kind of light,
remember, only just invented – while in the background the band plays
the "Marseillaise." It is a sublime moment in history, and Wilson evokes
and orchestrates it with marvelous dramatic power.

And yet, somehow, we find ourselves putting up more resistance than
Wilson – or even we ourselves – might expect. And if we do, Wilson has
no one to blame but himself. He wants us to see the scene at the Finland
Station as the fulfillment of the great collective revolutionary dream. But
his own concrete portraits of the Bolsheviks, and in particular of Lenin,
come across sounding more like savage indictments – all the more effective because unintended – than like the uncritical adorations he seems to
be trying to write.

Lenin, as Wilson interprets and celebrates him here, is utterly devoid
of any sort of human feeling. He totally avoids personal arguments,
personal conflicts, personal expressions of anything – for anything might
interfere with Party business. He fears, envies, needs, loves – nobody. He
refuses to listen to Beethoven, because he fears the music will touch him
and make him soft, and so more vulnerable and less effective. He "is the
most male of reformers because he never weeps; his attitude begins with
impatience." Wilson's Lenin incarnates a grim, heartless masculine mystique, and founds his revolution on this hard rock.

But for those of us who were inspired by the original romantic revolutionary dream, as Wilson himself seized and expressed it, and who have
followed him so far to see the vision unfold and develop, the sudden cold
depersonalization of this Finland Station is – the last place we will want
to go – far better even to jump off the train! The real mystery is what a

romantic and a tragedian like Wilson is doing in a place like this.

We can find a clue in the title of his last chapter on Marx: "Karl Marx Dies at His Desk." It is as if Wilson has felt a great surge of anger toward the people he most loves, all the passionate, complex, radiant, tragic people who fill his book. It is as if he has said to himself: Of course, people like this are bound to die at their desks, stooped over, shut in, closed off from the life and action of the world outside. As if he thought that the only way to arise from the misery of his desk was to cut the emotional cords that bound him to these beautiful losers, and try instead to enlist himself in a corps of indomitable precision machines. Our hearts and souls offend us – they make us vulnerable, lead us in contradictory ways, generate tragic conflicts that hold us back – and therefore let us pluck them out. And so, it seems, Wilson arose from the desk of his despair, to make a desperate leap into a one-dimensional faith.

Wilson's Leninist faith and hope do not seem to have lasted long. Barely a year after *To the Finland Station* first appeared, he was definitively back at his desk, grappling with human complexities and tragedies again, bitter toward the false god that had led him briefly astray. He lived at his desk for thirty years more and produced many illuminating and beautiful books. But he was never able to recover the world-historical breadth and expanse, the visionary intensity and power, that made *To the Finland Station* so great. It may be that faith, even the grossest bad faith, acts as a kind of crude fuel, which the inner flame of genius must feed on in order to burn bright.

The most common form of bad faith thirty years ago was to identify oneself totally with History, to act as if it presented us with ready-made final solutions, as if we did not have to decide what to do or how to live on our own. The commonest bad faith today is to act as if we were born yesterday, to believe that by simply ignoring history we can conjure away its power to shape and define what we do and who we are. In an age of historical amnesia, *To the Finland Station* can remind us that our history is alive and open and rich with excitement and promise. It can remind today's radicals of their own roots, and so put them in touch with sources of life and nourishment that they badly need to keep their vision and energy from drying up. And it can today remind defenders of "tradition" how radical our cultural traditions really are.

The historical imagination, Wilson says, not only "makes us feel … that we have lived through and known so many generations of men," but "makes us feel something more: that we ourselves are the last chapter of the story, and that the next chapter is for us to create." *To the Finland Station* is a work of the historical imagination at its most creative: it puts us in touch with the revolutionary dreams and visions of our past. If we read it well, we can use it to teach ourselves how to keep the dreams alive in the present, and maybe even, in the future, how to make the visions real. It can help us learn to create ourselves.

4

Studs Terkel: Living in the Mural

One of the most poignant and powerful of American dreams is the dream signified by the expression "Popular Front." These words are ordinarily held to denote a political and cultural policy adopted by international communism from 1934 to 1939, and again, through the Second World War, from 1941 to 1946: a policy of de-emphasizing struggles for revolution, and striving instead to unite all liberal and democratic forces within each country in the face of the dangers of Fascism. As the Cold War began, the Comintern pulled the plug on the Popular Front, and American Communism became a conspiratorial sect again. But, in America at least, the Popular Front policy had liberated immense imaginative energies that no party directive could kill. It organized the American labor movement into a powerful national force. It developed new ways to con-

Review of Studs Terkel, *Working: People Talk About What They Do All Day and How They Feel About What They Do* (New York: Pantheon, 1974). It first appeared in the *New York Times Book Review*, March 24, 1974.

trol capitalism: anyone who has ever lived in a rent-controlled or stabilized apartment is a direct beneficiary of Popular Front housing policy. But its greatest achievements are probably in the world of images: it articulated a vision of a genuinely democratic community, perhaps the first such coherent vision in American history.

This ideal community differed radically from the draconically purified New Jerusalem with which our Puritan founders had begun, and from the Populist idyll of an agrarian Paradise Lost, of the garden before the machines – or the swarthy immigrants – arrived. It was meant to be modern, industrial, ethnically and culturally diverse, a community with room for people like our parents and ourselves. This is why, a generation after the Popular Front was liquidated as a Party policy, it lives on as vividly as ever as a vision in a great many Americans' minds – including many Americans who were unborn or barely alive for the real thing. All this is crucial to understand because it is one of Studs Terkel's most distinctive and appealing qualities to be the ablest spokesman and visionary of the Popular Front in our time.

Let us try for a moment to create the imaginary landscapes of the Popular Front. The structure of this landscape would be one of those great epic murals that the Front generation loved – shaped, of course, like a map of America. In the Southwest corner we see Ma and Pa Joad hitting the road for California in their battered Model T. Back East, Jimmy Stewart in *Mr. Smith Goes to Washington* is confounding the fat cats in the Senate by speaking truth to power. Up in Detroit we find workers occupying car factories, perched atop turbines, while beetle-browed Henry Ford, surrounded by his goons, shakes his fist and gnashes his teeth on the overpass outside. Down in the Delta, Leadbelly, in convict's stripes, leads a chain gang in a resolute song, as bloated straw bosses

uneasily finger their guns. Out in the Northwest, hearty, smiling jack-
hammer men are building the Grand Coulee Dam, Woody Guthrie is
mounted on the ramparts, smiling and strumming his guitar, and a chorus of ragged, soulful mountain folk look on in amazement and dawning
hope. And back home in New York, radical speakers compete with the
birds on a lovely spring day in Union Square, and Earl Browder smiles
benignly down from Communist Party headquarters upstairs while portraits of Jefferson and Lincoln smile down on him; in the crowd, Ethel
Greenglass and Julius Rosenberg listen raptly, clasping each other in
chaste but radiant love; down on the Lower East Side, Aaron Copland
and Martha Graham huddle together as her company of angelic, ano-
rexic Jewish girls rehearses his "Appalachian Spring"; up in Harlem, Ralph
Ellison, only a scrawny kid, visits old couples' austere but impeccable
apartments and transcribes their memories of slavery for the Federal
Writer's Project, while musicians ease their big instruments down tene-
ment stairs, ready to heat up the night.

At the center of the mural – and the center of Popular Front sentimentality – is a great river of humanity, flowing through the heart of the
country, America's primal source of life and energy. Like the Mississippi,
it is fed by a thousand streams: by masses of anonymous, ordinary men
and women, from every occupation (they carry their lunchboxes and
tools as they go), every race and color and ethnic group, every class –
except the very highest, the ones in top hats. We see them just as they
start to see each other, overcoming all the social barriers that have kept
them apart or antagonistic, celebrating their vast diversity yet recogniz-
ing their common plight and their common hopes for life, feeling empathy and pledging solidarity, undertaking to march arm in arm toward the
purple mountain majesties of the future, to take possession of America

in the name of the people: "This land," as Woody Guthrie sang it, "was made for you and me." Terkel has spent most of his life working this river, investigating the lives of the "common," "ordinary" people who fill our land, trying to make their stories seen and heard in the hope of showing the people how much we all have in common "deep down," and bringing us together to work to change a social system that strains and drains us all. He should be seen as part of a whole generation of great photographers (Dorothea Lange, Walker Evans, Helen Levitt) and documentary filmmakers (Pare Lorentz, Willard van Dyke, Ralph Steiner) and folklorists (B. A. Botkin, John and Alan Lomax, Harry Smith, Henrietta Yurchenko) who were inspired by the Popular Front ideal, and whose work we are only just beginning to understand as an organic whole.

Terkel was born Louis Terkel in New York in 1912 and grew up in Chicago in the depths of the Depression. He got a law degree, but never practiced, and he has spent most of his life in the mass media. At some time, I cannot tell when, he began to call himself Studs, after James T. Farrell's Studs Lonigan, protagonist of one of the great novels of the Depression. Somehow Terkel escaped the blacklist, and, since the mid-1950s, he has conducted a daily talk and interview show over Chicago radio station WFMT, generally ignoring celebrities, except for jazz and blues musicians, and focusing in depth on the lives of the sort of anonymous people whose lives do not ordinarily get examined by the rest of us. Over the years his program has become a great success, with both an intellectual and a mass audience.

Terkel's finest book, *Division Street: America,* revived one of the favorite literary forms of the Front period, what I will call the We-The-People-Talk book. This is a book, usually put together by an author who has traveled up and down the country, in which a variety of people – of every

age, class, race, creed, etc. – tell their life stories and "speak for themselves." Titles like *The People Talk* by Benjamin Appel and *The Road: In
Search of America* by Nathan Asch (brother of Moses Asch, creator of the
Folkways music label, another of the great surviving Popular Front institutions) should convey the idea. Some of the most famous and best
writers of the age – Sherwood Anderson, James Agee, Erskine Caldwell,
Edmund Wilson – worked in this vein. *Division Street,* appearing amid the
turmoil of 1967, was like a breath of fresh air. It was full of decent,
warm, generous, sympathetic folks. Yet after a while it felt rather too
much like the air of 1929: though Terkel's people are "socially conscious"
and legitimately angry at business, government, "the big boys," the book
keeps entirely on the sunny side of their psyches. Any dark, murky, irrational feelings that might complicate fraternity and solidarity are left out.
A little while after putting down the book, it is hard to remember who is
who, just as in many 1930s models of the genre, individuals are reduced
to ingredients in "the people."

Terkel's next book, *Hard Times: An Oral History of the Great Depression*
(1970), tried to explore people's memories of the Depression years. Although full of vivid and moving stories, it seemed to lack focus. It suggested important questions about the ways biographical and historical
memory transform human experience, but it did nothing to even try to
resolve them. Nevertheless, it showed Terkel's perspective getting deeper
and more complex.

In his new book, *Working,* Terkel returns, as his subtitle suggests, to
the classic format of the We-The-People-Talk book. He could have taken
his epigraph from Earl Robinson and John Latouche's archetypal Popular
Front composition, "Ballad for Americans." This passage, sung beautifully by Paul Robeson, at once describes the scope and conveys some-

thing of the spirit of Terkel's project: "I'm everybody who's nobody and the nobody who's everybody … I'm an engineer, musician, carpenter, streetcleaner, farmer, office clerk, mechanic, housewife, stenographer, union organizer, bartender, truckdriver. … All of 'em! I'm the 'Et cetera' and the 'And-so-forth' who do the work. … I am … America."

And yet if Terkel gets closer than ever to the Popular Front vision in this book, he also diverges from it more radically than ever – or else, maybe, carries the vision to new heights and depths. For the first time in Terkel's work, his people are present in the radiance and frightfulness of their individuality. He is learning to confront all the weird and explosive psychic realities that the Front generation did not care or could not bear to see.

Terkel has chosen a subject that is particularly timely. The wildcat strikes at GM's new Lordstown, Ohio, assembly plant, the HEW's *Work in America* report, the increasing intensity of bitterness expressed by workers in so many occupations – blue- and white-collar, unskilled and executive alike – should be enough to convince readers that Americans have come to perceive work as a central problem, maybe the central problem, in the 1970s. Terkel provides an enormous amount of exciting material indispensable for any full understanding of this problem. He uses the discussion of work to get at what is deepest and most intimate in many people's lives, to understand work as Freud understood it, as the individual's firmest connection with reality. He has learned, in the words of the psychoanalyst Theodor Reik, to listen with the third ear. His book is being promoted like a bestseller, and it deserves to be one.

It is hard to know how Terkel gets so close to all these people. Like many of the best reporters, anthropologists, documentary filmmakers and psychoanalysts, he obscures the issue by editing his own presence out of most of the interviews he has transcribed; as a result, his people's stories generally read as monologues instead of the dialogues and human encounters they obviously are. Still, it is clear that he is giving off something that encourages people to associate freely, to mention second thoughts that they would normally keep under wraps, to take emotional risks, to expose their often precarious and frightening inner lives. He may have learned something of this from the late psychoanalytically minded anthropologist Oscar Lewis, author of *The Children of Sanchez, La Vida,* and a great unfinished work on the *barrios* of Havana. Then, too, Americans have grown more expressive, more willing to let things out, since Terkel first started listening to people talking: this is part of the legacy of the Sixties. Whatever its sources, this book shows a rare and precious human gift – and a gift that, if his earlier books are any evidence, has come to him relatively late in life. This gives *Working* a surprising electricity and emotional power. Sometimes, it seems to have almost too much power: we want to drop the book, it is too hot.

The heat is on from the start. Here is "Mike Lefevre" (Terkel's people are pseudonymous, except where they are public figures), a 37-year-old steelworker. First he abuses intellectuals, complains that they denigrate workers. A moment later, however, he stereotypically denigrates himself: "A mule, an old mule, that's the way I feel." He is hurt and angry that his teenage son "lacks respect." And yet, "I want my kid to be an effete snob. ... I want him to tell me he's not gonna be like me." He talks about the anger and violence inside him: he goes to a bar, insults someone randomly, starts a brawl. "He's punching me and I'm punching him, because we really both want to punch somebody else." But who? Forty years ago, in Clifford Odets's play *Waiting for Lefty,* a worker punched out his boss, and the audience stood up and cheered. But Terkel's worker has the brains to see how things have changed: the structure of work is far more abstract and depersonalized today, and cathartic moments don't come easy. "Who you gonna sock? You can't sock General Motors, you can't sock anyone in Washington. You can't sock a system."[1]

This guy is a fascinating character, a maelstrom of rage and yearning, self-hate and ambivalence. Moreover, he is smart and sensitive enough to grasp the ways in which he's trapped. But his knowledge doesn't seem to give him power to break free. He can use his wit, but it looks like he does most of his talking to himself. His fellow workers laugh at him for reading or trying to think seriously. Sometimes his reading leads him to new people, but either they patronize him as a hick, which is pretty bad, or they idolize him for his brute strength, which he thinks is even worse. Now and then he sabotages what he works on, "to make it unique … just so I can say I did it. …" He fights in bars, reads (his current reading is *Violence in America*), and drinks himself to sleep.

Then there is Fritz Ritter, doorman for forty years in an apartment house on New York's Upper West Side. He knows the house has seen better days. "It was real high class," he says, mournfully. "Nice furniture, rugs on the floor," fancy uniforms. But "the tenants looked down on me … You only spoke when they spoke to you. Otherwise you didn't say nothin'." In the good old days, it would have been unthinkable for him to relax on a couch in the lobby, or to have a conversation, as he is having with Terkel now. As he thinks of this, it cheers him up. "Times change. Today it's different. Today is every day more liberal. … More on the equal side, more friendship." A great many of Terkel's people express this ambivalence: they are glad to see more equality, yet mourn the loss of old dignities, fearful that this new mutuality is a sign that our society is falling apart.

One of the most persistent themes among Terkel's people, young and old, high and low on the social scale, is the ways in which people's attitudes toward their work have changed. Older workers complain that younger ones lack what Thorstein Veblen called the "instinct of workmanship," a desire to do their job well. On the other hand – this usually comes out in second thoughts or free associations – they feel a grudging but intense admiration for young people's willingness to stand up both to arbitrary power and to work they fear may turn out to be meaningless.

All through the twentieth century, more and more of the work in industrial societies has come to belong to the huge category that the Census Bureau calls "service," in other words, work performing services for people and interacting with them, rather than growing food or fabricating things. All through the twentieth century, socialism has transformed modern politics, partly in the form of real parties and movements that have held power in many countries, but also in the form of "a spectre haunting Europe," and haunting America as well. Even in countries like the US, where socialism has never had a chance to attain power, a great deal of social policy has been formed in response to that great ghost. Here, as in all advanced industrial countries, a steadily increasing number and proportion of the labor force is employed in "health, education and welfare." Workers in these sectors are structurally forced to become "street-level bureaucrats,"[2] mediating between needy individuals and powerful governments, and identifying in different degrees and intensities with both. Workers in this sector (I am one, a college teacher) are often distinguished by their high level of sensitivity and awareness – one reason why TV loves dramas about doctors, teachers and policemen – but also by their anguish at the misery and brutality they have to deal with, where basically no degree of knowledge will do any good.

Terkel is very good in getting close to human-service workers and getting them to talk. Here is Rose Hoffman, for thirty-five years a teacher in a poor city neighborhood, once mostly Polish, now mostly Puerto Rican. She denounces her current students and their families in a familiar bitter litany: "There isn't any shame, there isn't any pride," and so on. She is especially disturbed by the way "they" use profanity. And yet, and yet: "I had a fight with my husband the other day," she stops to say. "You know what I said to him? 'Fuck you!' (She laughs.) And I never talked that way. (Laughs again.) I hear it all the time from the students. ... Now I'm brazen." She is clearly glad, even proud, to be able to say that to her husband. As she tells this story, she comes to realize that, without knowing it, "they" have helped her stand up to "him." Once she gets it, she identifies with them more strongly: she can be to him what they are to her. She is experiencing one of the thrills of the teaching vocation, when you can learn from your students, when – most of the time quite unawares – they can help you to grow. But now that she knows it, where does it leave her? What and how will this brazen woman teach tomorrow? How will she get "them" to read the books and do their homework? And how will she act tomorrow night with "him," at the dinner table or in bed? The best moments in *Working* are moments of self-revelation, breaking in on workers when they least expect it. And Terkel is like a marvelous shrink who doesn't talk much, but who has a knack for getting people to talk to themselves in ways that will lead them to self-discovery.

As we follow Terkel's people's life stories, we learn how self-conscious so many people have become, how they have learned to ask intricate and sophisticated and tough questions about their work – both about its organization and patterns of authority and about what it ultimately means. This "existential" question, which not long ago was said (by President

Nixon among others) to be of interest only to pampered middle-class students, turns out to be crucial to a great many workers of all ages, including plenty with little education and less ideology but lots of passion and intelligence. A young proofreader speaks of trouble in his shop: the workers, particularly the young ones, have begun to ask why things are organized in a particular way. The boss, who has never been asked such questions, feels threatened, panics, overreacts, creates a crisis that disrupts the rhythm and flow on which his own profits depend. (During the 1960s, many senior professors also went through the roof when students asked – most of the time, without hostility – why the course was taught in this way and not that.) "Nobody refused to do anything," the proofreader says, "but we want to know why." The most significant legacy of the Sixties may turn out to be an enriched vocabulary for asking why.

And yet, some of the most humanly attractive people in this book don't seem to want to ask why, or anything else. They are people who have been working forever at the sort of grungy low-wage jobs we call "dead-end." But they don't seem to mind; indeed, they sound, more than anyone else here, existentially content. Take Alfred Pommier, forty-nine, a proud parking-lot attendant: "They call me Lovin' Al the Wizard, One-Swing Al – I'm known from Peking to Hong Kong, from West Coast to Pecos." He tells his story in a riff full of bluesy *double entendre*: "In my younger days I used to be a wizard, I could really roll. I could spin a car with one hand, and never miss a hole. … I could drive any car like a baby, like a woman change her baby's diaper. … I was so good, I make that swing with one hand, never need two." Or take Babe Secoli, a supermarket checker. She cultivates and practices her rhythm like a dancer, strives to keep her body in tune with her machine – "It's like playin' a piano." She claims she knows every can and every package in her store, and she

tries to know every customer. She seeks to turn the briefest, most innocu-
ous scene into an authentic human encounter. If she is away for even a
couple of days, "I'm very lonesome for this place. ... I look forward to
comin' to work. It's a great feelin'. I enjoy it somethin' terrible." How
should we feel about these people? On one level, they are drowning in
what Georg Lukács called "false consciousness": they don't even know
they're being exploited! On another level, they are the salt of the earth.

Karl Marx is the greatest theorist of work. He had distinctive insight
into the troubled and contradictory life of "the proletariat, the modern
working class." Marx saw work as an arena where, potentially, a worker
could not only "create an objective world by his practical activity," but
also "freely develop his physical and mental energy." On the other hand,
in real work in the bourgeois society he lived in, the worker "mortifies his
body and ruins his mind ... he does not affirm himself, but denies himself
... he feels himself only outside his work, and in his work he feels outside
himself." ("Alienated Labor," *MER*, 74–8). Marx thought that even as
work insulted and injured the workers, it made them smart enough to
see what was going on, angry enough and disciplined enough to organize
and revolt against a social system that turned work into a travesty of what
it could be. This revolutionary vision was not only thrilling and terrifying, but *plausible*. When it was not fulfilled – and, all through the twentieth century, it remained unfulfilled – people have wanted to know why. In
the 1890s, various writers developed a menu of reasons. The main arguments were that the workers were too comfortable (Werner Sombart), or
else too dumb (Georges Sorel, the Frankfurt School). Sombart, a German professor trying to explain "why there is no socialism in America,"
argued that America's spectacular abundance gave workers everything
they might possibly need. The second argument, often advanced by peo-

ple on the Left, was that the workers' minds had been numbed by liberalism, democracy, the mass media, etc., so they were were abject and pious and lacking the courage and virtue of their critics. Both these ideas have been recycled endlessly throughout the twentieth century, but haven't changed much. Neither of them has been very satisfying for long to people with open eyes and minds. It could be interesting to pose this question to Terkel, who offers a spectacular ethnographic knowledge of workers in America today.

Terkel would probably disparage both of these explanations of workers' failure to save the world. *Working* and his earlier books are full of stories of working class oppression and misery. And *Working*, more than any of his earlier studies, is full of workers who are as smart, as deep, and as free as anyone in the house. The idea implicit in *Working*, as a kind of subtext, is something like this: the workers know they are being screwed, but they do not revolt, because what they do instead is to use all their brains and all their sensitivity to give their work *meaning*, to drench it with beauty and excitement, to make it their own.

Terkel has dramatized brilliantly our workers' capacity to overcome misery by telling stories that give their misery meaning. But he himself has told a story that puts all their miseries and all their meanings together, and enables us to imagine a greater meaning. By locating the workers, their lives and their stories alongside each other, Terkel has created the sketch for a new mural, a new Popular Front, and for a new community that America might someday conceivably become. The new mural will be more honest, more authentically inclusive than the first, and it will have a new inwardness and self-scrutiny and psychic depth. Maybe now, after the American people emerge from the crises that have been choking us, it will be possible to start that river flowing again.

Notes

1. [1999] Well, yes and no. The Watergate scandal, developing just as this book appeared, showed that, yes, the people *could* "sock someone in Washington." On the other hand, the democratic power to remove individual politicians from office within any state doesn't give the people of the world much help in controlling a multinational corporate *system*. They need to learn how to think and feel as globally as modern capital itself.

2. See Michael Lipsky, *Street-Level Bureaucracy* (New York: Russell Sage, 1980), an important book that sheds much light on conflicts in everyday city life.

5

The People in *Capital*

None of the year-end lists of the best and most important books of 1977 included the one that, had anyone asked, would have headed mine: Marx's *Capital*. The first volume of *Capital,* the only one published in Marx's lifetime, has just been reissued by Vintage Books in a joint arrangement with Penguin Books and the *New Left Review* in England – in a handsome new edition, splendidly translated by Ben Fowkes. In the last few years, Penguin and Vintage have been bringing out a multivolume edition that will eventually include virtually all of Marx's and Engels's works in contemporary translations. This is an excellent project, but one that so far hasn't had the cultural impact it deserves. It isn't that there aren't plenty of people reading and discussing Marx; but they tend to be small sectarian groups speaking in tongues intelligible only to them-

This essay first appeared in the *Bennington Review,* April 1978.

selves, cut off from our culture as a whole. And yet Marx is one of the most communicative writers who ever lived; even his most complex ideas are presented vividly and dramatically; he didn't write in any esoteric, private language – as those who write about him tend to do – but as a man speaking to men.

Even when Marx is studied in universities – and he is studied far more today than when I was in college twenty years ago – his thought gets chopped up into various theories to be verified or refuted, and methods to be followed or discarded; what gets left out is what is most alive and exciting, Marx's vision of the world as a whole. A writer's vision of life is less tangible than his politics, economics, religion, ideology; but it goes deeper, and it is what makes his work last long after his causes have won or lost or faded away. Literate people understand this in general: they know that the truth and power in Plato doesn't depend on the validity of his theory of ideas, that Dante can change our lives even if Thomism doesn't, that Dostoevsky's hold on our souls doesn't stand or fall with his claims for the divine power of the Russian soul. But so many ordinarily sophisticated people become crude when they come to Marx: they observe acidly that workers are often nasty and brutish, or that capitalism hasn't collapsed, or that, in places where it has collapsed, the state hasn't withered away; they note these things, rather impatiently, then slam the book closed and walk away fast without looking back. They forget, or repress, something that they normally know: that it's possible for a writer to be wrong about all sorts of things, and yet to tell the truth about life.

What makes *Capital* so exciting is that, more than anything else Marx wrote, it brings to life his vision of modern life as a totality. This vision is spread out on an immense canvas: more than a thousand pages in the first volume alone; hundreds of characters – shopkeepers and sharecroppers,

miners and millowners, poets and publicists, doctors and divines, philosophers and politicians, the world-famous and the anonymous – speaking in
their own voices. The amazing multiplicity of real voices that Marx brings
forth, and the skill with which he propels and deploys them, carry us back
to the glorious days of the nineteenth-century novel, back to *Lost Illusions*
and *Bleak House* and *War and Peace*. Some of the most vivid characters
appear for only a moment; others stay with us for long stretches and
engage Marx in long passionate argument; others disappear for hundreds
of pages, only to return transformed. The people in *Capital* have a life that
will outlive capitalism itself.

Some of the mill, mine and factory owners and their apologists,
whose voices (for example, before the Parliamentary Factory Commissions) we hear for longer than we care to, make it clear that Dickens's
most grotesque caricatures, his Carkers and Podsnaps and Gradgrinds,
were remarkably close to life. We are introduced to Dr. Andrew Ure, "the
Pindar of the automatic factory," for whose work Marx feels a perverse
affection, "not only because of its undisguised cynicism, but because of
the undisguised naïveté with which it blurts out the contradictions of the
capitalist brain." Ure, in his landmark *Philosophy of Manufactures* (1835),
"preaches a long sermon to show how advantageous the rapid development of machinery is to the workers"; in the very next sentence, "he
warns them that by their obstinacy and their strikes they hasten that
development." Marx loves to quote Ure: "Violent revulsions of this nature [strikes, etc.] display shortsighted man in the vile character of a self-
tormentor." Few novelists could top that voice. Here it is again, with a
rhapsody on the capitalist factory:

a vast automaton, composed of various mechanical and intellectual organs, acting in the uninterrupted concert for the production of a common object, all of them being subordinated to a self-regulated moving
force . ... In these spacious halls the benignant power of steam summons
around him his myriads of willing menials.

Marx isn't adding much when he points out that in capitalism's industrial
vision, "the automaton itself is the subject, and the workers are merely
conscious organs, ... [all] subordinated to the central controlling force" to
capital; and that, in these spacious halls, "the central machine [is] not only
an automaton but an autocrat." With friends like Ure, we might ask, does
the bourgeoisie need enemies?

In fact, in the world of capital – and of *Capital* – Ure isn't so special.
There are the directors of the "Cyclops Steel and Iron Works" – what
novelist could get away with that? – explaining to the Factory Commission why twelve-year-old boys must work twelve-hour shifts through the
night. It's simple enough: they can't find any grown men who'll do it. But
why, the commissioners ask, should anybody have to do it? Can't the
steelmakers confine their operations to daylight hours? They ask one E. F.
Sanderson, whose firm produces steel rolling-mills and forges. Sanderson
is aghast: "But then there would be the loss of so much expensive machinery lying idle half the time. ..." The really striking thing, once again, is the
mixture of cynicism and naiveté. It is a mixture that a great many of us
have had jammed down our throats – especially those of us who work in
the "human-service" sector, where the squeeze to maximize labor "pro-
ductivity" has just begun. Once again, Marx's gloss is rather on the conservative side: "Messrs. Sanderson have something to make besides steel.
Steel-making is merely a pretext for surplus-value making. The steel fur-
naces, rolling-mills, iron, coal, etc., have something more to do than to

transform themselves into steel. They are there to absorb surplus-labour, and they naturally absorb more in 24 hours than in 12." For them, "the worker is nothing other than labor-power for the duration of his whole life, ... to be devoted to the self-expansion of capital." Notice how much of Marx's distinctive vocabulary – capital, labor-power, surplus-value – emerges very directly from this concrete situation. These expressions aren't arcane at all – in fact they're pretty simple, aren't they? In case we forget what they mean, Sanderson is right there to remind us. In the early 1960s, when I first read these pages, his voice seemed quite remote; now it sounds remarkably close to home. Much of Marx's achievement in *Capital* consists in making the words flesh, in bringing the voices of capital to life. This achievement has a special resonance for us over a century later: although so much of the world has changed, we can appreciate how much a part of our life these voices still are.

The voices in *Capital* are not all so grating. Many belong to industrial and agricultural workers, some barely ten years old, who come before the Factory Commissions, often at great personal risk, to give accounts of their work and their lives. For the most part, these workers do not speak the language of militancy, or even of moral indignation; their over-all stance seems to be one of stoical endurance. They don't fit the formulas of the *Communist Manifesto,* but Marx listens intently to them and lets them speak at length to us. Their voices remind us of stoicism's human strengths: its refusal to be cowed or conned, its determination to look things in the face and speak the truth. We're impressed, too, with their austere intelligence, their instinctive grasp of the complex technologies, industrial processes, divisions of labor and organizations in which they move and live. They may not be, at this point – and maybe not at any point – a revolutionary class; but they are permanently above and beyond the dumb docility in which their bosses have tried to immure them; they have attained the pride and dignity of spirit from which any material revolution must begin.

Marx often idealizes the working class, but here he makes it clear that they hold no monopoly on dignity or virtue. Some of the most impressive voices in *Capital* come from English factory inspectors, public health investigators, housing and sanitation commissioners – middle-class civil servants who are not only highly competent, but "free from partisanship and respect for persons." They don't have the power to transform capitalism – only a revolutionary mass movement led by the working class could do that-but they are free to think and talk straight about it, to discover and declare the truth about what it does to people from day to day. Marx pays tribute to them and builds his work on theirs. Indeed, although he is proud to sign his name to *Capital,* he presents it as a collective and collaborative enterprise, growing out of the works of thousands of people, as befits production in an industrial age.

Marx brings us admirable voices even from the heart of the bourgeoisie. They are not all Cyclopean Sandersons and Ures. Josiah Wedgewood, for instance, speaks on behalf of factory legislation: of course, he says, he overworks and underpays his workers; if he were to give them the wages they were worth, or working conditions worthy of human beings, he would go bankrupt in a week, undersold by competitors who cut costs by treating men like swine. Marx accepts Wedgewood's sympathy and good intentions at face value; but he uses them to show that, in bourgeois society, sympathy and good will are devoid of market value. It is irrelevant to hope, as Victorian moralists hoped, for changes of heart within the ruling class. It does a capitalist no good to have a noble heart because, as Marx says, "Capital has no heart." Within a capitalist system, goodness counts for nothing; in order to make it count, we must transform our social system as a whole. The comic irony of this situation is that our very sympathy for the bourgeoisie, for their plight as human beings, will work as an argument for their overthrow as a ruling class.

Along with this plenitude of real voices that carries us back to the golden years of the nineteenth-century novel, *Capital* contains another species of voices that pull us forward into the world of twentieth-century modernism. These are voices from mythology and poetry, from sorcery and theology, from every country and culture under the sun. They belong to Greek and Hindu gods, to foxes and cats from fairy tales, obscure theologians, epic heroes, Shakespearean kings and beggars; they speak in a dozen languages, and play havoc with the book's typography; they are likely to pop up at any moment, comment on the narrative, often in bizarre or cryptic ways, and then sink back into whatever limbo they came from, sometimes to reappear for a moment hundreds of pages later, sometimes never to be heard from again at all. We will find this cacophony of voices, languages, epochs and cultures half a century later in the *Cantos* and "The Waste Land"; but Marx's erudition and internationalism are a lot more genuine, less willed and forced, than Eliot's or Pound's. (He is not under their pressure to prove to "Europe" that they are cultured people and not hicks from the colonies.) Marx's point in presenting this immense and bizarre chorus is to show capitalism as a maelstrom that sweeps the whole world into its flood, past and present, reality and mythology, East and West: everything and everyone is caught up and whirled in the world market, nothing and no one has the power to hold back. We the readers – along, of course, with the writer – are part of it; as we respond, our voices are incorporated into the chorus; the audience finds itself onstage. This may be one reason why, like many great modernist works, *Capital* never really comes to an end: it reaches out to us in the audience, and challenges us to give the work an ending, by bringing an end to capitalism itself.

One of the surprising things about *Capital* is that, considering all the horrors it reveals, it isn't more depressing to read. It isn't depressing because, for all the misery Marx brings to light, the source of light in all his works is a vision of the thrill and promise of modern life. True, enormous changes must be made – the power of the bourgeoisie, original agents of modernization, must be broken – before the promise of modernity can be fulfilled. Nevertheless, the promise is there for us, it infuses Marx's writing with a dynamism, an excitement that pulls us along with him and makes us share his hopes.

I lack the space to unfold this vision in the detail and depth it deserves. (If they asked me, I could write a book.) But I can present a couple of passages from *Capital* that show the vision in action. Here is one from Chapter 24, "The Transformation of Surplus-Value into Capital":

> It is not use-values and their enjoyment, but exchange-value and its increase, that spur [the capitalist] into action. Fanatically intent on making value expand itself, he ruthlessly forces the human race to produce for production's sake. In this way he spurs on the development of society's productive forces, and the creation of those material conditions of production that alone can form the basis of a higher form of society, a society in which the full and free development of every individual forms the ruling principle.

Marx's language here enacts the furious onward movement it describes, from capitalist accumulation to human liberation. To get from the beginning to the end will require tremendous struggle and sacrifice. But the energy and flow of Marx's language grab the individual reader, and make him feel that these struggles and sacrifices can actually lead somewhere, can bring him somewhere he wants to be.

Our second passage comes from Chapter 15, "Machinery and Modern Industry." It proclaims a basic contradiction between "modern industry," which is inherently revolutionary and liberating, and "its capitalist form," the form in which it first comes into the world.

Modern industry never views or treats the existing form of a production process as the definitive one. Its technical basis is therefore revolutionary, whereas all earlier modes of production were essentially conservative. By means of machinery, chemical processes and other methods, it is continually transforming not only the technical basis of production, but also the functions of the worker and the social combinations of the labor process. At the same time, it thereby also revolutionizes the division of labor, and incessantly throws masses of capital and of workers from one branch of production to another. Thus large-scale industry, by its very nature, necessitates variation of labor, fluidity of functions, and mobility of the worker in all directions. ...

Now, "in its capitalist form," modern industry, through its very progress, inflicts immense suffering on its working class:

We have seen how this absolute contradiction [between modern industry and its capitalist form] does away with all repose, all fixity and all security as far as the worker's life-situation is concerned; how it constantly threatens, by taking away the instruments of labor, to snatch from his hands the means of subsistence, and, by suppressing his specialized function, to make him superfluous. We have seen, too, how this contradiction bursts forth without restraint in the ceaseless human sacrifices required from the working class, in the reckless squandering of labor-powers, and in the devastating effects of social anarchy. This is the negative side.

Thus the capitalist form in which modernity has been encased till now forces workers to fight modernity, to cling for dear life to jobs and divisions of labor that are not only oppressive and alienated, but obsolete. But capitalism is not the only way for mankind to be modern. If modern industry and society were reorganized for the sake of human beings instead of profits, the progress that presently generates mass misery could become a source of personal growth:

> This possibility of varying labor must become a general law of social production, and existing relationships must be adapted to permit its realization in practice. That monstrosity, the disposable working population held in reserve, in misery, for the changing requirements of capitalist exploitation, must be replaced by the individual man who is absolutely available for different kinds of labor; the partially developed individual, who is merely the bearer of one specialized social function, must be replaced by the totally developed individual, fit for a variety of labors, ready to face any change in production, for whom the different social functions he performs are only so many modes of giving free scope to his own natural and acquired powers.

Now there are plenty of questions that could be asked about this paradigm of a "totally developed individual." Would such a man – or such a woman – be devoted to anything or anyone, except insofar as that devotion furthered his own development? Is that enough? Could the totally developed individual be a citizen, a member of any sort of community? There's something strangely, familiarly American about this model. Indeed, Marx's one illustration of his paradigm is drawn from America – in fact, from California in the Gold Rush days! But Marx's American romance is another story.

The big story here is the sense of conflict and contradiction that pervades Marx's vision of modern life. His feeling for contradictions infuses the whole of *Capital* with vitality and excitement, and makes us feel modern life as an adventure. An adventure is not an idyll: much of its excitement springs from its risks, from the chance that it could end horribly; but we go on, because we are moving in an ambience of life and hope. This ambience could be a great gift to us today. It is right there, in *Capital*: the book lies open and open-ended, waiting only for us to give ourselves.

6

All That Is Solid Melts into Air:
Marx, Modernism and Modernization

I am the spirit that negates all ...
– MEPHISTOPHELES, IN *Faust*

Innovative Self-Destruction!
– AD FOR MOBIL OIL, 1978

I spent the 1960s in universities – Columbia, Oxford, Harvard – that I found intellectually exciting, but socially lonely. They all catered to the rich, to the current and the wannabe ruling class, and I felt I didn't fit in. At the end of the 1960s, I moved to the City College, City University of New York. I thought I would feel more at home with students who come from the working class, as I did, and who grew up on the streets of New York. It turned out I was right. Over the years, CCNY and CUNY have

---

The earliest version of this essay appeared in *Dissent*, Fall 1978.

been afflicted with plenty of troubles (that's another story), but never for a minute have I had to wonder why I was there. In my first decade or so at CCNY/CUNY, I identified myself strongly as a member of the New Left. (I should say, I'm still happy to identify myself this way, except that after thirty years I'd have to say *Used* Left now.) What this meant in practice was that I was involved in endless protests against the endlessly expanding Vietnam War and in various campaigns for racial justice. What it meant in theory was far less clear. There were direct, practical human reasons for resisting the war, and for helping black and Latin people to get a better deal in life. I was perfectly happy to explain this to my students. But I couldn't explain, and my connection to the New Left didn't help me understand, what kind of society we lived in. The early SDS had a vision something like Marxist Humanism. But as the Sixties went on, nobody seemed to be working to deepen and develop that vision, and dreadful events seemed to be working to shatter and scramble it into something very different and not so nice.

After the assassinations of 1968 and Nixon's victory, life on the New Left got increasingly crazy.[1] (This was just around the time when Patrick Buchanan, a youthful prodigy in Nixon's White House, was counseling his boss: "If we tear the country in half, we can pick up the bigger half.")[2] After SDS disintegrated in 1969, people I thought I knew – we had been in study groups, put out leaflets, got arrested together – drifted toward a primitivist romance that idealized any form of life that looked different from our own. Smart people seemed to be using their brains to dumb themselves down. The nuanced skepticism with which they confronted America totally vanished when they looked at – or rather imagined – heroic Others. Maoist mobs, Central American shamans, peasants from anywhere, tribesmen of any tribe, men in prison for any crime (guilty or not, it didn't matter), all were charged with a magical aura. Intellectuals who had rejected official liberalism because it was insufficiently complex now started talking a new language that seemed wonderfully simple: the keywords were "hate," "burn," "pig," "kill." Sensitive souls who had become Freedom Riders after reading Albert Camus were now standing up for Charles Manson. And my dear CCNY students – kids whose parents were butchers and cabdrivers and bookkeepers and telephone operators – raged against "our country clubs and our swimming pools," which the peoples of the world were about to righteously destroy. I said, "Wait a minute, guys, *whose* country clubs and *whose* swimming pools? Do you really think they're yours?" I also said most of the Third World had a pretty hot climate; didn't they think its peoples might enjoy a swim? But nobody laughed. I started to worry. These kids came from poverty, or somewhere very close to poverty. I was supposed to be helping them become doctors, lawyers, teachers, social workers, architects, and to put together decent lives for themselves. Their official civics lessons had taught them that they were free Americans and could do anything, the world was theirs. But now, as the left disintegrated, it emitted a nihilistic countercivics lesson: Americans were simply "negations of humanity" (Franz Fanon); "the white race is the cancer of history" (Susan Sontag); anything these kids could ever do in the world was depraved and monstrous. William Blake had a word for both these polarized visions: "the mind-forg'd manacles I hear." What could I do as a teacher to help my kids break their chains and grow up?

It was around this time that I started reading Marx again. I felt a desperate need for a radical criticism that didn't explode into primitive self-hate, and that wasn't nihilistic toward the whole modern world. Marx seemed like a good place to start. Also, I remembered that some of

Marx's *very* early writing, earlier than the 1844 essays that had knocked me out in 1959, really *was* self-abusive and self-hateful. In a way I could see in faint outline but couldn't yet grasp in detail or depth, he had evolved. Whenever I taught Marx, I had to deal with this. My students never failed to notice lines like these, written in 1843:

> What is the profane basis of Judaism? Practical need, self-interest. What is the worldly cult of the Jew? Peddling. What is his worldly god? Money. ...
>
> We discern in Judaism, therefore, a universal antisocial element. ... In the final analysis, the emancipation of the Jews is the emancipation of mankind from Judaism. (*Marx-Engels Reader,* 48–9)

This awful stuff is from Marx's second essay on the Jewish Question (*MER,* 47–52).

His first essay (*MER,* 26–46), written a little earlier, sounds nothing like this. It is a *critique* of the anti-Semitism of Marx's friend, the Young Hegelian philosopher Bruno Bauer. It advocates civil rights and full citizenship for Jews. It offers a critique of the inner contradictions of political democracy; it quotes Tocqueville, and shows his influence; it is one of the best things Marx ever wrote. This makes its companion piece all the more appalling, but strange as well. If this was Marx's level of awareness, why did he cave in to Bauer? We may never know; but we do know that it didn't last long.

Within a year, in *The Holy Family* and *The German Ideology,* Marx and Engels launched ferocious polemics against Bauer and his crowd. In these arguments, Marx returns to the perspective of his first Jewish Question essay, where he stays for the rest of his life.

In the brief period when Marx denounced the Jews, what did they signify for him? What was their primal crime, which made them "a universal antisocial element"? It seems that the primal Jewish sin is a sense of self: "practical need, self-interest." It's hard to know what to make of this. Is he saying that Jews should have no selves, or material needs? Maybe they should live on air? (And when you prick them, they shouldn't bleed?) Or is he saying something even stronger: that it is wrong for *anyone* to have practical needs and interests and a sense of self? Of course, this is one of the oldest living Platonic and Christian clichés: the self is evil; virtue means total self-sacrifice and self-annihilation.[3] In the twentieth century, this cliché would be reinvented by Stalinist communism. (In the 1970s, Maoists told me that the Chairman's Little Red Book said, right in the beginning, "The self is nothing, the collective is everything." I have never been able to find this epigram in that book, but I know it was ardently believed by the faithful.) Did Marx himself ever believe anything like this? I can't swear he didn't, but if he did, it wasn't for long. Very soon, and in all his great works, he would affirm practical need and self-interest as primal forces that make life go on.[4] And he wasn't allied for long with the medieval Church, and with modern reactionaries, in their primitivist hate for money and trade. He grew, he learned, he overcame. He came to believe that money became a sinister force only with "the transformation of money into capital" (*Capital* Volume 1, Chapters 4–6; *MER*, 329–42), and that the owners of capital are a very small cadre of high financiers and "industrial millionaires, the leaders of whole industrial armies" (*Communist Manifesto*, in *MER*, 474), not a mass of Jewish peddlers with their goods on their backs.

It was important to see that Marx was not attacking money, which everyone in modern societies needed to live, but capital, a distinctively modern social force, owned and controlled by a very few. But as I read on, I saw the story was more complex: even as Marx attacked capital, simultaneously he praised it in lyrically extravagant ways.

> The bourgeoisie ... has been the first to show what man's activity can
> bring about. It has accomplished wonders far surpassing Egyptian pyra-
> mids, Roman aqueducts and Gothic cathedrals. It has conducted expedi-
> tions that put all former Exoduses and Crusades in the shade. ...
>
> The bourgeoisie, through the exploitation of the world market, has
> given a cosmopolitan character to production and distribution in every
> country. ...
>
> The bourgeoisie, by the rapid improvement of all instruments of pro-
> duction, by the immensely facilitated means of communication ...
>
> The bourgeoisie, in its rule of hardly a hundred years, has created more
> massive and more colossal productive forces than have all preceding gen-
> erations together. ... (*Communist Manifesto,* in MER, 476–7)

Comparing this vision with the ones in Marx's essays of 1844 and before,
it is clear that he came to see capitalism in a far more complicated and
sympathetic light. Marx always considered himself as an enemy of capitalism, but his enmity got more interesting, more tinged with celebration,
more dialectical. I saw how Marx came to see the whole process of the
development of capitalism – its triumphs and horrors, its inescapable
inner conflicts and clashes, and its incubation of a socialist movement that
could gather the vision and power to overcome it – as a grand narrative.
The overarching subject of that story, it seemed to me, was MODERNITY.

For many years, without ever thinking about it, I had held *avant-garde*
prejudices: the greatest books will never be bestsellers, the greatest art
will never be shown in museums, the greatest music will never be played
on radio. So when I discovered Marx, it made sense that I should focus on
the *1844 Manuscripts* and ignore the *Manifesto.* But now I thought I could
see one of the primary sources of the *Manifesto*'s power: not only did it

unfold a luminous vision of the drama of modern life; it *communicated* that vision in a language that all modern men and women could grasp.

My reading of the *Manifesto* in the early 1970s turned out to be the core of *All That Is Solid Melts into Air*, my big book of the 1980s. In that book, Goethe's *Faust* comes first in the table of contents, but the *Communist Manifesto* came first in my mind. It helped me see how the bad things and the good things in the world could spring from the same place, how suffering could be a source of growth and joy, how radical thought could escape doldrums and dualisms and gather vision and energy for better times.

This essay has existed in several forms. The one below is based on its first publication, in the Summer 1978 issue of *Dissent* magazine, and on an expanded version in *All That Is Solid Melts into Air*.

In Part I of *All That Is Solid Melts into Air*, I showed how Goethe's *Faust*, universally regarded as a prime expression of the modern spiritual quest, reaches its fulfillment – but also its tragic catastrophe – in the transformation of modern material life. We will soon see how the real force and originality of Marx's "historical materialism" is the light it sheds on modern spiritual life. Both writers share a perspective that was far more widely shared in their time than it is in our own: a belief that "modern life" comprises a coherent whole. This sense of wholeness underlies Pushkin's judgment of *Faust* as "an *Iliad* of modern life." It presupposes a unity of life and experience that embraces modern politics and psychology, modern industry and spirituality, the modern ruling classes and the modern working classes. This chapter will attempt to recover and reconstruct Marx's vision of modern life as a whole.

It is worth noting that this sense of wholeness goes against the grain of contemporary thought. Current thinking about modernity is broken into two different compartments, hermetically sealed off from one another: "modernization" in economics and politics, "modernism" in art, culture and sensibility. If we try to locate Marx amid this dualism, we will find that, not surprisingly, he bulks large in the literature on modernization. Even writers who claim to refute him generally recognize his work as a primary source and point of reference for their own.[4] On the other hand, in the literature on modernism, Marx is not recognized in any way at all. Modernist culture and consciousness are often traced back to his generation, the generation of the 1840s – to Baudelaire, Flaubert, Wagner, Kierkegaard, Dostoevsky – but Marx himself does not rate even a branch in the genealogical tree. If he is even mentioned in this company, it is as a foil, or sometimes as a survival of an earlier and more innocent age – the Enlightenment, say – whose clear vistas and solid values modernism has supposedly destroyed. Some writers (like Vladimir Nabokov) depict Marxism as a dead weight that crushes the modernist spirit; others (like Georg Lukács in his communist years) see it as far saner, healthier and more "real" than those of the modernists; but everybody seems to agree that he and they are worlds apart.[5]

And yet, the closer we get to what Marx actually said, the less this dualism makes sense. Take an image like this: "Alles Staendische und Stehende verdampft," which Marx's friend Samuel Moore translated freely, but not outrageously, as "All that is solid melts into air." The cosmic scope and visionary grandeur of this image, its highly compressed and dramatic power, its vaguely apocalyptic undertones, the ambiguity of its point of view – the heat that destroys is also superabundant energy, an overflow of life – all these qualities are supposed to be hallmarks of the modernist imagination. They are just the sort of thing we are prepared to find in Rimbaud or Nietzsche, Rilke or Yeats – "Things fall apart, the center does not hold." In fact, this image comes from Marx, and not from any esoteric long-hidden early manuscript, but from the heart of the *Communist Manifesto*. It comes as the climax of Marx's description of "modern bourgeois society." The affinities between Marx and the great modernists are even clearer if we look at the whole of the dramatic images I brought up a moment ago: "All that is solid melts into air, all that is holy is profaned, and men at last are forced to face with sober senses the real conditions of their lives and their relations with their fellow men." Marx's second clause, which proclaims the destruction of everything holy, is more complex and more interesting than the standard nineteenth-century materialist assertion that God does not exist. Marx is moving in the dimension of time, working to evoke an ongoing historical drama and trauma. He is saying that the aura of holiness is suddenly missing, and that we cannot understand ourselves in the present until we confront what is absent. The final clause – "and men at last are forced to face ..." – not only describes a confrontation with a perplexing reality but acts it out, forces it on the reader – and, indeed, on the writer too, for "men," "die Menschen" as Marx says, are all in it together, at once subjects and objects of the pervasive melting process.

If we follow this modernist "melting vision," we will find it throughout Marx's works. Everywhere it pulls like an undertow against the more "solid" Marxian visions we know so well. It is especially vivid and striking in the *Communist Manifesto*. Indeed, it opens up a whole new perspective on the *Manifesto* as the archetype of a century of modernist manifestos and movements to come. The *Manifesto* expresses some of modernist culture's deepest insights and, at the same time, dramatizes some of its deepest inner contradictions.

At this point it would not be unreasonable to ask, Aren't there already more than enough interpretations of Marx? Do we really need a modernist Marx, a kindred spirit of Eliot and Kafka and Schoenberg and Gertrude Stein and Artaud? I think we do, not only because he's there, but because he has something distinctive and important to say. Marx, in fact, can tell us as much about modernism as it can tell us about him. Modernist thought, so brilliant in illuminating the dark side of everyone and everything, turns out to have some repressed dark corners of its own, and Marx can shine new light on these. Specifically, he can clarify the relationship between modernist culture and the bourgeois economy and society – the world of "modernization" – from which it has sprung. We will see that they have far more in common than either modernists or bourgeoisie would like to think. We will see Marxism, modernism and the bourgeoisie caught up in a strange dialectical dance, and if we follow their movements we can learn some important things about the modern world we all share.

1. The Melting Vision and Its Dialectic

The central drama for which the *Manifesto* is famous is the development of the modern bourgeoisie and proletariat, and the struggle between them. But we can find a play going on within this play, a struggle inside the author's consciousness over what is really going on and what the larger struggle means. We might describe this conflict as a tension between Marx's "solid" and his "melting" visions of modern life.

The *Manifesto*'s first section, "Bourgeois and Proletarians" (*MER*, 473–83), sets out to present an overview of what is now called the process of modernization, and sets the stage for what Marx believes will be its revolutionary climax.[6] Here Marx describes the solid institutional core of modernity. First of all, there is the emergence of a world market. As it spreads, it absorbs and destroys whatever local and regional markets it touches. Production and consumption – and human needs – become increasingly international and cosmopolitan. The scope of human desires and demands is enlarged far beyond the capacities of local industries, which consequently collapse. The scale of communications becomes worldwide, and technologically sophisticated mass media emerge. Capital is concentrated increasingly in a few hands. Independent peasants and artisans cannot compete with capitalist mass production, and they are forced to leave the land and close their workshops. Production is increasingly centralized and rationalized in highly automated factories. (It is no different in the country, where farms became "factories in the field," and the peasants who do not leave the countryside are transformed into agricultural proletarians.) Vast numbers of the uprooted poor flood into cities, which grow almost magically – and cataclysmically – overnight. In order for these great changes to go on with relative smoothness, some legal, fiscal and administrative centralization must take place; and it does take place wherever capitalism goes. National states arise and accumulate great power, although that power is continually undermined by capital's international scope. Meanwhile, industrial workers gradually awaken to some sort of class consciousness and activate themselves against the acute misery and chronic oppression in which they live. As we read this, we find ourselves on familiar ground; these processes are still going on around us, and a century of Marxism has helped to establish a language in which they make sense.

As we read on, however, if we read with our full attention, strange things begin to happen. Marx's prose suddenly becomes luminous, incandescent; brilliant images succeed and blend into one another; we are hurtled along with a reckless momentum, a breathless intensity. Marx is not only describing but evoking and enacting the desperate pace and frantic rhythm that capitalism imparts to every facet of modern life. He makes us feel that we are part of the action, drawn into the stream, hurtled along, out of control, at once dazzled and menaced by the on-ward rush. After a few pages of this, we are exhilarated but perplexed; we find that the solid social formations around us have melted away. By the time Marx's proletarians finally appear, the world stage on which they were supposed to play their part has disintegrated and metamorphosed into something unrecognizable, surreal, a mobile construction that shifts and changes shape under the players' feet. It is as if the innate dynamism of the melting vision has run away with Marx and carried him – and the workers, and us – far beyond the range of his intended plot, to a point where his revolutionary script will have to be radically reworked.

The paradoxes at the heart of the *Manifesto* are manifest almost at its very start: specifically, from the moment Marx starts to describe the bourgeoisie. "The bourgeoisie," he begins, "has played a most revolutionary role in history." What is startling about Marx's next few pages is that he seems to have come not to bury the bourgeoisie, but to praise it. He writes an impassioned, enthusiastic, often lyrical celebration of bourgeois works, ideas and achievements. Indeed, in these pages he manages to praise the bourgeoisie more powerfully and profoundly than its members have ever known how to praise themselves.

What have the bourgeois done to deserve Marx's praise? First of all, they have "been the first to show what man's activity can bring about" (476). Marx does not mean that they have been the first to celebrate the idea of *vita activa,* an activistic stance toward the world. This has been a

central theme of Western culture since the Renaissance; it has taken on
new depths and resonances in Marx's own century, in the age of romanticism and revolution, of Napoleon and Byron and Goethe's *Faust*. Marx
himself will develop it in new directions, and it will go on evolving into
our own era. Marx's point is that what modern poets, artists and intellectuals have only dreamed of the modern bourgeoisie has actually done.
Thus it has "accomplished wonders that far surpass Egyptian pyramids,
Roman aqueducts, Gothic cathedrals"; it has "conducted expeditions that
put all former migrations of nations and crusades in the shade." Its genius for activity expresses itself first in great projects of physical construc-
tion-mills and factories, bridges and canals, railroads, all the public works
that constitute Faust's final achievement – these are the pyramids and
cathedrals of the modern age. Next there are the immense movements
of peoples – to cities, to frontiers, to new lands – which the bourgeoisie
has sometimes inspired, sometimes brutally enforced, sometimes subsi-
dized, and always exploited for profit. Marx, in a stirring, evocative paragraph, transmits the rhythm and drama of bourgeois activism:

> The bourgeoisie, in its reign of barely a hundred years, has created more
> massive and more colossal productive power than have all previous gen-
> erations put together. Subjection of nature's forces to man, machinery,
> application of chemistry to agriculture and industry, steam navigation,
> railways, electric telegraphs, clearing of whole continents for cultivation,
> canalization of rivers, whole populations conjured out of the ground –
> what earlier century had even an intimation that such productive power
> slept in the womb of social labor? (475)

Marx is neither the first nor the last writer to celebrate the triumphs
of modern bourgeois technology and social organization. But his paean

is distinctive both in what it emphasizes and in what it leaves out. Although Marx identifies himself as a materialist, he is not primarily interested in the material objects that the bourgeoisie creates. What matters to him is the processes, the powers, the expressions of human life and energy: men working, moving, cultivating, communicating, organizing and reorganizing nature and themselves – the new and endlessly renewed modes of activity that the bourgeoisie brings into being. Marx does not dwell much on particular inventions and innovations in their own right (in the tradition that runs from Saint-Simon through McLuhan); what stirs him is the active and generative process through which one thing leads to another, dreams metamorphose into blueprints and fantasies into balance sheets, the wildest and most extravagant ideas get acted on and acted out ("whole populations conjured out of the ground") and ignite and nourish new forms of life and action.

The irony of bourgeois activism, as Marx sees it, is that the bourgeoisie is forced to close itself off from its richest possibilities, possibilities that can be realized only by those who break its power. For all the marvelous modes of activity the bourgeoisie has opened up, the only activity that really means anything to its members is making money, accumulating capital, piling up surplus value; all their enterprises are merely means to this end, in themselves of no more than transient and intermediary interest. The active powers and processes that mean so much to Marx appear as incidental by-products in the minds of their producers. Nevertheless, the bourgeois have established themselves as the first ruling class whose authority is based not on who their ancestors were but on what they themselves actually do. They have produced vivid new images and paradigms of the good life as a life of action. They have proved that it really is possible, through organized, concerted action, to change the world.

Alas, to the bourgeois's embarrassment, they cannot afford to look down the roads they have opened up: the great vistas may turn into abysses. They can go on playing their revolutionary role only by denying its full extent and depth. But radical thinkers and workers are free to see where the roads lead, and to take them. If the good life is a life of action, why should the range of human activities be limited to those that are profitable? And why should modern men, who have seen what man's activity can bring about, passively accept the structure of their society as it is given? Since organized and concerted action can change the world in so many ways, why not organize and work together and fight to change it still more? The "revolutionary activity, practical-critical activity" that overthrows bourgeois rule will be an expression of the energies that the bourgeoisie itself has set free.[7] Marx began by praising the bourgeoisie, not by burying it; but if his dialectic works out, it will be the virtues for which he praised the bourgeoisie that will bury it in the end.

The second great bourgeois achievement has been to liberate the human capacity and drive for development: for permanent change, for perpetual upheaval and renewal in every mode of personal and social life. This drive, Marx shows, is embedded in the everyday workings and needs of the bourgeois economy. Everybody within reach of this economy finds himself under pressure of relentless competition, whether from across the street or across the world. Under pressure, every bourgeois, from the pettiest to the most powerful, is forced to innovate, simply in order to keep his business and himself afloat; anyone who does not actively change on his own will become a passive victim of changes draconically imposed by those who dominate the market. This means that the bourgeoisie, taken as a whole, "cannot exist without constantly revolutionizing the means of production." But the forces that shape and drive the modern economy cannot be compartmentalized and cut off from the totality of life. The intense and relentless pressure to revolutionize production is bound to spill over and transform what Marx calls "conditions of production" (or, alternately, "productive relationships") as well, "and, with them, all social conditions and relationships."

At this point, propelled by the desperate dynamism he is striving to grasp, Marx makes a great imaginative leap:

> Constant revolutionizing of production, uninterrupted disturbance of all social relations, everlasting uncertainty and agitation, distinguish the bourgeois epoch from all earlier times. All fixed, fast-frozen relationships, with their train of venerable ideas and opinions, are swept away, all new-formed ones become obsolete before they can ossify. All that is solid melts into air, all that is holy is profaned, and men at last are forced to face with sober senses the real conditions of their lives and their relations with their fellow men. (476)

Where does all this leave us, the members of "modern bourgeois society"? It leaves us all in strange and paradoxical positions. Our lives are controlled by a ruling class with vested interests not merely in change but in crisis and chaos. "Uninterrupted disturbance ... everlasting uncertainty and agitation," instead of subverting this society, actually serve to strengthen it. Catastrophes are transformed into lucrative opportunities for redevelopment and renewal; disintegration works as a mobilizing and hence an integrating force. The one spectre that really haunts the modern ruling class, and that really endangers the world it has created in its image, is the one thing that traditional elites (and, for that matter, traditional masses) have always yearned for: prolonged solid stability. In this world, stability can only mean entropy, slow death, while our sense of progress and growth is our only way of knowing for sure that we are alive. To say that our society is falling apart is only to say that it is alive and well.

What kinds of people does this permanent revolution produce? In order for people, whatever their class, to survive in modern society, their personalities must take on the fluid and open form of this society. Modern men and women must learn to yearn for change: not merely to be open to changes in their personal and social lives, but positively to demand them, actively to seek them out and carry them through. They must learn not to long nostalgically for the "fixed, fast-frozen relationships" of the real or fantasized past, but to delight in mobility, to thrive on renewal, to look forward to future developments in their conditions of life and their relations with their fellow men.

Marx absorbs this developmental ideal from the German humanist culture of his youth, from the thought of Goethe and Schiller and their romantic successors. This theme and its development, still very much alive in our own day – Erik Erikson is its most distinguished recent exponent – may be Germany's deepest and most lasting contribution to world culture. Marx is perfectly clear about his links to these writers, whom he is constantly citing and alluding to, and to their intellectual tradition. But he understands, as most of his predecessors did not – the crucial exception is the aged Goethe, the author of *Faust,* Part Two – that the humanistic ideal of *self-development* grows out of the emerging reality of bourgeois *economic development.* Thus, for all Marx's invective against the bourgeois economy, he embraces enthusiastically the personality structure that this economy has produced. The trouble with capitalism is that, here as elsewhere, it destroys the human possibilities it creates. It fosters, indeed forces, self-development for everybody; but people can develop only in restricted and distorted ways. Those traits, impulses and talents that the market can use are rushed (often prematurely) into development and squeezed desperately till there is nothing left; everything else within us, everything nonmarketable, gets draconically repressed, or withers away for lack of use, or never has a chance to come to life at all.

The ironic and happy solution to this contradiction will occur, Marx says, when "the development of modern industry cuts from under its feet the very grounds on which the bourgeoisie produces and appropriates products." The inner life and energy of bourgeois development will sweep away the class that first brought it to life. We can see this dialectical movement as much in the sphere of personal as in economic development: in a system where all relationships are volatile, how can capitalist forms of life – private property, wage labor, exchange value, the insatiable pursuit of profit – alone hold still? Where the desires and sensibilities of people in every class have become open-ended and insatiable, attuned to permanent upheavals in every sphere of life, what can possibly keep them fixed and frozen in their bourgeois roles? The more furiously bourgeois society agitates its members to grow or die, the more likely they will be to outgrow it itself, the more furiously they will eventually turn on it as a drag on their growth, the more implacably they will fight it in the name of the new life it has forced them to seek. Thus capitalism will be melted by the heat of its own incandescent energies. After the Revolution, "in the course of development," after wealth is redistributed, class privileges are wiped away, education is free and universal, and workers control the ways in which work is organized, then – so Marx prophesies at the *Manifesto*'s climactic moment – then, at last,

> In place of the old bourgeois society, with its classes and class antago-
> nisms, we will have an association in which the free development of each
> will be the condition for the free development of all. (491)

Then the experience of self-development, released from the demands and distortions of the market, can go on freely and spontaneously; instead of the nightmare that bourgeois society has made it, it can be a source of joy and beauty for all.

I want to step back from the *Communist Manifesto* for a moment to emphasize how crucial the developmental ideal is to Marx, from his earliest writings to his last. His youthful essay "Alienated Labor" proclaims, as the truly human alternative to estranged labor, work that will enable the individual to "freely develop his physical and spiritual [or mental] energies" (*MER*, 74). In *The German Ideology* (1845–46), the goal of communism is "the development of a totality of capacities in the individuals themselves." For "only in community with others has each individual the means of cultivating his gifts in all directions; only in the community, therefore, is personal freedom possible" (*MER*, 191, 197). In *Capital Volume 1* in the chapter "Machinery and Modern Industry," it is essential to communism that it transcend the capitalist division of labor:

... the partially developed individual, who is merely the bearer of one specialized social function, must be replaced by the fully developed individual, fit for a variety of labors, ready to face any change in production, for whom the different social functions he performs are only so many modes of giving free scope to his own natural and acquired powers. (413–14)

This vision of communism is unmistakably modern, first of all in its individualism, but even more in its ideal of development as the form of the good life. Here Marx is closer to some of his bourgeois and liberal enemies than he is to traditional exponents of communism, who, since Plato and the Church Fathers, have sanctified self-sacrifice, distrusted or loathed individuality, and yearned for a still point at which all strife and all striving will reach an end. Once again we find Marx more responsive to what is going on in bourgeois society than are the members and supporters of the bourgeoisie themselves. He sees in the dynamics of capitalist development – both the development of each individual and of society as a whole – a new image of the good life: not a life of definitive perfection, not the embodiment of prescribed static essences, but a process of continual, restless, open-ended, unbounded growth. Thus he hopes to heal the wounds of modernity through a fuller and deeper modernity.[8]

2. Innovative Self-Destruction

We can see now why Marx gets so excited and enthusiastic about the bourgeoisie and the world it has made. Now we must confront something even more perplexing: next to the *Communist Manifesto,* the whole body of capitalist apologetics, from Adam Ferguson to Irving Kristol, is remarkably pale and empty of life. The celebrants of capitalism tell us surprisingly little of its infinite horizons, its revolutionary energy and audacity, its dynamic creativity, its adventurousness and romance, its capacity to make men not merely more comfortable but more alive. The bourgeoisie and its ideologists have never been known for their humility or modesty, yet they seem strangely determined to hide much of their light under a bushel. The reason, I think, is that there is a dark side to this light that they cannot blot out. They are dimly aware of this, and deeply embarrassed and frightened by it, to the point that they will ignore or deny their own strength and creativity rather than look their virtues in the face and live with them.

What is it that the members of the bourgeoisie are afraid to recognize in themselves? Not their drive to exploit people, to treat them purely as means or (in economic rather than moral language) as commodities. The bourgeoisie, as Marx sees it, doesn't lose much sleep over this. After all, they do it to one another, and even to themselves, so why shouldn't they do it to everybody else? The real source of trouble is the bourgeois claim to be the "Party of Order" in modern politics and culture. The immense amounts of money and energy put into building, and the self-consciously monumental character of so much of this building – indeed, throughout Marx's century, every table and chair in a bourgeois interior resembled a monument – testify to the sincerity and seriousness of this claim. And yet, the truth of the matter, as Marx sees, is that everything that bourgeois society builds is built to be torn down. "All that is solid" – from the clothes on our backs to the looms and mills that weave them, to the men and women who work the ma-chines, to the houses and neighborhoods the workers live in, to the firms and corporations that exploit the workers, to the towns and cities and whole regions and even nations that embrace them all – all these are made to be broken tomorrow, smashed or shredded or pulverized or dissolved, so they can be recycled or replaced next week, and the whole process can go on again and again, hopefully forever, in ever more profitable forms.

The pathos of all bourgeois monuments is that their material strength and solidity actually count for nothing and carry no weight at all, that they are blown away like frail reeds by the very forces of capitalist development that they celebrate. Even the most beautiful and impressive bourgeois buildings and public works are disposable, capitalized for fast depreciation and planned to be obsolete, closer in their social functions to tents and encampments than to "Egyptian pyramids, Roman aqueducts, Gothic cathedrals." (Engels, just a few years before the *Manifesto*, in the *Condition of the Working Class in England in 1844,* was appalled to find that workers' housing, built by speculators for fast profits, was constructed to last only forty years. He little suspected this would become the archetypal pattern of construction in bourgeois society. Ironically, even the most splendid mansions of the richest capitalists would be gone in less than forty years, not just in Manchester, but in virtually every capitalist city – leased or sold off to developers, pulled down by the same insatiable drives that threw them up. New York's Fifth Avenue is a vivid example, but there are modern instances everywhere.) Considering the rapidity and brutality of capitalist development, the real surprise is not that so much of our architectural and urban heritage has been destroyed, but that there is anything left to preserve.

If we look behind the sober scenes these bourgeoisie create to see how they really work and act, we find that these solid citizens would tear down the world if it paid to do so. Even as they frighten everyone with fantasies of proletarian rapacity and revenge, they themselves, through their inexhaustible dealing and developing, hurtle masses of men, materials and money up and down the earth, and erode or explode the foundations of everyone's lives as they go. Their secret – a secret they have managed to keep even from themselves – is that, behind their facades, they are the most violently destructive ruling class in history. All the anarchic, measureless, explosive drives that a later generation will baptize by the name of "nihilism" – drives that Nietzsche and his followers will ascribe to such cosmic traumas as the Death of God – are located by Marx in the seemingly banal everyday working of the market economy. He unveils the modern bourgeois as consummate nihilists on a far vaster scale than modern intellectuals can conceive.

Actually, the term *nihilism* springs from Marx's own generation: it was coined by Turgenev as a motto for his radical (but, really, rather "positive") hero Bazarov in the novel *Fathers and Sons* (1861). It is elaborated in a more serious way by Dostoevsky in *Notes from Underground* (1864) and *Crime and Punishment* (1866–67). The theme pervades all Nietzsche's writing, but it is explored in greatest detail and depth in *The Will to Power* (1885–88), especially in Book One, "European Nihilism." It is rarely mentioned, but worth noting, that Nietzsche considered modern politics and economics profoundly nihilistic in their own right. See Section I, an inventory of the roots of contemporary nihilism. Some of Nietzsche's images and analyses here have a surprisingly Marxist ring. Section 63, for instance, discusses the spiritual consequences, both negative and positive, of "the fact of credit, of worldwide trade and means of transportation" on the "breaking up of landed property ... newspapers (in place of daily prayers), railway, telegraph. Centralization of a tremendous number of interests in a single soul, which for that reason must be very strong and protean."[9] But these connections between the modern soul and the modern economy are never worked out by Nietzsche, and (with very rare exceptions) never even noticed by his followers.

Nietzsche vilifies the modern bourgeois for lacking the courage to look into the nihilistic abyss. Marx can help us see the human costs of looking away: this is a supremely creative class that is cutting itself off from its own creativity. But Marx wants us all to have the strength to look into that abyss, and some of his most vivid and striking images are meant to direct us that way. Thus, "Modern bourgeois society, a society that has conjured up such mighty means of production and exchange, is like the sorcerer who can no longer control the powers of the underworld that he has called up by his spells" (478). This image evokes the spirits of that dark medieval past that our modern bourgeoisie is supposed to have buried. Its members present themselves as matter-of-fact and rational, not magical; as children of the Enlightenment, not of darkness. When Marx depicts the bourgeois as sorcerers – remember, too, their enterprise has "conjured whole populations out of the ground," not to mention "the spectre of communism" – he is pointing to depths they deny. Marx's imagery projects, here as ever, a sense of wonder over the modern world: its vital powers are dazzling, overwhelming, beyond anything the bourgeoisie could have imagined, let alone calculated or planned. But Marx's images also express what must accompany any genuine sense of wonder: a sense of dread, for this miraculous and magical world is also demonic and terrifying, swinging wildly out of control, menacing and destroying blindly as it moves. The members of the bourgeoisie repress both wonder and dread at what they have made: these possessors don't want to know how deeply they are possessed. They learn only at moments of personal and general ruin – only, that is, when it is too late.

Marx's bourgeois sorcerer descends from Goethe's Faust, of course, but also from another literary figure who haunted the imagination of his generation: Mary Shelley's Frankenstein. These mythical figures, striving to expand human powers through science and rationality, unleash demonic powers that erupt irrationally, beyond human control, with horrifying results. In the second part of Goethe's *Faust*, the consummate underworld power, which finally makes the sorcerer obsolete, is a whole modern social system. Marx's bourgeoisie moves within this tragic orbit. He places its underworld in a worldly context and shows how, in a million factories and mills, banks and exchanges, dark powers work in broad daylight, social forces are driven in dreadful directions by relentless market imperatives that not even the most powerful bourgeois can control. Marx's vision brings this abyss close to home.

Thus, in the first part of the *Manifesto,* Marx lays out the polarities that will shape and animate the culture of modernism in the century to come: the theme of insatiable desires and drives, permanent revolution, infinite development, perpetual creation and renewal in every sphere of life; and its radical antithesis, the theme of nihilism, insatiable destruction, the shattering and swallowing up of life, the heart of darkness, the horror. Marx shows how both these human possibilities are infused into the life of every modern man by the drives and pressures of the bourgeois economy. In the course of time, modernists will produce a great array of cosmic and apocalyptic visions, visions of the most radiant joy and the bleakest despair. Many of the most creative modernist artists will be simultaneously possessed by both and driven endlessly from pole to pole; their inner dynamism will reproduce and express the inward rhythms by which modern capitalism moves and lives. Marx plunges us into the depths of this life process, so that we feel ourselves charged with a vital energy that magnifies our whole being – and are simultaneously seized by shocks and convulsions that threaten at every instant to annihilate us. Then, by the power of his language and thought, he tries to entice us to trust his vision, to let ourselves be swept along with him toward a climax that lies just ahead.

The sorcerer's apprentices, the members of the revolutionary proletariat, are bound to wrest control of modern productive forces from the Faustian-Frankensteinian bourgeoisie. When this is done, they will transform these volatile, explosive social forces into sources of beauty and joy for all, and bring the tragic history of modernity to a happy end. Whether or not this ending should ever really come to pass, the *Manifesto* is remarkable for its imaginative power, its expression and grasp of the luminous and dreadful possibilities that pervade modern life. Along with everything else that it is, it is the first great modernist work of art.

But even as we honor the *Manifesto* as an archetype of modernism, we must remember that archetypal models serve to typify not only truths and strengths but also inner tensions and strains. Thus, both in the *Manifesto* and in its illustrious successors, we will find that, against the creator's intentions and probably without his awareness, the vision of revolution and resolution generates its own immanent critique, and new contradictions thrust themselves through the veil that this vision weaves. Even as we let ourselves be carried along by Marx's dialectical flow, we feel ourselves being carried away by uncharted currents of uncertainty and unease, We are caught up in a series of radical tensions between Marx's intentions and his insights, between what he wants and what he sees.

Take, for instance, Marx's theory of crises: "crises that by their periodic return put the existence of the whole bourgeois society in question, each time more threateningly" (478). In these recurrent crises "a great part, not only of existing products, but of previously created productive forces, are repeatedly destroyed." Marx appears to believe that these crises will increasingly cripple capitalism and eventually destroy it. And yet, his own vision and analysis of bourgeois society show how well this society can thrive on crisis and catastrophe: "on one hand, by enforced destruction of a mass of productive forces; on the other, by conquest of new markets and more thorough exploitation of the old ones." The crises can annihilate people and companies that are, by the market's definitions, relatively weak and inefficient; they can open up empty spaces for new investment and redevelopment; they can force the bourgeoisie to innovate, expand and combine more intensively and ingeniously than ever: thus they may act as unexpected sources of capitalist strength and resiliency. It may be true that, as Marx says, these forms of adaptation only "pave the way for more extensive and more destructive crises." But, given the bourgeois capacity to make destruction and chaos pay, there is no apparent reason why these crises can spiral on endlessly, smashing people, families, corporations, towns, but leaving the structures of bourgeois social life and power intact.

Next we might take Marx's vision of the revolutionary community. Its foundations will be laid, ironically, by the bourgeoisie itself. "The progress of industry, whose inadvertent promoter is the bourgeoisie, replaces the isolation of the workers through competition with their union through association" (483). The immense productive units inherent in modern industry will throw large numbers of workers together, will force them to depend on each other and to cooperate in their work – the modern division of labor requires intricate cooperation from moment to moment on a vast scale – and so will teach them to think and act collectively. The workers' communal bonds, generated inadvertently by capitalist production, will generate militant political institutions, unions that will oppose and finally overthrow the private, atomistic framework of capitalist social relations. So Marx believes.

And yet, if his overall vision of modernity is true, why should the forms of community produced by capitalist industry be any more solid than any other capitalist product? Might not these collectivities turn out to be, like everything else here, only temporary, provisional, built for obsolescence? Marx in 1856 will speak of the industrial workers as "new-fangled men ... as much an invention of modern times as machinery itself" (578).[10] But if this is so, then their solidarity, however impressive at any given moment, may turn out to be as transient as the machines they operate or the products they turn out. The workers may sustain each other today on the assembly line or the picket line, only to find

themselves scattered tomorrow among different collectivities with different conditions, different processes and products, different needs and interests. Once again the abstract forms of capitalism seem to subsist –
capital, wage labor, commodities, exploitation, surplus value – while
their human contents are thrown into perpetual flux. How can any lasting human bonds grow in such loose and shifting soil?

Even if the workers do build a successful communist *movement,* and
even if that movement generates a successful revolution, how, amid the
flood tides of modern life, will they ever manage to build a solid communist *society*? What is to prevent the social forces that melt capitalism from
melting communism as well? If all new relationships become obsolete
before they can ossify, how can solidarity, fraternity and mutual aid be
kept alive? A communist government might try to dam the flood by
imposing radical restrictions, not merely on economic activity and enterprise (every socialist government has done this, along with every capitalist welfare state), but on personal, cultural and political expression. But
insofar as such a policy succeeded, wouldn't it betray the Marxist aim of
free development for each and all? Marx looked forward to communism
as the fulfillment of modernity; but how can communism entrench itself
in the modern world without suppressing those very modern energies
that it promises to set free? On the other hand, if it gave these energies
free rein, mightn't the spontaneous flow of popular energy sweep away
the new social formation itself?

Thus, simply by reading the *Manifesto* closely and taking its vision of
modernity seriously, we arrive at serious questions about Marx's answers.
We can see that the fulfillment Marx sees just around the bend may be a
long time coming, if it comes at all; and we can see that even if it does
come, it may be only a fleeting, transitory episode, gone in a moment,

obsolete before it can ossify, swept away by the same tide of perpetual change and progress that brought it briefly within our reach, leaving us endlessly, helplessly floating on. We can see, too, how communism, in order to hold itself together, might stifle the active, dynamic and developmental forces that have brought it into being, might betray many of the hopes that have made it worth fighting for, might reproduce the inequities and contradictions of bourgeois society under new names – names like "People's Republic," names like *soviet*. Ironically, then, we can see Marx's dialectic of modernity re-enacting the fate of the society it describes, generating energies and ideas that melt it down into its own air.

3. Nakedness: The Unaccommodated Man

Now that we have seen Marx's "melting" vision in action, I want to use it to explicate some of the *Manifesto*'s most powerful images of modern life. In the passage below, Marx is trying to show how capitalism has transformed people's relationships with each other and with themselves. Although in Marx's syntax "the bourgeoisie" is the subject – its economic activities that bring the big changes about – modern men and women of every class are objects, for all are changed:

> The bourgeoisie has torn apart the many feudal ties that bound men to their "natural superiors," and left no other bond between man and man than naked interest, than callous cash payment. It has drowned the heavenly ecstasies of pious fanaticism, of chivalrous enthusiasm, of philistine sentimentalism, in the icy water of egotistical calculation. ... The bourgeoisie has stripped of its halo every occupation hitherto honored and looked up to with reverent awe. ... The bourgeoisie has torn away from the family its sentimental veil, and turned the family relation into a pure

money relation.... In place of exploitation veiled by religious and political illusions, it has put open, shameless, direct, naked exploitation. (475–6)

Marx's basic opposition here is between what is open or naked and what is hidden, veiled, clothed. This polarity, perennial in Eastern as well as Western thought, symbolizes everywhere a distinction between a "real" world and an illusory one. In most ancient and medieval speculative thought, the whole world of sensuous experience appears illusory – the Hindu "veil of Maya" – and the true world is thought to be accessible only through transcendence of bodies, space and time. In some traditions, reality is accessible through religious or philosophical meditation; in others, it will be available to us only in a future existence after death: the Pauline "for now we see through a glass darkly, but then face to face."

The modern transformation, beginning in the age of the Renaissance and Reformation, places both these worlds on earth, in space and time, filled with human beings. Now the false world is seen as a historical past, a world we have lost (or are in the process of losing), while the true world is in the physical and social world that exists for us here and now (or is in the process of coming into being). At this point a new symbolism emerges. Clothes become an emblem of the old, illusory mode of life; nakedness comes to signify the newly discovered and experienced truth; and the act of taking off one's clothes becomes an act of spiritual liberation, of becoming real. Modern erotic poetry elaborates this theme, as generations of modern lovers have experienced it, with playful irony; modern tragedy penetrates its awesome and fearsome depths. Marx thinks and works in the tragic tradition. For him, the clothes are ripped off, the veils are torn away, the stripping process is violent and brutal; and yet, somehow, the tragic movement of modern history is supposed to culminate in a happy end.

The dialectic of nakedness that culminates in Marx is defined at the very start of the modern age, in Shakespeare's *King Lear*. For Lear, the naked truth is what a man is forced to face when he has lost everything that other men can take away, except life itself. We see his voracious family, aided by his own blind vanity, tear away its sentimental veil. Stripped not only of political power but of even the barest traces of human dignity, he is thrown out of doors in the middle of the night at the height of a torrential and terrifying storm. This, he says, is what human life comes down to in the end: the solitary and poor abandoned in the cold, while the nasty and brutish enjoy all the warmth that power can provide. Such knowledge seems to be too much for us: "man's nature cannot carry / Th' affliction, nor the fear." But Lear is not broken by the storm's icy blasts, neither does he flee them; instead, he exposes himself to the storm's full fury, looks it in the face and affirms himself against it even as it tosses and tears him. As he wanders with his royal fool (Act III, Scene 4), they meet Edgar, disguised as a crazy beggar, stark naked, apparently even more wretched than he. "Is man no more than this?" Lear demands. "Thou art the thing itself: unaccommodated man." Now, at the climactic moment of the play, he tears off his royal robes – "Off, off you lendings" – and joins "poor Tom" in naked authenticity. This act, which Lear believes has placed him at the very nadir of existence – "a poor, bare, forked animal" – turns out, ironically, to be his first step toward a full humanity, because, for the first time, he recognizes a connection between himself and another human being. This recognition enables him to grow in sensitivity and insight, and to move beyond the bounds of his self-absorbed bitterness and misery. As he stands and shivers, it dawns on him that his kingdom is full of people whose whole lives are consumed by the abandoned, defenseless suffering that he is going through right now. When he was in power he never noticed, but now he stretches his vision to take them in:

> Poor naked wretches, wheresoe'er you are,
> That bide the pelting of this pitiless storm,
> How shall your houseless heads and unfed sides,
> Your loop'd and window'd raggedness defend you
> From seasons such as these? O,I have ta'en
> Too little care of this! Take physic, pomp;
> Expose thyself to feel what wretches feel,
> That thou mayst shake the superflux to them,
> And show the heavens more just. (III, 4, 28–36)

It is only now that Lear might be fit to be what he claims to be, "every inch a king." His tragedy is that the catastrophe that redeems him humanly destroys him politically: the experience that makes him genuinely qualified to be a king (to the extent that any human being can be) makes it impossible for him to be one. His triumph lies in becoming something he never dreamt of being, a human being. Here a hopeful dialectic lights up the tragic bleakness and blight. Alone in the cold and the wind and the rain, Lear develops the vision and courage to break out of his loneliness, to reach out to his fellow men for mutual warmth. Shakespeare is telling us that the dreadful naked reality of the "unaccommodated man" is the point from which accommodation must be made, the only ground on which real community can grow.

In the eighteenth century, the metaphors of nakedness as truth and stripping as self-discovery take on a new political resonance. In Montesquieu's *Persian Letters,* the veils that Persian women are forced to wear symbolize all the repressions that traditional social hierarchies inflict on people. By contrast, the absence of veils in the streets of Paris symbolizes a new kind of society where "liberty and equality reign," and where, as a consequence, "everything speaks out, everything is visible, everything is audible. The heart shows itself as clearly as the face."[11] Rousseau, in his *Discourse on the Arts and Sciences,* denounces "the uniform and deceptive veil of politeness" that covers his age, and says that "the good man is an athlete who loves to wrestle stark naked; he despises all those vile ornaments that cramp the use of his powers."[12] Thus the naked man will be not only a freer and happier man, but a better man. The liberal revolutionary movements that bring the eighteenth century to a climax act out this faith: if hereditary privileges and social roles are stripped away, so that all men can enjoy an unfettered freedom to use all their powers, they will use them for the good of all mankind. We find here a striking absence of worry as to what the naked human being will do or be. The dialectical complexity and wholeness that we found in Shakespeare have faded away, and narrow polarizations have taken their place. The counter-revolutionary thought of this period shows the same narrowing and flattening of perspective. Here is Burke on the French Revolution:

> But now all is to be changed. All the pleasing illusions that made power gentle, and obedience liberal, which harmonized the different shades of life ... are to be dissolved by this new conquering empire of light and reason. All the decent drapery of life is to be rudely torn off. All the super-added ideas, which the heart owns, and the understanding ratifies, as necessary to cover the defects of our weak and shivering nature, and to raise it to a dignity in our own estimation, are to be exploded as a ridiculous, absurd and antiquated fashion.[13]

The *philosophes* imagined nakedness as idyllic, opening new vistas of beauty and happiness for all; for Burke it is counter-idyllic, an unmitigated disaster, a fall into nothingness from which nothing and no one can rise. Burke cannot imagine that modern men might learn something, as Lear learns, from their mutual vulnerability in the cold. Their only hope lies in their capacity to construct mythic draperies heavy enough to stifle their dreadful knowledge of who they are.

For Marx, writing in the aftermath of bourgeois revolutions and reactions, and looking forward to a new wave, the symbols of nakedness and unveiling regain the dialectical depth that Shakespeare gave them two centuries before. The bourgeois revolutions, in tearing away veils of "religious and political illusion," have left naked power and exploitation, cruelty and misery, exposed like open wounds; at the same time, they have uncovered and exposed new options and hopes. Unlike the common people of all ages, who have been endlessly betrayed and broken by their devotion to their "natural superiors," modern men, washed in "the icy water of egoistical calculation," are free from deference to masters who destroy them, animated rather than numbed by the cold. Because they know how to think of, by and for themselves, they will demand a clear account of what their bosses and rulers are doing for them – and doing to them – and be ready to resist and rebel where they are getting nothing real in return.

Marx's hope is that once the unaccommodated men of the working class are "forced to face ... the real conditions of their lives and their relations with their fellow men," they will come together to overcome the cold that cuts through them all. Their union will generate the collective energy that can fuel a new communal life. One of the *Manifesto*'s primary aims is to point the way out of the cold, to nourish and focus the common yearning for communal warmth. Because the workers can come through the affliction and the fear only by making contact with the self's deepest resources, they will be prepared to fight for collective recognition of the self's beauty and value. Their communism, when it comes, will appear as a kind of transparent garment, at once keeping its wearers warm and setting off their naked beauty, so that they can recognize themselves and each other in all their radiance.

Here, as so often in Marx, the vision is dazzling but the light flickers if we look hard. It isn't hard to imagine alternate endings to the dialectic of nakedness, endings less beautiful than Marx's but no less plausible. Modern men and women might well prefer the solitary pathos and grandeur of the Rousseauean unconditioned self, or the collective costumed comforts of the Burkean political masque, rather than the Marxian attempt to fuse the best of both. Indeed, the sort of individualism that scorns and fears connections with other people as threats to the self's integrity, and the sort of collectivism that seeks to submerge the self in a social role, may be more appealing than the Marxian synthesis, because they are intellectually and emotionally so much easier.

There is a further problem that might keep the Marxian dialectic from even getting under way. Marx believes that the shocks and upheavals and catastrophes of life in bourgeois society enable moderns, by going through them, as Lear does, to discover who they "really are." But if bourgeois society is as volatile as Marx thinks it is, how can its people ever settle on any real selves? With all the possibilities and necessities that bombard the self and all the desperate drives that propel it, how can anyone define, definitively, which ones are essential and which merely incidental? The nature of the newly naked modern man may turn out to be just as elusive and mysterious as that of the old, clothed one – maybe even more elusive, because there will no longer be any illusion of a real self underneath the masks. Thus, along with community and society, individuality itself may be melting into the modern air.

4. The Metamorphosis of Values

The problem of nihilism emerges again in Marx's next line: "The bourgeoisie has resolved all personal honor and dignity into exchange-value; and in place of all the freedoms that men have fought for, it has put one unprincipled freedom – free trade." The first point here is the immense power of the market in modern men's inner lives: they look to the price list for answers to questions not merely economic but metaphysical-questions of what is worthwhile, what is honorable, even what is real. When Marx says that other values are "resolved into" exchange-value, his point is that bourgeois society does not efface old structures of value but subsumes them. Old modes of honor and dignity do not die; instead, they get incorporated into the market, take on price tags, gain a new life as commodities. Thus, any imaginable mode of human conduct becomes morally permissible the moment it becomes economically possible, becomes "valuable"; anything goes if it pays. This is what modern nihilism is all about. Dostoevsky, Nietzsche and their twentieth-century successors will ascribe this predicament to science, rationalism, the Death of God. Marx would say that its basis is far more concrete and mundane: it is built into the banal everyday workings of the bourgeois economic order – an order that equates our human value with our market price, no more, no less, and that forces us to expand ourselves in pushing our price up as far as we can make it go.

Marx is appalled by the destructive brutalities that bourgeois nihilism brings to life, but he believes that it has a hidden tendency to transcend itself. The source of this tendency is the paradoxically "unprincipled" principle of free trade. Marx believes that the bourgeois really believe in this principle – that is, in an incessant, unrestricted flow of commodities in circulation, a continuous metamorphosis of market values. If, as he believes, the members of the bourgeoisie really do want a free market, they will have to enforce the freedom of new products to enter the market. This in turn means that any full-fledged bourgeois society must be a genuinely open society, not only economically but politically and culturally as well, so that people will be free to shop around and seek the best deals, in ideas, associations, laws and social policies, as well as in things. The unprincipled principle of free trade will force the bourgeoisie to grant even communists the basic right that all businessmen enjoy, the right to offer and promote and sell their goods to as many customers as they can attract.

Thus, by virtue of what Marx calls "free competition within the realm of knowledge" (489), even the most subversive works and ideas – like the *Manifesto* itself – must be allowed to appear, on the grounds that they may sell. Marx is confident that once the ideas of revolution and communism become accessible to the masses they *will* sell, and communism as a "self-conscious, independent movement of the immense majority" (482) will come into its own. Thus he can live with bourgeois nihilism in the long run, because he sees it as active and dynamic, what Nietzsche would call "a nihilism of strength."

"Nihilism ... is ambiguous," Nietzsche said in *The Will to Power*, Sections 22 and 23. There is a nihilism of strength and a nihilism of weakness. In Type A, nihilism of strength, "a sign of increased power of the spirit," here "the spirit may have grown so strong that previous goals [convictions, articles of faith] have become incommensurate ... It reaches its maximum of relative strength as a violent force of destruction – as active nihilism." Marx understood far better than Nietzsche the nihilistic strength of bourgeois society. Propelled by its nihilistic drives and energies, the bourgeoisie will open the political and cultural floodgates through which its revolutionary nemesis will flow.

This dialectic presents several problems. The first concerns the bourgeoisie's commitment to the unprincipled principle of free trade, whether in economics, politics or culture. In fact, in bourgeois history this principle has generally been more honored in the breach than in the observance. The members of the bourgeoisie, especially the most powerful, have generally fought to restrict, manipulate and control their markets. Indeed, much of their creative energy over the centuries has gone into arrangements for doing this – chartered monopolies, holding companies, trusts, cartels and conglomerates, protective tariffs, patents, price-fixing, open or hidden subsidies from the state – all accompanied by paeans in praise of the free market. Moreover, even among the few who really do believe in free exchange, there are fewer still who would extend free competition to ideas as well as things.

Interestingly, the most trenchant statement of this principle – that free trade and competition entail free thought and culture – may be found, surprisingly, in Baudelaire. His *Preface to the Salon of 1846*, dedicated "To the Bourgeois," asserts a special affinity between modern enterprise and modern art: both are striving "to realize the idea of the future in its most diverse forms – political, industrial, artistic," both are thwarted by "the aristocrats of thought, the monopolists of things of the mind," who would stifle the energy and progress of modern life.[14] Arguments like Baudelaire's make perfect sense in dynamic and progressive periods like

the 1840s – or the 1960s. On the other hand, in periods of reaction and
stagnation, like the 1850s or the Reagan age, this sort of argument is apt
to sound unthinkably bizarre, if not monstrous, to many bourgeois who
embraced it enthusiastically just a few years before. We must keep in
mind that Wilhelm von Humboldt, J. S. Mill, and Justices Holmes and
Brandeis and Douglas and Black have been still, small voices in bourgeois
society, embattled and marginal at best. A more typical bourgeois pattern
is to praise freedom when in opposition and to repress it when in power.
Here Marx may be in danger – a surprising danger for him – of getting
carried away by what bourgeois ideologues say, and losing touch with
what the men with money and power actually do. This is a serious problem, because if the members of the bourgeoisie really don't give a damn
about freedom, then they will work to keep the societies they control
closed against new ideas, and it will be harder than ever for communism
to take root. Marx would say that their need for progress and innovation
will force them to open up their societies even to ideas they dread. Yet
their ingenuity might avoid this through a truly insidious innovation: a
consensus of mutually enforced mediocrity, designed to protect each
individual bourgeois from the risks of competition, and bourgeois society as a whole from the risks of change.

   In the climactic chapter of the first volume of *Capital*, "The Historical
Tendency of Capitalist Accumulation," Marx says that when a system of
social relations acts as a fetter on "the free development of productive
forces," that social system has simply got to go: "It must be annihilated; it
is annihilated." But what would happen if, somehow, it didn't get annihilated? Marx lets himself imagine this for barely an instant, only to dismiss
the possibility. "To perpetuate" such a social system, he says, would be
"to decree universal mediocrity" (*MER*, 437). This is perhaps the one

thing that Marx is utterly incapable of imagining.

Another problem in Marx's dialectic of the free market is that it entails a strange collusion between bourgeois society and its most radical opponents. This society is driven by its unprincipled principle of free exchange to open itself to movements for radical change. The enemies of capitalism may enjoy a great deal of freedom to do their work – to read, write, speak, meet, organize, demonstrate, strike, elect. But their freedom to move transforms their movement into an enterprise, and they find themselves cast in the paradoxical role of merchants and promoters of revolution, which necessarily becomes a commodity like everything else. Marx does not seem to be disturbed by the ambiguities of this social role – maybe because he is sure that it will become obsolete before it can ossify, that the revolutionary enterprise will be put out of business by its rapid success. A century later, we can see how the business of promoting revolution is open to the same abuses and temptations, manipulative frauds and wishful self-deceptions, as any other promotional line.

Finally, our skeptical doubts about promoters' promises must lead us to question one of the primary promises in Marx's work: the promise that communism, while upholding and actually deepening the freedoms that capitalism has brought us, will free us from the horrors of bourgeois nihilism. If bourgeois society is really the maelstrom Marx thinks it is, how can he expect all its currents to flow only one way, toward peaceful harmony and integration? Even if a triumphant communism should someday flow through the floodgates that free trade opens up, who knows what dreadful impulses might flow in along with it, or in its wake, or impacted inside? It is easy to imagine how a society committed to the free development of each and all might develop its own distinctive varieties of nihilism. Indeed, a communist nihilism might turn out to be far more explosive and disintegrative than its bourgeois precursor – though also more daring and original – because, while capitalism cuts the infinite possibilities of modern life with the limits of the bottom line, Marx's communism might launch the liberated self into immense unknown human spaces with no limits at all.

5. The Loss of a Halo

All the ambiguities in Marx's thought are crystallized in one of his most luminous images: "The bourgeoisie has stripped of its halo every activity hitherto honored and looked up to with reverent awe. It has transformed the doctor, the lawyer, the priest, the poet, the man of science into its paid wage-laborers" (476). The halo, for Marx, is a primary symbol of religious experience, the experience of something holy. For Marx, as for his contemporary Kierkegaard, experience, rather than belief or dogma or theology, forms the core of religious life. The halo splits life into sacred and profane: it creates an aura of holy dread and radiance around the figure who wears it; the sanctified figure is torn from the matrix of the human condition, split off inexorably from the needs and pressures that animate the men and women who surround it.

Marx believes that capitalism tends to destroy this mode of experience for everybody: "all that is holy is profaned"; nothing is sacred, no one is untouchable, life becomes thoroughly desanctified. In some ways, Marx knows, this is frightful: modern men and women may well stop at nothing, with no dread to hold them back; free from fear and trembling, they are free to trample down everyone in their way if self-interest drives them to it. But Marx also sees the virtue of a life without auras: it brings about a condition of spiritual equality. Thus the modern bourgeoisie may hold vast material powers over the workers and everybody else, but it will never achieve the spiritual ascendancy that earlier ruling classes could take for granted. For the first time in history, all confront themselves and each other on a single plane of being.

We must remember that Marx is writing at a historical moment when, especially in England and France (the *Manifesto* really has more to do with them than with the Germany of Marx's time), disenchantment with capitalism is pervasive and intense, and almost ready to flare up in revolutionary forms. In the next twenty years or so, the bourgeoisie will prove remarkably inventive in constructing halos of its own. Marx will try to strip these away in the first volume of *Capital,* in his analysis of "The Fetishism of Commodities" – a mystique that disguises the intersubjective relations between men in a market society as purely physical, "objective," unalterable relations between things. In the climate of 1848, this bourgeois pseudo-religiosity had not yet established itself. Marx's targets here are, for both him and us, a lot closer to home: those professionals and intellectuals – "the doctor, the lawyer, the priest, the poet, the man of science" – who think they have the power to live on a higher plane than ordinary humanity, to transcend capitalism in life and work.

Why does Marx place that halo on the heads of modern professionals and intellectuals in the first place? To bring out one of the paradoxes of their historical role: even though they tend to pride themselves on their emancipated and thoroughly secular minds, they turn out to be just about the only moderns who really believe that they are called to their vocations and that their work is holy. It is obvious to any reader of Marx that in his commitment to his work he shares this faith. And yet he is suggesting here that in some sense it is a bad faith, a self-deception. This passage is so arresting because, as we see Marx identifying himself with the critical force and insight of the bourgeoisie, and reaching out to tear the halos from modern intellectuals' heads, we realize that in some sense it is his own head he is laying bare.

The basic fact of life for these intellectuals, as Marx sees them, is that they are "paid wage-laborers" of the bourgeoisie, members of "the modern working class, the proletariat." They may deny this identity – after all, who wants to belong to the proletariat? – but they are thrown into the working class by the historically defined conditions under which they are forced to work. When Marx describes intellectuals as wage earners, he is trying to make us see modern culture as part of modern industry. Art, physical science, social theory like Marx's own, all are modes of production; the bourgeoisie controls the means of production in culture, as in everything else, and anyone who wants to create must work in the orbit of its power.

Modern professionals, intellectuals and artists, insofar as they are members of the proletariat,

> live only so long as they find work, and ... find work only so long as their labor increases capital. These workers, who must sell themselves piecemeal, are a commodity like every other article of commerce, and are consequently exposed to all the vicissitudes of competition, to all the fluctuations of the market. (479)

Thus they can write books, paint pictures, discover physical or historical laws, save lives, only if someone with capital will pay them. But the pressures of bourgeois society are such that no one will pay them unless it pays to pay them – that is, unless their works somehow help to "increase capital." They must "sell themselves piecemeal" to an employer willing to exploit their brains for profit. They must scheme and hustle to present themselves in a maximally profitable light; they must compete (often brutally and unscrupulously) for the privilege of being bought, simply in order to go on with their work. Once the work is done they are, like all other workers, separated from the products of their labor. Their goods and services go on sale, and it is "the vicissitudes of competition, the fluctuations of the market," rather than any intrinsic truth or beauty or value – or, for that matter, any lack of truth or beauty or value – that will determine their fate. Marx does not expect that great ideas and works will fall stillborn for want of a market: the modern bourgeoisie is remarkably resourceful in wringing profit out of thought. What will happen instead is that creative processes and products will be used and transformed in ways that will dumfound or horrify their creators. But the creators will be powerless to resist, because they must sell their labor power in order to live.

Intellectuals occupy a peculiar position in the working class, one that generates special privileges but also special ironies. They are beneficiaries of the bourgeois demand for perpetual innovation, which vastly expands the market for their products and skills, often stimulates their creative audacity and imagination, and – if they are shrewd enough and lucky enough to exploit the need for brains – enables them to escape the chronic poverty in which most workers live. On the other hand, because they are personally involved in their work – unlike most wage laborers, who are alienated and indifferent – the fluctuations of the marketplace strike them in a far deeper way. In "selling themselves piecemeal," they are selling not merely their physical energy but their minds, their sensibilities, their deepest feelings, their visionary and imaginative powers, virtually the whole of themselves. Goethe's *Faust* gave us the archetype of a modern intellectual forced to "sell himself" in order to make a difference in the world. Faust also embodied a complex of needs endemic to intellectuals: they are driven not only by a need to live, which they share with all men, but by a desire to communicate, to engage in dialogue with their fellow men. But the cultural commodity market offers the only media in which dialogue on a public scale can take place: no idea can reach or change moderns unless it can be marketed and sold to them. Hence they turn out to be dependent on the market not for bread alone but for spiritual sustenance – a sustenance they know the market cannot be counted on to provide.

It is easy to see why modern intellectuals, trapped in these ambiguities, would imagine radical ways out: in their situation, revolutionary ideas would spring from the most direct and intense personal needs. But the social conditions that inspire their radicalism also serve to frustrate it. We saw that even the most subversive ideas must manifest themselves through the medium of the market. Insofar as these ideas attract and arouse people, they will expand and enrich the market, and so "increase capital." Now, if Marx's vision of bourgeois society is at all accurate, there is every reason to think that it will generate a market for radical ideas. This system requires constant revolutionizing, disturbance, agitation; it needs to be perpetually pushed and pressed in order to maintain its elasticity and resilience, to appropriate and assimilate new energies, to drive itself to new heights of activity and growth. This means, however, that men and movements that proclaim their enmity to capitalism may be just the sort of stimulants capitalism needs. Bourgeois society, through its insatiable drive for destruction and development, and its need to satisfy the insatiable needs it creates, inevitably produces radical ideas and movements that aim to destroy it. But its very capacity for development enables it to negate its own inner negations: to nourish itself and thrive on opposition, to become stronger amid pressure and crisis than it could ever be in peace, to transform enmity into intimacy and attackers into inadvertent allies.

In this climate, then, radical intellectuals encounter radical obstacles: their ideas and movements are in danger of melting into the same modern air that decomposes the bourgeois order they are working to overcome. To surround oneself with a halo in this climate is to try to destroy danger by denying it. The intellectuals of Marx's time were particularly susceptible to this sort of bad faith. Even as Marx was discovering socialism in the Paris of the 1840s, Gautier and Flaubert were developing their mystique of "art for art's sake," while the circle around Auguste Comte was constructing its own parallel mystique of "pure science." Both these groups – sometimes in conflict with each other, sometimes interfused – sanctified themselves as avant-gardes. They were at once perceptive and trenchant in their critiques of capitalism, and, at the same time, absurdly complacent in their faith that they had the power to transcend it, that they could live and work freely beyond its norms and demands.

Marx's point in tearing the halos from their heads is that nobody in bourgeois society can be so pure or safe or free. The networks and ambiguities of the market are such that everybody is caught up and entangled in them. Intellectuals must recognize the depths of their own dependence – spiritual as well as economic dependence – on the bourgeois world they despise. It will never be possible to overcome these contradictions unless we confront them directly and openly. This is what stripping away the halos means.

This image, like all the great images in the history of literature and thought, contains depths that its creator could not have foreseen. First of all, Marx's indictment of the nineteenth-century artistic and scientific *avant-gardes* cuts just as deeply against the twentieth-century Leninist "vanguards" who make an identical – and equally groundless – claim to transcend the vulgar world of need, interest, egoistical calculation and brutal exploitation. Next, however, it raises questions about Marx's own romantic image of the working class. If being a paid wage laborer is the antithesis of having a halo, how can Marx speak of the proletariat as a class of new men, uniquely equipped to transcend the contradictions of modern life? Indeed, we can carry this questioning a step further. If we have followed Marx's unfolding vision of modernity, and confronted all its endemic ironies and ambiguities, how can we expect *anybody* to transcend all this?

Once again we encounter a problem we have met before: the tension between Marx's critical insights and his radical hopes. My emphases in this essay have leaned toward the skeptical and self-critical undercurrents in Marx's thought. Some readers may be inclined to take only the criticism and self-criticism to heart, and throw out the hopes as utopian and naive. To do this, however, would be to miss what Marx saw as the essential point of critical thinking. Criticism, as he understood it, was part of an ongoing dialectical process. It was meant to be dynamic, to drive and inspire the person criticized to overcome both his critics and himself, to propel both parties toward a new synthesis. Thus, to unmask phony claims of transcendence is to demand and fight for real transcendence. To give up the quest for transcendence is to put a halo on one's own stagnation and resignation, and to betray not only Marx but ourselves. We need to strive for the precarious, dynamic balance that Antonio Gramsci, one of the great communist writers and leaders of our century, described as "pessimism of the intellect, optimism of the will."[15]

Conclusion: Culture and the Contradictions of Capitalism

I have been trying in this essay to define a space in which Marx s thought and the modernist tradition converge. First of all, both are attempts to evoke and to grasp a distinctively modern experience. Both confront this realm with mixed emotions, awe and elation fused with a sense of horror. Both see modern life as shot through with contradictory impulses and potentialities, and both embrace a vision of ultimate or ultra modernity – Marx's "new-fangled men … as much the invention of modern time as machinery itself" ; Rimbaud's "Il faut être absolument moderne" – as the way through and beyond these contradictions.

In the spirit of convergence, I have tried to read Marx as a modernist writer, to bring out the vividness and richness of his language, the depth and complexity of his imagery – clothes and nakedness, veils, halos, heat, cold – and to show how brilliantly he develops the themes by which modernism will come to define itself: the glory of modern energy and dynamism, the ravages of modern disintegration and nihilism, the strange intimacy between them; the sense of being caught in a vortex where all facts and values are whirled, exploded, decomposed, recombined; a basic uncertainty about what is basic, what is valuable, even what is real; a flaring up of the most radical hopes in the midst of their radical negations. At the same time, I have tried to read modernism in a Marxist way, to suggest how its characteristic energies, insights and anxieties spring from the drives and strains of modern economic life: from its relentless and insatiable pressure for growth and progress; its expansion of human desires beyond local, national and moral bounds; its demands on people to exploit not only their fellow men but also themselves; the volatility and endless metamorphosis of all its values in the maelstrom of the world market; its pitiless destruction of everything and everyone it cannot use – so much of the premodern world, but so much of itself and its own modern world as well – and its capacity to exploit crisis and chaos as a springboard for still more development, to feed itself on its own self-destruction.

I don't pretend to be the first to bring Marxism and modernism together. In fact, they have come together on their own at several points over the past century, most dramatically at moments of historical crisis and revolutionary hope. We can see their fusion in Baudelaire, Wagner, Courbet, as well as in Marx, in 1848; in the expressionists, futurists, dadaists and constructivists of 1914–25; in the ferment and agitation in Eastern Europe after Stalin's death; in the radical initiatives of the 1960s, from Prague to Paris and throughout the US. But as revolutions have been suppressed or betrayed, radical fusion has given way to fission; both Marxism and modernism have congealed into orthodoxies and gone their separate and mutually distrustful ways.[16] So-called orthodox Marxists have at best ignored modernism, but all too often worked to repress it, out of fear, perhaps, that (in Nietzsche's phrase) if they kept looking into the abyss the abyss would start looking back into them. Orthodox modernists, meanwhile, have spared no expense of spirit in refashioning for themselves the halo of an unconditioned "pure" art, free from society and history. This essay tries to close off an exit route for orthodox Marxists by showing how the abyss they fear and flee opens up within Marxism itself. But Marxism's strength has always lain in its willingness to start from frightening social realities, to work through them and work them through; to abandon this primary source of strength leaves Marxism with little but the name. As for the orthodox modernists who avoid Marxist thought for fear that it might strip them of their halos, they need to learn that it could give them back something better in exchange: a heightened capacity to imagine and express the endlessly rich, complex and ironic relationships between them and the "modern bourgeois society" that they try to deny or defy. A fusion of Marx with modernism should melt the too-solid body of Marxism – or at least warm it up and thaw it out – and, at the same time, give modernist art and thought a new solidity and invest its creations with an unsuspected resonance and depth. It would reveal modernism as the realism of our time.

I want in this concluding section to bring the ideas I have developed here to bear on some contemporary debates concerning Marx, modernism and modernization. I will begin by considering the conservative indictments of modernism that developed at the end of the 1960s, and that have flourished in the reactionary ambience of the past decade. According to Daniel Bell, the most serious of these polemicists, "Modernism has been the seducer," enticing contemporary men and women (and even children) to desert their moral, political and economic stations and duties.[17] Capitalism, for writers like Bell, is wholly innocent in this affair: it is portrayed as a kind of Charles Bovary, unexciting but decent and dutiful, working hard to fulfill his wayward wife's insatiable desires and to pay her insupportable debts. This portrait of capitalist innocence has a fine pastoral charm; but no capitalist could afford to take it seriously if he hoped to survive for even a week in the real world that capitalism has made. (On the other hand, capitalists can certainly enjoy this picture as a fine piece of public relations, and laugh all the way to the bank.) Then, too, we must admire Bell's ingenuity in taking one of the most persistent of modernist orthodoxies – the autonomy of culture, the artist's superiority to all the norms and needs that bind the ordinary mortals around him – and turning it against modernism itself.

But what is masked here, by modernists and anti-modernists alike, is the fact that these spiritual and cultural movements, for all their eruptive power, have been bubbles on the surface of a social and economic cauldron that has been teeming and boiling for more than a hundred years. It is modern capitalism, not modern art and culture, that has set and kept the pot boiling – reluctant as capitalism may be to face the heat. The drug-crazed nihilism of William Burroughs, a favorite *bête noire* in anti-modernist polemics, is a pale reproduction of his ancestral trust, whose profits financed his avant-garde career: the Burroughs Adding Machine Company, now Burroughs International, sober nihilists of the bottom line.

In addition to these polemical attacks, modernism has always elicited objections of a very different order. Marx in the *Manifesto* took up Goethe's idea of an emerging "world literature," and explained how modern bourgeois society was bringing a world culture into being:

> In place of the old wants, satisfied by the productions of the country, we find new wants, requiring for their satisfaction the products of distant lands and climes. In place of the old local and national self-sufficiency, we have intercourse in every direction, universal interdependence. And as in material, so in spiritual *[geistige]* production. The spiritual creations of individual nations become common property. National one-sidedness and narrow-mindedness become more and more impossible, and from the numerous national and local literatures there arises a world literature. (476–7)

Marx's scenario can serve as a perfect program for the international modernism that has flourished from his era to our own: a culture that is broad-minded and many-sided, that expresses the universal scope of modern desires, and that, despite the mediations of the bourgeois economy, is the "common property" of mankind. But what if this culture were not universal after all, as Marx thought it would be? What if it turned out to be an exclusively and parochially Western affair? This possibility was first proposed in the middle of the nineteenth century by various Russian populists. They argued that the explosive atmosphere of modernization in the West – the breakdown of communities and the psychic isolation of the individual, mass impoverishment and class polarization, a cultural creativity that sprang from desperate moral and spiritual anarchy – might be a cultural peculiarity rather than an iron necessity inexorably awaiting the whole of mankind. Why should not other nations and civilizations achieve more harmonious fusions of traditional ways of life with modern potentialities and needs? In short, sometimes this belief was expressed as a complacent dogma, sometimes as a desperate hope – it was only in the West that "all that is solid melts into air."

The twentieth century has seen a great variety of attempts to realize nineteenth-century populist dreams as revolutionary regimes have come to power all over the underdeveloped world. These regimes have all tried, in many different ways, to achieve what nineteenth-century Russians called the leap from feudalism to socialism: in other words, by heroic exertions, to attain the heights of modern community without ever going through the depths of modern fragmentation and disunity. This is not the place to explore the many different modes of modernization that are available in the world today. But it is relevant to point out the fact that, in spite of the enormous differences among political systems today, so many seem to share a fervent desire to wipe modern culture off their respective maps. Their hope is that if only the people can be protected from this culture, then they can be mobilized in a solid front to pursue common national aims instead of going off in a multitude of directions to pursue volatile and uncontrollable aims of their own.

Now it would be stupid to deny that modernization can proceed along a number of different roads. (Indeed, the whole point of modernization theory is to chart these roads.) There is no reason that every modern city must look and think like New York or Los Angeles or Tokyo. Nevertheless, we need to scrutinize the aims and interests of those who would protect their people from modernism for their own good. If this culture were really exclusively Western, and hence as irrelevant to the Third World as most of its governments say, would these governments need to expend as much energy repressing it as they do? What they are projecting onto aliens and prohibiting as "Western decadence" is in fact their own people's energies and desires and critical spirit. When government spokesmen and propagandists proclaim their various countries to be free of this alien influence, what they really mean is merely that they have managed to keep a political and spiritual lid on their people so far. When the lid comes off, or is blown off, the modernist spirit is one of the first things to come out: it is the return of the repressed.

It is this spirit, at once lyrical and ironical, corrosive and committed, fantastic and realistic, that has made Latin American literature the most exciting in the world today – though it is also this spirit that forces Latin American writers to write from European or North American exile, on the run from their own censors and political police. It is this spirit that speaks from the dissident wall posters in Peking and Shanghai, proclaiming the rights of free individuality in a country that – so we were told only yesterday by China's Maoist mandarins and their comrades in the West – isn't even supposed to have a word for individuality. It is the culture of modernism that inspires the hauntingly intense electronic rock music of the Plastic People of Prague, music that is played in thousands of barricaded rooms on bootlegged cassettes even as the musicians languish in prison camps. It is modernist culture that keeps critical thought and free imagination alive in much of the non-Western world today.

Governments don't like it, but it is likely that in the long run they can't help it. So long as they are forced to sink or swim in the maelstrom of the world market, forced to strive desperately to accumulate capital, forced to develop or disintegrate – or rather, as it generally turns out, to develop *and* disintegrate – so long as they are, as Octavio Paz says, "condemned to modernity," they are bound to produce cultures that will show them what they are doing and what they are. Thus, as the Third World is increasingly caught up in the dynamics of modernization, modernism, far from exhausting itself, is only just beginning to come into its own.

In closing, I want to comment briefly on two indictments of Marx, by Herbert Marcuse and Hannah Arendt, which raise some of the central issues of this book. Marcuse and Arendt formulated their critiques in America in the 1950s, but seem to have conceived them in the 1920s, in the milieu of German romantic existentialism, when both were students (and one was more than a student) of Martin Heidegger. I'm not sure that Heidegger ever actually read Marx's writings, but he seems to have sympathized with their critical thrust. However, he thought they did not go far enough: Marx's primal error, from his perspective, was to believe that modern society and modern life had lasting human value, when in truth they were hollow and empty of value. (Readers unfamiliar with Heidegger might think of Ezra Pound and T. S. Eliot.) Neither Marcuse nor Arendt offers a total repudiation of modern life, as their master did, but both maintain that Marx uncritically celebrates the values of labor and production, and that he neglects other human activities and modes of being that are ultimately at least as important. Their criticism might be summed up by an epigram of Adorno's (which he never put in print) that Marx wanted to turn the whole world into a giant workhouse.[18] They all reproach Marx for a failure of moral imagination.

Marcuse's most trenchant criticism of Marx occurs in *Eros and Civilization*, in which Marx's presence is evident on every page, but strangely never mentioned by name. However, in a passage like the one that follows, where Marx's favorite culture hero, Prometheus, is attacked, it is obvious what is being said between the lines:

> Prometheus is the culture-hero of toil, productivity, and progress through repression ... the trickster and (suffering) rebel against the gods, who creates culture at the price of perpetual pain. He symbolizes productiveness, the unceasing effort to master life. ... Prometheus is the archetypal hero of the performance-principle.

Marcuse proceeds to nominate alternate mythological figures, whom he considers more worthy of idealization: Orpheus, Narcissus and Dionysus – and Baudelaire and Rilke, whom Marcuse sees as their modern votaries.

> [They] stand for a very different reality. ... Theirs is the image of joy and fulfillment, the voice that does not command but sings, the deed which is peace and ends the labor of conquest: the liberty from time that unites man with god, man with nature ... the redemption of pleasure, the halt of time, the absorption of death: silence, sleep, night, paradise – the Nirvana-principle not as death but life.[19]

What the Promethean/Marxian vision fails to see is the joys of peacefulness and passivity, sensual languor, mystical rapture, a state of oneness with nature rather than achieved mastery over it.

There is something to this – certainly "luxe, calme et volupté" is far from the center of Marx's imagination – but less than there may at first seem to be. If Marx is fetishistic about anything, it is not work and production but rather the far more complex and comprehensive ideal of *development* – "the free development of physical and spiritual energies" (*1844 Manuscripts*); "development of a totality of capacities in the individuals themselves" (*German Ideology*); "the free development of each will be the condition for the free development of all" (*Manifesto*); "the universality of individual needs, capacities, pleasures, productive forces, etc." (*Grundrisse*); "the fully developed individual" (*Capital*). The experiences and human qualities that Marcuse values would certainly be included in this agenda, though there is no guarantee that they would head the list. Marx wants to embrace Prometheus *and* Orpheus; he considers communism worth fighting for, because for the first time in history it could enable men to have both. He might also argue that it is only against a background of Promethean striving that Orphic rapture gains moral or psychic value; "luxe, calme et volupté" by themselves are merely boring, as Baudelaire knew well.[20]

Finally, it is valuable for Marcuse to proclaim, as the Frankfurt School has always proclaimed, the ideal of harmony between man and nature. But it is equally important for us to realize that, whatever the concrete content of this balance and harmony might be – a difficult enough question in its own right – it would take an immense amount of Promethean activity and striving to create it. Moreover, even if it could be created, it would still have to be maintained; and given the dynamism of the modern economy, mankind would have to work incessantly – like Sisyphus, but constantly striving to develop new measures and new means – to keep its precarious balance from being swept away and melting in foul air.

Arendt, in *The Human Condition*, understands something that liberal critics of Marx generally miss: the real problem in his thought is not a draconic authoritarianism but its radical opposite, the lack of a basis for any authority at all. "Marx predicted correctly, though with an unjustified glee, the 'withering away' of the public realm under the conditions of the unhampered development of 'the productive forces of society.'" The members of his communist society would find themselves, ironically, "caught in the fulfillment of needs that nobody can share and which nobody can fully communicate." Arendt understands the depth of the individualism that underlies Marx's communism, and understands, too, the nihilistic directions in which that individualism may lead. In a communist society where the free development of each is the condition for the free development of all, what is going to hold these freely developing individuals together? They might share a common quest for infinite experiential wealth; but this would be "no true public realm, but only private activities displayed in the open." A society like this might well come to feel a sense of collective futility: "the futility of a life which does not fix or realize itself in any permanent subject that endures after its labor is past."[21]

This critique of Marx poses an authentic and urgent human problem. But Arendt comes no closer than Marx to resolving the problem. Here, as in many of her works, she weaves a splendid rhetoric of public life and action, but leaves it quite unclear what this life and action are supposed to consist of-except that political life is *not* supposed to include what people do all day, their work and production relationships. (These are consigned to "the cares of the household," a subpolitical realm which Arendt considers to be devoid of the capacity to create human value.) Arendt never makes it clear what, besides lofty rhetoric, modern men can or ought to share. She is right to say that Marx never developed a theory of political community, and right that this is a serious problem. But the problem is that, given the nihilistic thrust of modern personal and social development, it is not at all clear what political bonds modern men can create. Thus the trouble in Marx's thought turns out to be a trouble that runs through the whole structure of modern life itself.

I have been arguing that those of us who are most critical of modern life need modernism most, to show us where we are and where we can begin to change our circumstances and ourselves. In search of a place to begin, I have gone back to one of the first and greatest of modernists, Karl Marx. I have gone to him not so much for his answers as for his questions. The great gift he can give us today, it seems to me, is not a way out of the contradictions of modern life but a surer and deeper way into these contradictions. He knew that the way beyond the contradictions would have to lead through modernity, not out of it. He knew we must start where we are: psychically naked, stripped of all religious, aesthetic, moral halos and sentimental veils, thrown back on our individual will and energy, forced to exploit each other and ourselves in order to survive; and yet, in spite of all, thrown together by the same forces that pull us apart, dimly aware of all we might be together, ready to stretch ourselves to grasp new human possibilities, to develop identities and mutual bonds that can help us hold together as the fierce modern air blows hot and cold through us all.

Notes

1. See the later chapters of Todd Gitlin, *The Sixties: Years of Hope, Days of Rage* (New York: Bantam 1987), for a vivid personal account of this process.

2. Quoted in Jonathan Schell, *Time of Illusion* (New York: Simon & Schuster, 1976).

3. Half a century after Marx, the French philosopher Simone Weil built a whole metaphysics and ontology on the desire for self-abasement. For her, too, this desire is linked with anti-Semitism. She believed that it was the Jews' primal sin to have inflicted the self on the world. Weil is the most brilliant Jewish anti-Semite in modern history. She was drawn to a mystical Catholicism, and worked to convert other Jews, but herself refused baptism, on the ground that she refused to accept the Old Testament as part of the Bible. Weil petitioned the Nazis to be exempt from wearing the Yellow Star on the grounds that she shared their view of the Jews. (The Nazis were not impressed.) She starved herself to death in England in 1943.

4. See W. W. Rostow, *The Stages of Economic Growth: A Non-Communist Manifesto* (Cambridge: Cambridge University Press, 1960). Alas, Rostow's account of Marx is garbled and shallow, even for an opponent. A more perceptive account of the relationship between Marx and recent studies of modernization can be found in Robert C. Tucker, *The Marxian Revolutionary Idea* (New York: Norton, 1969), Chapter 5. See also Shlomo Avineri, *The Social and Political Thought of Karl Marx* (Cambridge: Cambridge University Press, 1968), and Anthony Giddens, *Capitalism and Modern Social Theory* (Cambridge: Cambridge University Press, 1971), especially Parts 1 and 4.

5. There are two outstanding exceptions, to whom I owe a lot, Harold Rosenberg and Henri Lefebvre. For Rosenberg, see especially "The Resurrected Romans" (1949), reprinted in his *The Tradition of the New* (Horizon, 1959), and "The Pathos of the Proletariat" (1949) and "Marxism: Criticism and/or Action" (1956), both reprinted in *Act and the Actor: Making the Self* (New York: Meridian, 1972). See also Henri Lefebvre, *Introduction to Modernity*, trans. John Moore (London: Verso 1995 [1963]).

6. Most of my citations from the *Manifesto* are drawn from Samuel Moore's classic translation (London, 1888), authorized and edited by Engels, and universally reprinted. I have sometimes deviated from Moore, in the direction of more literalism and concreteness, and of a diction less Victorian and more vivid. These changes are generally but not always indicated by bracketed citations from the German. For a convenient edition of the German text, see *Karl Marx-Friedrich Engels Studienausgabe,*

4 volumes, edited by Irving Fetscher (Frankfurt am Main: Fischer Bucherci, 1966). The *Manifesto* is in Band III, 59–87.

7. *Theses on Feuerbach*, #1; reprinted in *MER*, 143. These are notes written by Marx sometime in the spring of 1845 and then forgotten. Engels salvaged them after Marx's death and published them under the present name. They have always been loved for their prophetic language.

8. In the *Grundrisse*, the 1857–58 notebooks that became the basis for *Capital*, Marx makes a distinction between "the modern epoch" or "the modern world" and "its limited bourgeois form." In communist society, the narrow bourgeois form will be "stripped away," so that the modern potentiality can be fulfilled. He begins this discussion with a contrast of classical (specifically Aristotelian and modern views of economy and society. "The old view, in which the human being appears as the aim of production ... seems to be very lofty when contrasted with the modern world, where production appears as the aim of *mankind* and wealth as the aim of production. "In fact, however," Marx says, "when the limited bourgeois form is stripped away, what is wealth other than the universality of individual needs, capacities, pleasures, productive forces etc., created through universal exchange? The full development of human mastery over the forces of nature, those of so-called nature as well as of humanity's own nature? The absolute working-out of his creative potentialities, with no presupposition other than the previous historic development, which makes this totality of development, i.e. the development of all human powers as such the end in itself, not as measured on a *predetermined* yardstick? Where he does not reproduce himself in one specificity, but produces his totality? Strives not to remain something he has become, but is in the absolute movement of becoming?" In other words, Marx wants a truly infinite pursuit of wealth for everyone: not wealth in money – "the limited bourgeois form" – but wealth of desires, of experiences, capacities, sensitivities, of transformations and developments. The fact that Marx follows these formulations with question marks may suggest a certain hesitancy about this vision (*Grundrisse: Foundations of the Critique of Political Economy*, trans. Martin Nicolaus (London: Pelican, 1973), 488).

9. *The Will to Power*, ed. and trans. Walter Kaufmann and R. J. Hollingdale (New York: Vintage, 1978).

10. See "Speech at the Anniversary of the *People's Paper*," delivered in April 1856, apparently Marx's first speech in English (*MER*, 577–8).

11. *The Persian Letters* (1721), Letters 26, 63, 88 (New York: Meridian, 1961).

12. *Discourse on the Arts and Sciences* (New York: Dutton, 1950), 146–9.

13. *Reflections on the Revolution in France* (1790), reprinted in a joint edition with Thomas Paine's *Rights of Man* (New York: Dolphin, 1961), 90.

14. In Baudelaire, *Art in Paris, 1845–62*, ed. and trans. Jonathan Mayne (Phaidon, 1965), 41–3.

15. From Gramsci's posthumous manuscript, "The Modern Prince." Reprinted in his *Prison Notebooks*, selected, edited and translated by Quintin Hoare and Geoffrey Nowell Smith (New York: International Publishers, 1971), 173.

16. Marxism and modernism may also come together as a utopian fantasy in an age of political quiescence: cf. surrealism and its offshoots in the 1920s or the work of American thinkers like Paul Goodman and Norman O. Brown in the 1950s. Herbert Marcuse spans both generations, especially in his most original work, *Eros and Civilization* (1955). Other modes of convergence animate the writings of Brecht, Benjamin, Adorno and Sartre.

17. Bell, *The Cultural Contradictions of Capitalism* (New York: Basic Books, 1975). See also "Modernism and Capitalism," *Partisan Review* 45 (1978), which became the preface to the paperback edition of *Cultural Contradictions*.

18. Quoted by Martin Jay in his history of the Frankfurt School, *The Dialectical Imagination* (New York: Little, Brown, 1973), 57.

19. Marcuse, *Eros and Civilization: A Philiosophical Inquiry into Freud* (New York: Vintage, 1962), 146–7, and all of Chapter 8, "Orpheus and Narcissus."

20. Compare two of Marx's statements about life in communist society. First, from the "Critique of the [German Social-Democratic Party] Gotha Program," 1875: "In a higher phase of communist society, after the enslaving subordination of the individual to the division of labor, and thereby the antithesis between mental and physical labor, has vanished; after labor has become not only a means of life, but life's prime want; after productive forces have also increased, along with the all-around development of the individual, and all the springs of cooperative wealth flow more abundantly – only then can the narrow horizon of bourgeois right be crossed in its entirety, and society inscribe on its banner: From each according to his ability, to each according to his needs!" (*MER*, 531). Marx doesn't say so, but he and his audience both know that this ideal is inspired by the New Testament vision of the primitive Church, in which, according to the Book of Acts, all believers "had all things in common. ... Neither were there any among them that lacked: for as many as were possessors of lands or houses sold them, and brought the prices of the things that were sold, and

laid them at the apostles' feet, and distribution was made unto every man according as he had need" (*Acts* 4:32–5). The Book of Acts gives us no details about the nature of human needs in that primitive communist community; but all we can tell from the context suggests that the believers' needs were small and didn't grow.

Compare this with the vision in the *Grundrisse*, in which communism will realize the modern ideal of the infinite pursuit of wealth, "stripping the limited bourgeois form [of wealth] away"; thus communist society will liberate "the universality of needs, capacities, pleasures, productive forces ... the development of all human powers as the end in itself"; man will "produce his totality" and live "in the absolute movement of becoming." This vision is thrilling, and far closer to home than the vision in the Bible; but if we try to imagine it becoming real in this time and that place, won't everybody's universal needs be, I wouldn't say impossible to fulfill, but at least a problem? And isn't the pursuit of infinite development for everybody – and the insistence that it must be infinite, and that it must be for everybody, with nobody's needs swept under the rug – bound to produce serious stresses and strains? They may differ from the class conflicts endemic to bourgeois society, but they are likely to be at least as deep. Marx acknowledges the possibility of this sort of trouble only in the most oblique way, and says nothing about how a communist society might deal with it. On the other hand, we know that Marx is no utopian socialist. He tells us why he thinks people who grow up under capitalism will have the inner strength to live according to communist norms, and why those norms will make them happier and more fulfilled; but he never tells us just how the new society will run. Marx is one of the great theorists of work, but he is often gruelling to work with.

21. Arendt, *The Human Condition: A Study of the Central Dilemmas Facing Modern Man* (New York: Anchor, 1959), 101–2, 114–16.

7

The Signs in the Street

Perry Anderson's discussion of my book *All That Is Solid Melts into Air* is both welcome and perplexing. He is so appreciative and generous at the beginning, so dismissive and scornful at the end – not merely toward my book, but toward contemporary life itself. What happens in the middle? I can't figure it out. There is an interesting historical analysis, building on Arno Mayer's work, of the political and social conditions that underlay the great modernist breakthroughs of 1890 to 1920. This analysis makes fascinating reading, but Anderson loads his history with far more weight than it can bear. He argues that "the intersection between a semi-aristocratic ruling order, a semi-industrialized capitalist economy, and a semi-emergent or insurgent labour movement" nourished the creative triumphs of cubism, relativity, psychoanalysis, the *Rites of Spring, Ulysses,*

Response to Perry Anderson, "Modernity and Revolution," *New Left Review* 144 (March–April 1984).

etc. This is perfectly plausible, though there are a number of other equally plausible ways to tell this story. (My own would place more emphasis on the experience of marginal groups like Jews and homosexuals.) Anderson then makes a bizarre leap: he seems to say that the absence of *these* conditions since the end of World War II must lead to the absence of *any* creative triumphs. But why shouldn't other conditions inspire other triumphs, today, tomorrow, or any other day?

This pretzel logic gets another perverse twist toward the paper's end, where Anderson claims that the current disappointment of our hopes for socialist revolution in the West means the doom of all Western spiritual and cultural life: "What marks the situation of the Western artist is ... the closure of horizons: without an appropriable past, or an imaginable future, in an interminably recurrent present." Doesn't he realize how much human creativity grows, and always has grown, out of disappointment? Disappointment with democratic Athens led to *The Trojan Women* and Plato's *Republic*; disappointment in Jesus of Nazareth (who, remember, was supposed to bring about the end of the world) led to most of what's morally creative in Christianity – specifically, the revaluation of values that glorified suffering, lowliness and defeat; disappointment with the French Revolution led to the creative breakthroughs of romanticism, which nourished (and continue to nourish) a legion of new revolutions. So it goes. When people are faced with the closing of familiar horizons, we open up new horizons; when we are disappointed in some of our hopes, we discover or create new visions that inspire new hopes. That's how our species has survived so much sadness and ruin through the ages. If humanity had ever accepted *a priori* foreclosures of history, our history would have ended long ago.

Does Anderson really believe the Sex Pistols' verdict of "NO FUTURE!"?

(Even Johnny Rotten, as he screamed it, was trying in his way to change it.) If Anderson's horizon really looks closed, maybe he should think of this as a problem, rather than as the human condition. Maybe his theoretical framework has pressed him into a corner, and he needs to turn around and look the other way, where there may be plenty of trouble but at least there's light and space.

All That Is Solid Melts into Air unfolds a dialectic of modernization and modernism. "To be modern," as I define it at the book's beginning and end, "is to experience personal and social life as a maelstrom, to find one's world in perpetual disintegration and renewal, trouble and anguish, ambiguity and contradiction: to be part of a universe in which all that is solid melts into air. To be a modernist is to make oneself somehow at home in this maelstrom, ... to grasp and confront the world that modernization makes, and to strive to make it our own." Modernism aims "to give modern men and women the power to change the world that is changing them, to make them the subjects as well as the objects of modernization." Anderson is willing to accept this as a vision of nineteenth-century culture and politics, but he thinks that it is irrelevant to our century, let alone to our day. When he criticizes my failure to "periodize," his point is that the liberating force of modernism is confined to an earlier period. It isn't quite clear when that period ended (World War I? World War II?), but the main point is that it ended long ago. The hope of making ourselves at home in the maelstrom, of becoming subjects as well as objects, of making the modern world our own – these hopes have forever melted into air, at least for Anderson, and he thinks it's futile for me to try to recreate them.

I could assail Anderson's reading of modern and contemporary history in plenty of ways, but it wouldn't do anything to advance our common understanding. I want to try something different. Anderson's view of the current horizon is that it's empty, closed; mine is that it's open and crowded with creative possibilities. The best way to defend my vision might be to show what this horizon looks like, what's actually out there as I see it. For the next few pages, I want to present a few scenes from everyday life, and from an art and culture that are part of this life, as it is going on right now. These scenes do not lead logically to one another; nevertheless, they are connected, as figures in a collage. My point in introducing them is to show how modernism is still happening, both in our streets and in our souls, and how it still has the imaginative power to help us make this world our own.

Modernism has its traditions, and they are there to be used and developed. Baudelaire tells us how to see the present: "All centuries and all peoples have their beauty, so inevitably we have ours. That's the order of things. ... The life of our city is rich in poetic and marvelous subjects. The marvelous envelops and soaks us like an atmosphere, only we don't see it. ... We need only open our eyes to recognize our heroism." He wrote this in 1846, in an essay entitled "The Heroism of Modern Life."

Faces in the Crowd

A CUNY (City University of New York) graduate student comes to see me about his dissertation and his life: Larry, a big, muscular redhead, usually jovial, occasionally menacing, looking a little like the Wild Man in medieval art. He comes from the steel mills near Pittsburgh. After a dreadful childhood, abandoned by alcoholic parents, brought up by a series of indifferent and impoverished relatives, he escaped to a big state university on a football scholarship. Quite by accident, as he tells it, he discovered that he loved to read, think, dream. Now he dreams vast, epic, neo-Idealist visions, communing with Fichte and Schelling and Hegel as he drives a taxi all night to make the rent. I ask him what he wants to do with his life; he says he wants to become a thinker so he can search for the ultimate truth and, if he finds it, proclaim it to the world.

I am moved by his ambition, which I shared at his age – and still do share, though I wouldn't be likely to put it as directly and honestly as he. But I tell him that part of the truth about life in Reagan's America is that it contains no job openings for independent, humanistic thought. I say that if he wants to pursue the truth, he's going to have to use all his intelligence to learn to lie, to disguise his enterprise as something else that he can get a job doing. The question then becomes, what is the best disguise? I feel like hell as I say this, but I see no way around it.

I suggest he do an ethnographic and political study of his steel town. He recoils in horror, and tells me that world is crumbling. Mills are closing down; more than half the jobs in his town have recently disappeared and the others could go at any moment; men are running away or disintegrating, families are breaking up, complex social networks are ripping apart at the seams. He visits his old local bars, and men who used to taunt him for loving books and hanging out with kikes, niggers, fags and commies in New York now envy him for having a lifeline to a world outside. Larry grew up hating this town, and the hate helped him learn who he was. Now he pities it and he's got to learn about himself all over again.

As I write this, they're playing a song on the radio that comes straight from Larry's world, "Making Thunderbirds," by Bob Seger, a hard rocker from Detroit. It has a slashing guitar attack, a driving beat, and it's sung with an intensity that doesn't come through on the radio very often these

days. The narrator is a middle-aged, unemployed (or about-to-be-unem-
ployed) autoworker, who pines for his youth: "Back in '55 we were making Thunderbirds":

> We were making Thunderbirds, we were making Thunderbirds.
> They were long and low and sleek and fast and all you've ever heard.
> We were young and strong, we were making Thunderbirds.

The car, a splendid new model of the 1950s, is a symbol of the world we
have lost: when a worker could identify himself, his youth and sexual
energy, with the thing he produced; when "the big line moved" and it was
a thrill to be part of its momentum; when the young workers of Detroit
could feel like the vanguard of America and America could feel like
Number One in the world. The symbolic power rides on the music as
much as the text; the beat and tempo and guitar echo the music of 1955,
when rock-and-roll was young and the world was all before it. "Thunderbirds" connects especially to Chuck Berry, whose "Maybelline" defined a
classic American myth – that the workingman could be really manly,
manlier than his social superiors, in and through his car – and who tried
to create a music that would be the moral equivalent of that car.

Seger takes us back to those songs and those cars, to make us feel the
depths of what we have lost. For the world those workers were building,
or thought they were building, is gone with the wind; no longer young or
strong or proud, no longer even working, they are junked, along with
their old cars, along with Detroit – maybe even along with America itself.
The song's text seems to say "NO FUTURE!" but the music pulls against the
text with desperate urgency. The narrator may well feel he's got nothing
left; the singer-songwriter knows and shows that he's got more than he
thinks. What he's got above all is the passion and depth and guts to rock

and rage against the dying of the light.

It is a frozen Saturday afternoon just before Christmas. I am walking across Houston Street on Manhattan's Lower East Side, blinded by the low sun in my face. This is a poor neighborhood, full of abandoned tenements, small workshops, lumberyards, auto supply and body shops, junkyards and storage dumps. Near the East River, gathering around small bonfires, winos and junkies are almost the only people on the street; not even the kids are out, it's too cold to play. As I get further west, a few young families emerge – Hispanic, white-bohemian, interracial – heading across town on weekend shopping expeditions.

On a particularly desolate block, between an abandoned factory and a gas station, I walk into a jarring scene. In front of a yard full of broken furniture, old refrigerators and sinks, up against a Cyclone fence, ten figures are chained in a row. Up close, I see that they are sculpted, in plaster or papier-mâché, but their proportions are eerily real. The figures are covered with plastic trash bags; the bags are slit or torn in places, and rags, orange peels, old newspapers, packaging for food, drink, diapers, appliances, are beginning to leak out. Although the faces are covered up, the figures are subtly detailed and differentiated, and amazingly lifelike, and it is dreadful to see them facing me just inches away, slumping over or caving in, pressing against their ropes as they rot.

What is this, anyway? It is a work of environmental art, created for this particular space and time, for this site and this neighborhood and this public, by a young sculptor named David Finn who lives a few blocks away. He will dismantle and remove it in a few days, if it has not already decomposed, or if some lover or hater of art has not removed it first. It has special resonance for this neighborhood and its people, whose fate it may symbolize. (One of its strongest undertones is a bitter meditation on the meaning of "junk.") I ask a couple of local derelicts who are hovering about what they think of it, and one shakes his head sadly and says, "Somebody's got to pay. We know it." But it has wider reverberations as well. We've met these figures before. Was it in El Salvador, or Lebanon, or, … ? This piece fulfils brilliantly one of the Left's chief aims in the Vietnam era: *Bring the War Home!* Only which war is this, so close to home? The artist doesn't tell us; we've got to work it out for ourselves. But whatever we do with it, this work of art has put us, the spectators, into the picture, implicated us a lot more deeply than we may like. The figures will disappear from our street, but they won't be so easy to evict from our minds. They'll haunt us like ghosts, at least till we recognize them as *our* ghosts and deal with them face to face.

Another student comes by: Lena, seventeen years old, built like Marilyn Horne. Lena grew up in her family's Puerto Rican *bodega,* the adored only girl in an overwhelmingly male household, and in their storefront Pentecostal church, where she sang solos at an early age. She says her existence was untroubled until she entered college, when her mind came to life and her world split open. Suddenly she was alive to poetry, philosophy, psychology, politics, to sexuality, romance, feminism, the peace movement, socialism. Impulses, insights, ideas, all came pouring out of her torrentially; at first her family thought she might be under a spell. Before long, however, for her ideas on abortion, sexuality, and equal rights for women, she was excommunicated from the church. After that, her family was put up against the wall by their fellow-believers, who were a large portion of their customers: How long were they going to tolerate a damned soul who wore the mark of the beast in their house and in their store? Her family resisted the pressure, and bravely stood by her: they would die for her – but they couldn't even begin to understand her. In the midst of this crisis, her father was shot by robbers and almost killed. The family has had to pull together closer than ever around the store, and Lena may have to go on leave from school, at least for a few months, and work there full time. She would rather die than desert her family in an emergency. But she knows that when normal life returns, if it ever does, for their sake as well as her own, she's going to have to go. But go where? In the Hispanic immigrant working-class world that is the only world she knows and loves – a world that gave her much of the strength she has, though it turned on her as soon as she tried to use it – the only alternative to the family is the gutter. There are plenty of deviants in that world, but few rebels, and very, very few intellectual rebel girls. Moreover, she knows that in many ways she's still only a kid, far more frail and vulnerable than she looks, just beginning to figure out what she wants from life. I try to tell her that her fight for liberty and autonomy has a long and honorable history, that she can find many kindred spirits and comrades in books, and many more all over the city and the country, probably closer to home than she thinks, fighting battles like her own, creating and sustaining institutions for mutual support. She believes me, but says she isn't ready to meet them yet: she's got to cross that lonesome valley by herself, got to get over, before she can join hands with anyone else.

Carolee Schneeman is a painter, sculptor, dancer, collagist, film-maker and performance artist in New York; she has been active and innovative in many realms since the heyday of the Judson Dance Group twenty years ago. She is best known for her "body art" and performance pieces, which have shown her body, her sexuality and her inner life in daring and fruitful

ways, transforming autobiography into iconography. There was a moment, near the end of the sixties, when her sort of radical imagination
was chic; she is still as free a spirit as ever, but in the Reagan era it feels
lonelier and more exposed out there than it used to be. In the spring of
1982 Schneeman began a series of sexy and intimate collages that would
be called "Domestic Souvenirs." The work was going along smoothly
when suddenly, that June, Israel invaded Lebanon, and, as she later described it, "Lebanon invaded me." Work she eventually did that summer
and fall, and showed in New York a year later, looks radically different
from anything she has done before. Within these collages, images of
sexuality in an ambience of domestic tranquility and sweet communion
interact with frightful Expressionist visions of the disasters of war.
Schneeman's "Lebanon" incorporates many of the images that she has
been elaborating for years, but gives them darker and deeper meaning.
There is plenty of naked flesh, as always, but now many of the arms, legs,
breasts, etc., seem to be contorted in terror or twisted and maimed.
Nakedness, once (and still) a symbol of sexual joy and energy and personal authenticity, now expresses human frailty and vulnerability – "Is
man no more than this?" – as bodies sexually tense or post-coitally relaxed
are mounted among bodies tensed in fright or relaxed in death. Blood,
whose menstrual flow Schneeman once used to express both a woman's
fertility and a self's inner depths, now suggests the blasting away of body
and soul alike. Diaphanous garments, earlier images of erotic play, now
evoke shreds and shrouds. A central, obsessive image is a triangular tab-
leau of a woman rushing forward while two men move with her and hold
her from behind: reproduced in many different textures and tonalities, it
suggests both a romantic sexual dream and a political nightmare of
wounds, terror and hopeless flight. Throughout these works, the two

modes of meaning interpenetrate and deepen each other. In the midst of our domestic bliss, their homes are being blown away. On the other hand, the maiming and murdering over there are so dreadful precisely because their victims are men and women whose bodies are made to twine around each other and whose imaginations are made for love, just like our own.

In Schneeman's "Lebanon," politics invades the most intimate spaces of the self, envelops our bodies, thrusts into our dreams. From this intercourse, a terrible beauty is born. The artist started out to talk personally, not politically; she ended up showing that the political is personal, and that is why politics matters so much. Alas, her public doesn't seem to want to see what she has to show: this show has so far attracted no reviews and made no sales. Ironically, a fairly large public (for the art public) has been happy, over the years, to look into her most private spaces; but as soon as her vision opened outward and spilled over into public space, as soon as her art penetrated a political space that everybody shared, much of this public was quick to look away. One of the perennial romances of modern times is the fusion of personal with political life. We all dream of this, at least sometimes; but when it actually happens, as it happened to Schneeman last summer, it may be too much for most people to bear, too much even to look at, like looking directly into the sun. So just when – and probably just because – she has worked harder than ever to create dialogue, she is left talking to herself. Still, the works are there, and she and we can hope the dialogue will go on.

Every year or so I go back to the part of the Bronx where I was born. It's not an easy trip to make, though it's only about five miles northeast of where I live now. The South Bronx of my youth, a ghetto with fresh air and trees for second-generation immigrants, celebrated as an ultra-modern environment in the 1920s and 1930s, was written off as obsolete by capital in the 1960s. Abandoned by the banks, the insurance underwriters, the real estate industry, the federal government, and bulldozed and blasted by a superhighway through its heart, the Bronx wasted away fast. (I talk about this in the last chapter of *All That Is Solid Melts into Air;* living through it is one of the things that led me to think about the ambiguities of modernity in the first place.) In the 1970s its primary industry was probably arson for profit; for awhile it seemed that the very word "Bronx" had become a cultural symbol for urban blight and death. Every time I heard or read about the destruction of a building I had known, or saw it burn on the local news, I felt like a piece of my flesh was being ripped away.

I've always turned the old corner with dread: What if, when I reach the apartment house where I grew up, there's nothing there? It wouldn't be surprising: so many of the buildings in these parts have been sealed up or torn down; streets that were busy and noisy and too narrow for the crowds twenty years ago are as open and empty as deserts today. But it hasn't happened, at least not yet; the building looks surprisingly good, a little Art Deco jewel in the midst of devastation. A heroic superintendent and organized tenants have held it together; and its present landlord appears to have some interest in keeping it up rather than tearing it down. I feel a sense of metaphysical relief. As I explore further, I see that some of the buildings that were burnt-out hulks a few years ago have been, or are being, very nicely rehabbed today. It's very, very slow and fragile; under the Carter administration there was little money for rehabilitation, under Reagan there was even less, and private capital wrote off the Bronx more than twenty years ago. But it's happening, a little here, a little there, the beat and pulse of life beginning again.

I climb the steep hill on East 170th Street, our old shopping center. The quarter-mile stretch alongside our block is utterly lifeless, but the next quarter-mile has been kept up and partially rehabbed and, although dirty and gritty, it is bursting with life. The street is jammed with Black and Latin families – and now some Asian ones as well (where do they come from? when did they get here? who can I ask?) – loading themselves up with food, clothes, appliances, fabrics, toys and everything else they can carry away from the post-Christmas sales.

I board a bus heading south toward Manhattan. Just behind me, a massive black woman gets on, bent under numerous parcels; I give her my seat. Just behind her, her fifteen-or-so-year-old daughter undulates up the aisle, radiant, stunning in the skin-tight pink pants she has just bought. The mother won't look, buries her head in her shopping bags. They continue an argument that has clearly been going on since they left the store. The daughter says that, after all, she bought this with her own money that she made working; the mother replies that if this is all she can think of to buy, she isn't grown up enough to be trusted with her own money or to be out working. "Come on, Mama," the girl says, turning herself around and turning the heads of everybody in the bus, "look at that pink, ain't it beautiful, won't it be nice for spring?" It's January, and spring is a long way off. The mother still won't look, but after a while she lifts her eyes slowly, then shakes her head. "With that ass," she says, "you'll never get out of high school without a baby. And I ain't taking care of no more babies. You're my last baby." The girl squeezes her mother's arm: "Don't worry, Mama. We're modern. We know how to take care of ourselves." The mother sighs, and addresses her packages: "Modern? Just you take care you don't bring me no modern babies."

Soon I get off, feeling as happy and whole as the girl in the bus. Life is rough in the South Bronx, but the people aren't giving up: modernity is alive and well.

The Loss of a Halo

These are some of the people on my horizon. It's wider and more open than the one Perry Anderson sees, and it's crowded with human passion, intelligence, yearning, imagination, spiritual complexity and depth. It's also crowded with oppression, misery, everyday brutality and a threat of total annihilation. But the people in the crowd are using and stretching their vital powers, their vision and brains and guts, to face and fight the horrors; many of the things they do, just to get through the day and night, reveal what Baudelaire called "the heroism of modern life." The faces in the crowd today may be different from those in Baudelaire's age; but the forces that propel them haven't changed since modern times began.

Some of these people, in my book and in the vignettes above, are artists. They are caught up in the same chaos as the rest of us; they are special in their ability to give it expressive form, to light it up, to help us navigate and collect ourselves and find each other, so that we can survive and sometimes even thrive in the maelstrom's midst. These artists are like the poet in Baudelaire's prose poem "The Loss of a Halo":

> My friend, you know how terrified I am of horses and vehicles? Well, just now as I was crossing the boulevard in a great hurry, splashing through the mud, in the midst of a moving chaos, with death galloping at me from every side, I made a sudden move, and my halo slipped off my head, and fell into the mire of the macadam. I was much too scared to pick it up. I thought it was better to lose my insignia than to get my bones broken.

Besides, I said to myself, every cloud has a silver lining. Now I can walk around incognito, do low things, throw myself into every kind of filth, just like ordinary mortals. So here I am, just as you see me, just like yourself. ...

For artists and writers today, as much as for Baudelaire, this loss of a halo can be a step in the liberation of art; the reduction of the modern artist to an ordinary mortal can open up new lifelines and force fields through which both artists and their public can grow.

I am grateful to Perry Anderson for remembering *The Politics of Authenticity,* and for pointing out the continuities between that work and what I'm doing now. Then as now, I've been trying to develop a theoretical vision of the unifying forces in modern life. I still believe that it's possible for modern men and women who share the desire to "be themselves" to come together, first to fight against the forms of class, sexual and racial oppression that force everyone's identity into rigid molds and keep anyone's self from unfolding; and next, to create Marx's "association in which the free development of each is the condition for the free development of all." Nevertheless, *All That Is Solid,* and what I've written here, have a much thicker density and a richer atmosphere than my earlier work. This is because I've tried increasingly to situate my exploration of the modern self within the social contexts in which all modern selves come to be. I'm writing more about the environments and public spaces that are available to modern people, and the ones that they create, and the ways they act and interact in these spaces in the attempt to make themselves at home. I'm emphasizing those modes of modernism that seek to take over or to remake public space, to appropriate and transform it in the name of the people who are its public. This is why so much of *All That Is Solid* is taken up with public struggles and encounters, dialogues and confrontations in the streets; and why I've come to see the street and the demonstration as primary symbols of modern life.

Another reason that I've written so much about ordinary people and everyday life in the street, in the context of this controversy, is that Anderson's vision is so remote from them. He only has eyes for world-historical Revolutions in politics and world-class Masterpieces in culture; he stakes out his claim on heights of metaphysical perfection, and won't deign to notice anything less. This would be all right, I guess, except that he's so clearly miserable over the lack of company up there. It might be more fruitful if, instead of demanding whether modernity can still produce masterpieces and revolutions, we were to ask whether it can generate sources and spaces of meaning, of freedom, dignity, beauty, joy, solidarity. Then we would have to confront the messy actuality in which modern men and women and children live. The air might be less pure, but the atmosphere would be a lot more nourishing; we would find, in Gertrude Stein's phrase, a lot more *there* there. Who knows – it's impossible to know in advance – we might even find some masterpieces or revolutions in the making.

This isn't Anderson's problem alone. I think it's an occupational hazard for intellectuals, regardless of their politics, to lose touch with the stuff and flow of everyday life. But this is a special problem for intellectuals on the Left, because we, among all political movements, take special pride in noticing people, respecting them, listening to their voices, caring about their needs, bringing them together, fighting for their freedom and happiness. (This is how we differ – or try to differ – from the world's assorted ruling classes and their ideologues, who treat the people they rule as animals or machines or numbers or pieces on a chessboard, or who ignore their existence completely, or who dominate them all by playing them against each other, teaching them that they can be free and happy only at each other's expense.) Intellectuals can make a special contribution to this ongoing project. If our years of study have taught us anything, we should be able to reach out further, to look and listen more closely, to see and feel beneath surfaces, to make comparisons over a wider range of space and time, to grasp hidden patterns and forces and connections, in order to show people who look and speak and think and feel differently from each other – who are oblivious to each other, or fearful of each other – that they have more in common than they think. We can contribute visions and ideas that will give people a shock of recognition, recognition of themselves and each other, that will bring their lives together. That is what we can do for solidarity and class-consciousness. But we can't do it, we can't generate ideas that will bind people's lives together, if we lose contact with what those lives are like. Unless we know how to recognize people, as they look and feel and experience the world, we'll never be able to help them recognize themselves or change the world. Reading *Capital* won't help us if we don't also know how to read the signs in the street.

8

From Paris to Gdansk

Forty years have passed since the appearance of Edmund Wilson's magnificent study of the European revolutionary tradition, *To the Finland Station*. That book established itself almost instantly as a modern classic in the spirit of Stendhal, Carlyle and Tolstoy, making great literature out of history. Forty years later, Wilson's work challenges us to retell the story in ways of our own, to renew our perspective on where modern radicalism leads and what it means.

Much of the compelling force of Wilson's vision comes through in his title. Lenin's triumphal entry into revolutionary Petrograd in April 1917, where he was acclaimed at the Finland Station by an ecstatic crowd, appeared to be the point toward which all roads led – not merely the fulfillment of the revolutionary tradition that began in France in 1789 (at

Review of James H. Billington, *Fire in the Minds of Men: Origins of the Revolutionary Faith* (New York: Basic Books, 1980). This essay first appeared in the *New York Times Book Review*, Sept. 24, 1980.

the Finland Station a band played the "Marseillaise"), but the climactic moment of modern history as a whole. At the end of the 1930s, whether or not one approved of the Soviet order, this vision was at least plausible. Between then and now, however, radicalism has gone through gigantic metamorphoses all over the world, from the Gulag to the Prague Spring and the Polish shipyards, from British and Scandinavian social democracy to Mao and Castro, from worker self-management in Yugoslavia to the management of murder by the Red Brigades. After all this, and much more, the Finland Station appears as just one stop among many, within a system that contains a multitude of lines of force and rights of way. We need a history of radicalism that will open up its past and place the Finland Station in a wider and deeper perspective. But this history will also need a shaping vision that will give our enlarged perspective a new coherence.

James Billington is as qualified as anyone alive today to write this history. He has spent most of the past thirty years working as a historian; he taught for years at Princeton and currently directs the Woodrow Wilson International Center for Scholars in Washington. In 1966 he published *The Icon and the Axe: An Interpretation of Russian Culture*, probably the single finest American book on Russia, and one of the most impressive achievements of American scholarship since the end of World War II. In *The Icon and the Axe,* Billington embraces a thousand years of Russian history without spreading his resources thin. He writes as vividly and knowledgeably about literature as about land tenure; he explores the relationship of spatial and architectural forms to political forms; he has command of a dozen languages, and unravels Russia's indebtedness to the Poles, Germans, Italians, Jews, English, French, Dutch, but in ways that enrich rather then dilute Russia's distinctiveness. His writing at its best is both novelistic, bringing dozens of characters beautifully to life, and poetic, following images into their depths; and it shows how dedication to scholarship can nourish, rather than undermine, the powers of vision and imagination.

In *Fire in the Minds of Men,* Billington contracts his time frame, but expands his horizons in space, as he explores and tries to chart the amazingly rich profusion of radical men and women, movements and institutions that have burst into life from Italy to Poland, from Algeria to Idaho, over the past two hundred years.

This is "a story not of revolutions, but of revolutionaries, the innovative creators of a new tradition." Billington focuses on the intense modern "spiritual thirst" that generated a "revolutionary faith." This faith, he says, has become "the most successful ideological export of the West to the world," and has established itself as "the faith of our time." This revolutionary faith cuts across national, class, ethnic and religious boundaries, and unites people and groups that may be at each other's throats. Its core is the belief that, if only we can overthrow evil powers and institutions, a just and beautiful new world will spring into being. Billington's central symbol of this faith, taken from Dostoevsky, is the image of a fire that can both destroy and create.

Fire in the Minds of Men begins, as many histories of radicalism do, in Paris in the 1790s. But rather than focusing on the Bastille or the National Assembly, Billington takes us to an almost-forgotten urban environment that turns out to be perhaps even more rich and exciting. This is the network of cafés, plazas and pleasure-gardens created by the King's brother, the avaricious, reformist, decadent Duke of Orleans, on the grounds of the Palais-Royale. Here, where royal ownership protected customers from arrest, the most intense intellectual and political discus-

sions intertwined with sexual banter and commerce and assignation, and
with every form of theatrical self-display.

The Palais-Royale, where it was said that "all desires can be gratified as
soon as conceived," emerged in the 1780s as the closest thing in Paris to a
"forum of the people," and, increasingly, as an "anti-Versailles." It would
serve as the mobilization point for many of the great revolutionary dem-
onstrations and meeting grounds for an array of new radical clubs and
circles, the arena for emerging forms of revolutionary theater, the headquarters for a thriving and creative popular journalism. It may be the
place that gave birth to an important modern verb, *politiquer,* "to politic."

But the politics of the Palais-Royale were "a politics of desire," conducted in outrageous clothes and language, saturated with strong drink
and open sexuality. Jacobin politicians always distrusted and feared this
milieu, so alien to their modes of discipline, but it exerted a strong pull
on masses of Parisians for whom revolution meant not only life and
liberty but the pursuit of happiness. This was Danton's revolution, a
revolution of joy that was (as Büchner's "Danton's Death" makes clear)
just as serious, and just as tragic in the end, as Robespierre's revolution of
virtue. Billington brings this world unforgettably to life. He makes us see
how new forms of thought and action can evolve out of new forms, of
space – and then, dialectically, transform the spaces that made them what
they are.

After this brilliant beginning, Billington goes on to enfold a network
of new social forms that nineteenth-century radicalism brought to life.
He shows us dozens of secret revolutionary brotherhoods and orders:
Illuminati, Philadelphians, numerous variants of (and spinoffs from)
Freemasonry, Sublime Perfect Masters, Auguste Blanqui's Society of Sea-
sons (led by Spring), Irish Fenians, Italian Carbonari, the Polish League of

Scythebearers, the German League of Outlaws (which metamorphosed into the Communist League, for which Marx and Engels wrote their *Manifesto*). He is fascinated by the secret signs, the colorful and often menacing rituals, the intense psychosexual (as well as political) bonds.

Billington goes on to show the importance of music to radical life: how the "Marseillaise," the "Internationale," the IWW's "Solidarity Forever" (taken over in the 1930s by the CIO) helped to create communities; how opera played a crucial role in nineteenth-century struggles for national liberation (the performance of an anti-Hapsburg opera in Brussels in 1830 actually started the revolution that led to Belgium's independence).

Billington offers an exemplary discussion of the evolution of modern newspapers, which in their great periods have not only raised and deepened popular consciousness, and generated sparks for radical energy and action, but also have created human bonds – both inside the paper itself, in the newsroom and pressroom, and between writers and readers – that engendered visions of what a new society and a new life might be like.

One of Billington's central themes is the tragedy of radical creativity. It seems to be the fate of radical innovations – the brotherhoods, the ceremonies, the music, the popular journalism and graphics, the forms of fraternity and community – to be discovered and co-opted by various ruling classes, which coolly and cynically exploit them as instruments of mass manipulation, and use them to whip millions of people into the chauvinist and xenophobic frenzies whose political consequences and human costs are all too clear today.

Fire in the Minds of Men is full of all the good things we have come to expect from Billington: a sensibility with a global reach; vast erudition transformed into vivid drama; a feeling for spaces and environments;

lyrical and moving evocations of the Russian revolutionary movement, especially its populist phase, Billington's first love. He gives us a gallery of magnificent characters, many of whom we will never have heard of, but whom now we will never forget – Flora Tristan, the Franco-Peruvian feminist revolutionary idolized by Marx and Engels; James Fary, theorist of youth revolution, and later hero of Swiss democracy; Thomas Urbain, disciple of Saint-Simon, later Ismail, "the first Black Muslim"; and literally dozens more.

And yet, for all this, the book never comes together as a whole. If *To the Finland Station* is weakened by a constricting ideo-chronology, *Fire in the Minds of Men* has the opposite problem: it doesn't move in any direction at all. As a result, although it will be valuable for years as a treasury of radical history, biography and anthropology, it will be hard for anyone to read it through as a book in its own right.

It is easy to see how the sheer enormousness of Billington's project would be enough to make him – or any other writer – lose his way. But there are also large blind spots in his sensibility that serve to block his way.

Billington's biggest blind spot here is Karl Marx. He simply can't see any value whatever in the man or his works. Wherever Marx comes up, Billington's level of thought and writing drops precipitously to the level of the Cold War polemics of two and three decades ago. Sometimes Billington treats Marx as an abstract symbol of all the cold, hard, mechanical, heartless, impersonal forces in the modern world. Sometimes he portrays him as a sort of gangster: when Marx opposes the communist tailor Wilhelm Weitling, "the thumping of his fist did not stop until Weitling had been driven to America." He admires Rosa Luxemburg, her faith, her revolutionary martyrdom, he even calls her "Rosa," but he can't seem to grasp that she lived and died a Marxist. Billington's problem with

Marx also leads him to bathe any and all of Marx's opponents in a sentimental glow: thus, for instance,

> Marx was the modern Dominican ... of the revolutionary church; Proud-
> hon was its Saint Francis. The former spoke primarily to the intellect; the
> latter mainly to the emotions. Franciscans were always farther from
> power and closer to heresy; but it was the Dominicans who lit the fires of
> the Inquisition and Savonarola.

Not included in this scheme is Proudhon's response to Marx's criticism of
his economics, in *The Poverty of Philosophy* (1847). Marx's criticism was
just another part of the Jewish plot, said Proudhon. Marx, Rothschild,
Heinrich Heine, they were all the same – all embodiments of "the Jew,"
who was scheming to rule the world:

> The Jew [Proudhon writes] is the enemy of the human race. One must
> send this race back to Asia or exterminate it. ... By fire or fusion, or by
> expulsion, the Jew must disappear. *Work to be done.* [Proudhon's emphasis]
> What the peoples of the Middle Ages hate by instinct, I hate upon reflec-
> tion, and irrevocably.

Now this certainly speaks to the emotions, as Billington says, and it is very
fiery; but the spirit is a long way from Assisi. Can a writer who gets all this
hopelessly garbled be trusted with fire?

Billington's Marx problem may be part of a larger failing, a hostility to
theory. Even Proudhon and Bakunin, who hated Marx personally and
politically, held him in the highest esteem as a thinker. (Bakunin even
began a Russian translation of *Capital*.) Billington cannot for the life of
him understand why. The reason was, simply, that Marx showed an un-
equaled theoretical grasp of the forces that hold the modern world to-

gether, of its inner dynamics, contradictions and potentialities. Proudhon and Bakunin – and the best of their anarchist successors, from Kropotkin to Emma Goldman to Paul Goodman – recognized that there was much they could learn from Marx, even if they didn't like him.

Billington, unlike them, fails to see that there is something he is missing, and that Marx might help him to find it or work it out. Not that he, or anyone else, should admire Marx uncritically. But a serious encounter with *Capital* – or even with the theoretical (as distinct from the tactical) section of the *Communist Manifesto* – might force him to develop his own overall vision of the virtues and the perils of modernity, and the relationship between them, and his own idea of how to preserve the good and overcome the bad. This is what Edmund Wilson got from wrestling with Marx: it gave his book a center. Billington, disdaining Marx, produces an enormous middle without a center. Where structure, vision, ideas should be, there is only drift, and his fire is continually threatening to burn itself out.

There is one more big blind spot. Any reader who can remember the 1960s will make dozens of connections between Billington's scenes – the rituals, the clothes, the music, the sexual display, the expressive extravagance, the ambiance of intoxication, the political theater on the stage and in the streets – and our own. Berkeley in the heyday of the Free Speech Movement, the Pentagon in 1967, Haight Street and St. Mark's Place, Columbia, the streets of Paris in 1968 – "All power to the imagination" – these should be Billington's Finland Stations, or at least his Palais-Royales, and they should constitute the dramatic climax of his book. Alas, he doesn't like us. It's even worse than dislike: he freezes us out of history. In his book, the 1960s never happened at all. Feminism is the only contemporary radical project toward which he is even minimally polite. Billington's enormous range of sympathy, the vast scope and generosity of his vision, seems to fail him as soon as the fire gets close to home. This keeps him from giving his book the dramatic resolution and intellectual coherence it deserves. It's as if he would rather write an incoherent book than confront *people like us*. But then why write a book about the romantic left in the first place?

For all these difficulties, *Fire in the Minds of Men* is a fascinating and often delightful book. Billington's people, visions and scenes can help us grasp our past, to confront what we have become in the present, and to imagine an imaginable future.

For anyone who wants to keep the fire alive, and to make it a creative rather than a merely destructive force, Billington has whole worlds to give. It will be a pleasure to stand in his debt! As I write this, I can imagine him shuddering and wishing we'd just go away. But who else does he think will care about his treasure chest of radical history – who will even think it *is* a treasure chest – if not people who want to make radical history of their own?

9

Georg Lukács's Cosmic *Chutzpah*

... was that *your* "calling" or what ever?

– Max Weber to Lukács in prison, March 1920

Georg Lukács, one of the remarkable men of the twentieth century, began life in the age of Disraeli and Nietzsche and carried on into the age of the Beatles and walks on the moon. He is the author of two world-class masterpieces, *History and Class Consciousness* and *Theory of the Novel*, and of dozens of other books and thousands of articles, pamphlets, manifestos and other writings of nearly every genre on nearly every subject we can imagine. His ideas are central to the history of Marxism (this is widely recognized), but also of existentialism (which is hardly recognized at all). He spent the last half-century of his life as a committed commu-

---

Review of István Eörsi, ed., *Georg Lukács: Record of a Life. An Autobiographical Sketch.* Trans. Rodney Livingstone (London: Verso, 1985); and Judith Marcus and Zoltan Tar, eds., *Georg Lukács: Selected Correspondence 1902–1920* (New York: Columbia University Press, 1985). It first appeared in the *Village Voice Literary Supplement,* July 1985.

nist, participating in the revolutions of 1918–19, living through the horrors of Stalinism, emerging into political life again in the Hungarian
revolution of 1956, suffering imprisonment by a wide assortment of jailers but surviving his jailers, and being there to denounce both the bombs
over Hanoi and the tanks in Prague.

Record of a Life is a series of sketches and interviews that Lukács hastily
put together shortly before his death in 1971, when he realized that he
would never live to write his autobiography. There is a wonderful grandeur about Lukács as he emerges here. He is physically frail but intellectually powerful and spiritually intense, striving to grasp the meaning of
his life and work. He radiates the aura of those old men of Greek mythology Philoctetes with his wound and his bow, Oedipus at Colonus, the
androgynous prophet Tiresias who has foresuffered all. These comparisons are meant only to show what a problematical figure he was: his
intellectual and visionary powers were always intertwined with blindness, wounds and guilt.

I first encountered Lukács in Washington Square Park in the spring of
1958. I was a freshman at Columbia, out of the Bronx for the first time in
my life, enthralled by the sights and sounds of Manhattan and the books
and ideas of the world. As I wandered through the park one lovely afternoon, I saw, among the singers and players and hustlers and kibitzers, a
fellow I had known in high school, standing under the arch, declaiming
and handing out leaflets to the crowd. He had been a Communist Party
stalwart all through school, but 1956 had hit him hard, and after Budapest
he seemed to drop out of sight. Now here he was again, testifying that
capitalism was on its last legs, and that the international working class
and its vanguard party were alive and well. I greeted him and got him to
take a break; we walked around the park, gossiped about old school

friends, looked longingly at the girls, and started to worry about the world.

He remarked on the books I was carrying – Kierkegaard, Dostoevsky, Martin Buber – and wondered if I was becoming a junkie on that old opium of the people. I in turn wondered if he was still recruiting people to join the Red Army and see the world. Suddenly he turned dead serious: "Are you asking if I'm still a communist?" All right, I said: Was he, could he be, even now? He replied that he was more of a communist than ever. I must have looked dubious, or maybe just disgusted. He reached into his briefcase and pulled out a text, poorly mimeographed and heavily underlined. It was called "What Is Orthodox Marxism?" by a Georg Lukács. "Here," he ordered, "read this!" The text began with the proclamation that even if every single one of Marx's theses about the world were to be proved wrong, an orthodox Marxist could simply discard them "without having to renounce his orthodoxy for a single moment." I was instantly stunned: Who was this guy and what was he saying? I fell back on a reality I was sure of: "And those tanks in Budapest? Don't they prove something?" My friend hesitated for a moment, then drew himself up and answered decisively. "They prove," he said, "that the USSR is not orthodox."

I can still remember the way that first page of Lukács made my head spin. The cosmic *chutzpah* of the man was staggering. I'd known plenty of Marxists who were willing to admit that Marx might be wrong about many things; in spite of this, they said, he was right about the essential things, and that was why they were Marxists. Now here was a Marxist saying that Marx might be wrong about *everything,* and he couldn't care less; that the truth of Marxism was independent of anything that Marx said about the world, and hence that nothing in the world could ever refute it; and that this was the essence not merely of Marxist truth, but of Marxist orthodoxy – even if it was the orthodoxy of a single believer, shut out from the communion of the ecclesiastic party, keeping the faith alone in the park. When I thought about it later, it struck me that the Marxism of Lukács's "What Is Orthodox Marxism?" had more in common with the existential flights of the religious writers whose books I was carrying that day – Kierkegaard, Dostoevsky, Buber – than with the Stalinist dogmatics on which my friend had grown up. As I thought of Lukács in their company, it flashed on me that what I had just read was a Marxist *credo quia absurdum*. Could it be that Communism had found its St. Augustine at last?

I asked my teachers about Lukács and found out all I could. No one knew too much in those years, but everyone found him fascinating. He was a Hungarian Jew, son of a banker, born in Budapest in 1885. He had studied in Heidelberg with Max Weber and in Berlin with Georg Simmel; both considered him, though still in his twenties, one of the most brilliant and original minds of the age. He had begun his career as a writer on art and culture, a founder of magazines and a theater – he brought Ibsen and Strindberg to Budapest – but then, horrified and radicalized by the First World War, became a militant member of the Hungarian Communist Party. In 1919, during the brief life of the Soviet Republic of Hungary, he served as commissar of education and culture. After its overthrow, he escaped to Vienna and then to Berlin, where he became active and prominent in the Communist International. When Hitler came to power he found himself a refugee again, this time in Moscow, where he helped to discover, excavate and publish some of the buried writings of the young Marx. At the end of the Second World War he returned to Budapest, where he wrote and taught philosophy for the rest of his life.

Lukács's reputation rested above all on a work of philosophy, politics, and social theory that he published in German in 1923, *History and Class Consciousness.*[1] This book had been long out of print and very hard to get – and therein lies a tale. It began with the essay I had read that day in the park, "What Is Orthodox Marxism?" Ironically, although Lukács had been constantly preoccupied with establishing a Marxist orthodoxy, he became a prime victim once the Communist movement began to persecute internal heresy. In the Comintern in 1924 and 1928, in Moscow in 1934, in Budapest in 1949, he was subjected to campaigns of the crudest vilification; three generations of Stalinist hacks had stigmatized him as a symbol of all the dangers of "deviation." In all these cases (Morris Watnick chronicled them in *Soviet Survey* in 1958,[2] the first discussion of Lukács in English), he had submitted to his persecutors, repudiated his ideas, and begged forgiveness rather than be isolated from the world communist movement. In 1928 he was condemned by the Comintern for "premature antifascism" (he was vindicated later, but too late for him). He then withdrew from political activity and hoped for a quieter life, writing literary and cultural history. But it was not to be.

In 1934, *History and Class Consciousness* was condemned for the heresy of philosophical idealism. At this point, Lukács seemed to enlist actively in the fight against his life and thought. He confessed "not only the theoretical falsity of my book, but its practical danger." The diatribes against him "all the more strengthened my conviction that, in the intellectual sphere, the front of Idealism is the front of Fascist counter-revolution." He ended by praising Comrade Stalin and his henchmen for their "iron implacability and refusal to compromise with all deviations from Marxism-Leninism." He did not offer to burn *History and Class Consciousness* (or himself) in Red Square, but he did swear to do everything in his power to ensure that his masterpiece would never be reprinted anywhere again. ("In the fight between you and the world," Kafka once wrote, "back the world.")

When I read this, I felt confirmed in my sense of Lukács as a religious figure. His capacity for abjection and repentance, his drive to punish and mortify himself for the sake of sanctity, had more in common with the inner world of Augustine's *Confessions* than with the sensibility of Karl Marx. But this was a very modern Augustine, as he might have been imagined by Dostoevsky or Freud: endlessly reinventing himself, hoping to obliterate his past once and for all, only to trip over it – or maybe dig it up – again and again; persecuting and purging himself in a quest for pure orthodoxy, only to find himself inventing new modes of heresy, leading to new orgies of guilt, confession and self-recrimination.

In 1956, Lukács went through a stunning metamorphosis. That year, as the Stalinist system shook and crumbled, the Hungarian people rose up against their Soviet masters. Lukács participated enthusiastically in this revolution, and once again, after thirty-seven years, served as minister of education and culture in a Hungarian revolutionary government. When the USSR moved in, Lukács, as a member of Prime Minister Imre Nagy's cabinet, was one of the first to be arrested. Imprisoned in Count Dracula's old Transylvanian castle, he was interrogated by the Soviet secret police and put under pressure to submit, confess, recant, inform, denounce. Lukács had gone through these motions many times before over the previous thirty years. This time, however, he refused to betray his comrades, his people or himself. Pressed to denounce Imré Nagy, Lukács said that he would be glad to air his opinions about Nagy once the two of them were free men in the streets of Budapest, but he would never break solidarity with a fellow prisoner. After six months in prison,

Lukács was released and allowed to return to Budapest. It was understood that he would not agitate actively against the new government; neither, however, would he endorse it. At the age of seventy, this lifelong seeker after orthodoxy found himself an authentic heretical hero.

History and Class Consciousness appeared in French translation in 1960. Lukács protested its publication, but his objections only made the book more notorious and intriguing. My friends and I, and many intellectuals like us – members of the generation that would soon be called the New Left – opened the book with breathless anticipation, and found that it lived up to its advance notices. Whatever we might think about its many theories and arguments, *History and Class Consciousness* convinced us that socialist thought in our time could be carried on at the highest pitch of intellectual power, fused with the most passionate feeling, transformed into an inspired vision. Lukács gave us both a standard that challenges and a specter that haunts any radical who sits down to write today.

The heart of *History and Class Consciousness,* and the primary source of its power, is a 140-page essay, situated at the book's center, entitled "Reification and the Consciousness of the Proletariat." *Reification* is a poor Latinized equivalent for *Verdinglichung,* a German word that means "thingification," the process by which a person is transformed into a thing. The basic trouble with capitalism, Lukács argues, is that it treats people as if they were things, and treats human relationships as if they were between things. The particular sort of thing that people in modern capitalist societies get turned into is the *commodity.* Lukács takes Marx's idea of the "Fetishism of Commodities" *(Capital* Volume 1, Chapter 1), and extends it into a total vision of what capitalism does to human life.

He begins with an exploration of work, carrying Marx's discussion of "alienated labor" into the age of immense bureaucracies (private and public), efficiency experts, systems analysis and long-range planning. The process of labor is "progressively broken down into abstract, rational, specialized operations." Workers lose contact not only with the products or services they create, but with their own thoughts and feelings and actions. "Even the worker's psychological attributes are separated from his total personality, and placed in opposition to it, so as to facilitate their integration into specialized rational systems and their reduction to statistical units." This fragmentation of activity tends to generate a "fragmentation of the subject," so that a worker's personal qualities, talents or idiosyncrasies "appear as sources of error."

The worker is meant to be "a mechanical part incorporated into a mechanical system. He finds it already pre-existing and self-sufficient, it functions independently of him, and he has to conform to its laws whether he likes it or not. ... Here, too, the personality can do no more than look on helplessly while its own existence is reduced to an isolated particle and fed into an alien system." In such a system we feel passive and contemplative; we experience ourselves as spectators in processes that happen to us, rather than active participants shaping our lives.

Most of Marx's successors focused almost exclusively on the oppression of manual and industrial workers. Lukács shows how the force of Marx's analysis and indictment goes far beyond them. In fact, capitalism treats all men and women as interchangeable parts, as commodities exchangeable for other commodities. Administrators, soldiers, scientists, even entrepreneurs – everybody in modern society – is forced into the Procrustean bed of reification and systematically deprived of the freedom that everyone is supposed to enjoy. Even the modern capitalist "experiences the same doubling of personality, the same splitting up of man into an element of the movement of commodities and an objective and impotent observer of that movement." Capitalists are rewarded for their inner passivity and lack of integration; but it is urgent to see the human costs of this system, even to its ruling class. Lukács deepens the case against capitalism by showing us how, even in its mansions on the hill, no one is at home.

He puts much energy into a critique of early-twentieth-century forms of discourse that passed for social science. He attacks the attempt to formulate laws of human behavior that will have the static, timeless quality of physical laws about the behavior of matter and energy. Such an aim assumes that human realities and social relationships are unchangeable, inexorable as gravitational force, impervious to human will, beyond any kind of social or political control. This paradigm masks the enormous diversity of human relationships in different times and places – indeed, even within the same time and place – and the capacity of human beings, acting collectively, to change the world. Something is fundamentally wrong with modes of thought (whether they are called philosophy, history or science) whose main force is to convince people that there is no alternative to the way they live now. One of the most insidious powers of modern capitalism, Lukács believes, is its capacity to mobilize the energy of our intellects – and of our intellectuals – to blur our minds and paralyze our will, to reduce us to passive spectators of whatever fate the market inflicts on us.

The young Lukács often writes as a kind of Left neo-Kantian: in the face of the world we live in, to revolt is a categorical imperative. It is the only way to seize control of our fate, to assert ourselves as subjects, as people, against a social structure that treats us as things. In his model of Marxism, the crucial issue isn't one class oppressing another class, but one total *system* oppressing everybody. The ultimate end isn't economic justice, but personal *authenticity*. Lukács insists on the crucial importance of consciousness and self-awareness in political life. Capitalism may be breaking down, but there is no reason to think that it will give way to something better, unless the people are conscious that things *can be* better, that they have the power to transform and renew the world. If the workers can come to know themselves – to grasp the sources of their present weakness and self-alienation, of their potential freedom and power – then capitalism is doomed. Lukács connects the 1900 Marxist ideal of "revolutionary class-consciousness" with the ancient Socratic demand to "know thyself." But these aims require an arduous process of education and self-education, of struggle – both in theory and practice – of continual self-criticism and self-overcoming. One of the main reasons for having a Communist party, Lukács argues, is to focus and organize the work of self-knowledge, to transform it into a collective project. Equally important is the creation of a vibrant, dynamic, self-critical and self-renewing radical culture. Without culture and consciousness, the workers will not be able to grow up. If they don't grow, the reification-machine will go on running, and its victims won't ever know what's hit them or why they feel like hollow men inside.

If they do learn and grow, the *soviet* or worker's council will be an ideal expression of their new life. Government and politics won't be obscure processes enacted on behalf of remote or invisible interests, but activities that men and women do, on their own, in their everyday lives. The economy won't be a machine running on its own momentum toward its own goals, but a structure of concrete decisions that men and women freely make about how they want to live and fulfill their needs. Culture, instead of being a veil of mystification thrown over everyday life, will be created by ordinary people out of their real desires and needs and hopes. In a workers' democracy, the constraints of the exploitive economy, of the repressive state, of the culture of mystification, will all wither away. Then "the life of man as man in relation to himself, to his fellow men and to nature, can now become the authentic content of human life. Socially, man is now born as man."

History and Class Consciousness appeared in English at an ideal moment for an emerging generation of radical intellectuals. It helped us in the West to see how, even where capitalism was highly successful in economic terms (the 1960s, remember, was the climax of the greatest capitalist boom in history), it could still be humanly disastrous, inflicting insult and injury on the people in it by treating them as nothing more than commodities. Simultaneously, Lukács's book enabled intellectuals in the Soviet bloc to understand how the so-called workers' states had developed their own distinctive forms of reification. The 1960s spawned an amazing variety of eruptions and rebellions by people who were sick and tired of being treated as things, who fought to end reification and to assert themselves as subjects, as active participants in their everyday lives. For those of us who were trying to think this through, *History and Class Consciousness* was a rich source of ideas and energy. Moreover, for a generation accustomed to a Marxism of sterile formulas and rigid dogmas enforced by party hacks, this book brought Marxism back to its deepest sources as a vision and a theory of human liberation.

One of the most striking things about *History and Class Consciousness* was the religious language in it. First there was the theme of "orthodoxy" with which the book began; then the revolutionary party was supposed to bring "total absorption of the personality" of its members; then the goal of socialism was said to be "the redemption of man"; the transition from capitalism to socialism would be "a leap into the realm of freedom," after which "man is now born as man." No one knew enough about Lukács, back in the 1960s, to sort out these ideas and drives. But it was clear that one of his most important achievements was to bring together the body of Marxist theory and practice with the stream of *Innerlichkeit* and spiritual yearning, which, more than any economic analysis or attachment to the working class, has led countless men and women to "prove their ideas by action, by living and dying for the revolution."

This fusion was the primary source of Lukács's power and originality. But it had its dark side as well. One of the most disturbing of his religious ideas – an idea that has been deeply problematical whenever it has occurred in the history of religion – is the idea of *incarnation*. Thus, in the course of expounding on the Leninist idea of a "vanguard" Communist Party, Lukács gives it a twist that would have been unimaginable to a secular and pragmatic mind like Lenin's: "The Party," he says, "is the historical embodiment and active incarnation of revolutionary class consciousness," and, again, a little later, "the incarnation of the ethics of the fighting proletariat."

Lukács's doctrine of incarnation is as profound a mystery as anything ever proclaimed by any Christian church. But it poses special dangers all its own. If the Communist party, in some mysterious way, "is" the revolutionary working class, then it becomes impossible to imagine that, say, the party might betray the working class, or even to ask whether the party is serving the working class as well as it should: the party stands not only beyond doubt, but beyond question or scrutiny.

Similar problems arise around Lukács's notion of Marxist orthodoxy, equally impervious to any facts or events that might cast doubt on its truth. Finally, there is the idea of *totality*, according to which the question

of freedom becomes "purely tactical," because "freedom cannot represent a value in itself": the only real issue is whether the Communist Party,
incarnation of the working class, holds the "totality of power." If these
ideas were brought together – the trinity of totality, orthodoxy and incarnation – they could generate a theology of total submission, a metaphysical undertow that might well be strong enough to drown all Lukács's
dreams of liberation.

The radical contradictions that animate this book, and the strength and
depth with which its contradictory ideas are expressed, mark *History and
Class Consciousness* as one of the great modernist works of the century. To
young readers who discovered Lukács in the 1960s, he seemed to belong
in the company of great modern thinkers at war with themselves – Rousseau, Dostoevsky, Nietzsche – theorists and exponents of both liberation
and of domination. Although Lukács was in some obvious way a Marxist,
his kindred spirits were all a lot weirder than Marx.

We were just getting used to seeing Lukács as a great modernist when
he came out with a scurrilous, hysterical attack on modernism. This
essay, "The Ideology of Modernism," reads like an indictment at a Stalinist trial.[3] It puts together an amalgam in the defendant's box, consisting
of great twentieth-century writers (Kafka, Proust, Joyce, Faulkner, Musil,
Freud), utterly mediocre writers (Steinbeck, Thomas Wolfe), and assorted Nazi ideologues and hacks. It then assaults these "modernist"
subjects. In "their" writings, the personality is dissolved, the objective
world is inexplicable, there is no past and no history, perversity and idiocy
are the essence of the human condition. Modernism has no perspectives,
furthers the dissolution of the personality, destroys the complex tissue of
humanity's relations with the environment. Kierkegaard says that the self

is opaque to itself, and this furnishes a convenient alibi for Nazi murder-
ers. Kafka "substitutes his *Angst*-ridden view of the world for objective
reality." Freud is "obsessed with pathology" and sickens an otherwise
healthy audience; he lacks the sane wisdom of Pavlov, "who takes the
Hippocratic view that mental abnormality is a deviation from a norm."
So it goes.

"The Ideology of Modernism" is colossally, willfully ignorant. Or
maybe it is not exactly ignorance, but rather what Veblen called "trained
incapacity" to see what is there. This learning disability is a special embarrassment for those who like to think of themselves as Marxists. Marxists are supposed to be able to understand art in relation to historical and
material reality. Instead, Lukács speaks as if it were writers who autono-
mously *create* reality: as if Freud had created the twentieth century's
pathologies and Kafka its police states. (After his imprisonment in
Dracula's castle, Lukács was reported to have said, "I was wrong, Kafka
was a realist after all." But he never put this insight into print, or thought
it through.)

Lukács says that he is fighting in the name of "realism," whose basic
idea is that "reality can be known." What he really means, we see as we
read on, is that reality *is* known, and he knows it, and he doesn't want to
read any writing that doesn't tell him what he already knows. He totally
identifies with the aggressors, assaulting Kafka and Joyce and Freud in
exactly the language that Nazi and Stalinist hacks and thugs used to
assault them. It's as if he is hoping to destroy their masterworks in just
the way that his Soviet masters destroyed his own. Luckily, they were
beyond his power – though his diatribes probably kept some great writers
from being read. The one great modernist within his reach, whom he
violated and brutalized shamefully, was himself.

I remembered hearing that in *The Magic Mountain* Thomas Mann had used Lukács as a model for Leo Naphta, one of his most luminous characters, a Jewish-Jesuit-Communist who kills himself on the verge of the First World War.[4] I was glad that, unlike Naphta, Lukács was living on (and on). But if Mann was suggesting something about Lukács's need for rough trade with himself, this was hard to deny. Works like "The Ideology of Modernism" read like a kind of ritual self-murder. Why did Lukács keep throwing himself off the bridge? What crime or sin was he atoning for, and how long would his trial by ordeal last?

By the early 1970s, you could find people in American (and European and Australian) universities who had actually worked with Lukács. They were a pretty smart bunch; philosopher Agnes Heller is probably the most illustrious. I remember asking some *Lukácsniki* how one of the best minds of the century could sink so low. They said that I had to understand the political context: even as he assaulted modernism, Lukács also denounced socialist realism, the one form of literature that Stalin condoned. In fact, Lukács was the only writer in the Soviet bloc who had ever been able to get away with this. Did I think it had been easy, or without risks? By attacking the "Western orthodoxy" of modernism, Lukács was clearing space in which he would be free to attack the "Eastern orthodoxy" of socialist realism. Couldn't I see how, within the immense constraints of life in the Soviet bloc, Lukács had created space for literary and cultural freedom? Yes, I could see it. Still, I feared that the force of Lukács's cultural politics might well be to open the door for the free spirits of the 1860s, while keeping those of the 1960s locked out.

More of Lukács's writings were reissued and translated in the course of the 1960s. There were the works of literary criticism and cultural history written in the 1930s and 1940s: *Studies in European Realism, Goethe and His Age, The Historical Novel, The Young Hegel.* These books lacked the brilliance and originality of *History and Class Consciousness,* but moved on a level far above the antimodernist diatribes of the 1950s. The books were full of marvelous connections and insights, and full of nostalgia for the sweetness of life before the First World War. They showed Lukács as a conservative thinker: conservative in the best sense, striving to embrace, nourish and protect the heritage of bourgeois humanism even as the twin menaces of Nazism and Stalinism were closing in. Lukács's comrades in this preservationist enterprise were a generation of gifted Jewish scholars, scattered to the winds by Nazism – among them Ernst Cassirer, Erich Auerbach, Arnold Hauser and Erwin Panofsky. In these works, Lukács's communism often faded into the background. But he was surely right to say that any socialist movement that abandoned this heritage or let it die would be surrendering its soul.

As Lukács's historical works were being reissued, a number of his post-Stalin political essays were coming out, hot off the presses. (The *New Left Review* played a crucial role in getting this material to British and American readers.) These articles made it clear how thrilled Lukács was to see Stalinism unmasked, and how eagerly he embraced Khrushchev's promises of domestic liberalization and international détente. Some of this writing showed an unprecedented emotional openness, and readers could not help sharing the old man's unmediated joy that he had come through and outlived his jailers.

But even here shadows of ambiguity begin to close on the pure daylight. Lukács's invectives against Stalin cite many disastrous flaws but make only the briefest, most cryptic reference to his mass murders. And it is disturbing that, in his essays on Stalin, Lukács spends so much space and energy denouncing Trotsky – as if, just as in his attacks on modernism, he needs to prove his own orthodoxy, lest the force of his criticism place his loyalty in doubt. Often in this period, Lukács seems to be going out of his way to protest too much, to suggest inexhaustible ironic depths. This systematic ambiguity pervades the process of the republication of his early works, complete with recantations, official bans and underground printing. The wheels within wheels turned more frantically than ever in a 1967 preface to a new edition of *History and Class Consciousness,* an edition that Lukács had apparently fought to suppress. He testified it was a mistake for him to write the book, and advised readers it would be a mistake for them to read it – but in a language of enticement that ensured his advice would fail.

Lukács's death in 1971 was far from the end of his story. In the years since, an amazing array of his early writings has come to light, including much that Lukács himself believed lost; some of his most brilliant and original writing is just beginning to appear in print.[5] We are still in the process of discovering Lukács, running the movie backwards, and getting the first things last. In fact, we are discovering parts of the movie that Lukács clearly hoped to censor, faces he left on the cutting-room floor, the return of the repressed.

The most fascinating of Lukács's early works is *Theory of the Novel,* written in the midst of the horrors of the First World War, long suppressed by the author, finally republished (with another of those famous seductively self-denying prefaces) shortly before his death.[6] *Theory of the Novel* argues that every literary form expresses a particular "metaphysical dissonance," which springs from the inner contradictions of its historical and social milieu. It goes on to evoke, with great lyrical brilliance, the dissonances that were tearing the modern world apart in 1915. It tries to

imagine, and indeed to call into being, a true modernist art in which "all
the fissures and rents inherent in the historical situation [will] be drawn
into the form-giving process." *Theory of the Novel* is one of the great
works of romantic criticism, in the class of Wordsworth's Preface to the
Lyrical Ballads and Schiller's *Letters on the Aesthetic Education of Man*. It
concludes with a ringing declaration that the inner dialectic of the modern novel leads beyond the novel and, indeed, beyond the wretched and
alienated world whose spirit the novel expresses. The emergence of Tolstoy and Dostoevsky are distinctive "signs of the world to come." Their
interpretations of the modern world mark the start of a great wave of
change in this world, a "breakthrough into a new epoch," the dawn of a
"new unity" of soul and social institutions. Moreover, even before the
Russian Revolution and Lukács's conversion to Communism, he insisted
that backward, grungy Russia was fated to be the salvation of the corrupt
and decadent West.

Theory of the Novel is also fascinating in its religious anguish and longing. Lukács describes the modern novel as "an expression of transcenden-
tal homelessness"; the novel's typical environment as "a universe abandoned by God"; the epoch in which he writes as "an age of absolute
sinfulness"; the modern hero's predicament as "the torment of a creature
condemned to solitude and devoured by a longing for communion."
Here, and throughout the book, Lukács makes clear the sort of inner
needs that his commitment to communism, for a time at least, would
fulfill.

Recent scholarship has unearthed the way in which Lukács became a
Communist. In fact, it was a religious conversion, an upheaval of the
mind and heart, a second birth. It seems to have happened very suddenly,
in the last days of 1918. According to one of his intimate friends, it

happened "between one Sunday and the next, like Saul turning into Paul."

Even as he was turning, Lukács wrote two remarkable brief essays, perhaps the clearest and most candid things he ever wrote: "Bolshevism as a Moral Problem," a few days before his conversion, and "Tactics and Ethics," a few days after.[7] The "Bolshevism" essay, which was long believed lost and was rediscovered shortly before Lukács's death, makes it clear that he saw himself as making an existential "leap of faith" into Bolshevism, and moreover considered this revolutionary faith to be utterly absurd. The question at hand was whether the Bolshevik revolution would really "mean the end of *all* class domination" or "simply entail the reshuffling of classes" in which "the previous oppressors will become the new oppressed class"; whether the emerging socialist regime would in fact "bring about the salvation of humanity" or merely create "an ideological shell for class interests." Anywhere a Bolshevik regime comes to power, "the existing class oppression will ... be replaced by that of the proletariat." The Bolshevik regime will aim "to drive out Satan so to speak, with the help of Beelzebub – in the hope that this last and therefore most open and cruel of class oppression will finally destroy itself, and in so doing put an end to class oppression forever. "In order to become a Bolshevik," Lukács says,

> We have to believe true *credo quia absurdum est* – that no new class struggle will emerge out of this class struggle (resulting in the quest for a new oppression), which would provide continuance to the old sequence of meaningless and aimless struggles – but that oppression will effect the elements of its own destruction. It is, therefore, a question of belief – as it is in the case of any ethical question – of what the choice will be. Let me emphasize again: Bolshevism rests on the metaphysical assumption

that the bad can engender the good, or, as Razumikhin says, in Dostoevsky's *Crime and Punishment,* that it is possible to lie our way through to
the truth.

This author is unable to share this belief.

And yet, within a few days of this essay, Lukács had decided to make the
leap. What changed his mind? It's hard to say for sure. "Tactics and Ethics" offers a pragmatic argument that in East Central Europe in 1919, the
likely political alternatives are either a communist revolution or a fascist
dictatorship; at this time, in this place, liberal democracy is simply not in
the cards. This argument is plausible but has a limited force. It justifies
participating in a communist movement, on the grounds that it is the
lesser of two available evils. But Lukács invests far more emotion in
communism, and expects far more from it, than his pragmatic argumen-
tation could ever comprehend. We need to look between the lines of his
text and search out the emotional subtext. The most intense emotion in
the inner world of "Tactics and Ethics" is Lukács's sense of guilt. The
ethical rhetoric he speaks in at first sounds Kantian; we should act as if we
were universal legislators, ethically responsible for the whole world. But
if we listen for the feeling, it is less Kant than Dostoevsky, or Kant as he
might have been remembered by Raskolnikov.[8]

Thus, for Lukács, we really are responsible for all the oppression,
violence and murder in the world. If we become communists, we are
guilty of all the murders committed in the name of communism, not
only now but in the indefinite future, *"just as if we had killed them all"* (my
emphasis). If we refuse to commit ourselves to communism, and fascism
triumphs instead, we are guilty of all Fascist murders, now and to come.
No matter what happens, whatever we do or don't do, we are all murder-
ers, there is no way to escape the blood on our hands. What can a mur-

derer do? Is there any way to atone? These were the sorts of questions that were tormenting Lukács at the end of 1918. He seems to have concluded that if the criminal were to lean to the Left, his crimes might actually accomplish something, his murders might help to end (or at least diminish) murders, his lies might open the way to some sort of truth.

In his later years, Lukács disparaged the thinking that led to his conversion as "utopian," "messianic," "sectarian." It wasn't till later on, he said, that he became a "realist" and "materialist" and learned true Marxism. After digging deep into his early work, I would argue the exact opposite: that at the high tide of his messianic hopes, Lukács's moral and political thinking was clear, honest and deeply attuned to material realities, in the finest Marxist tradition. He said repeatedly, in 1919, that it was impossible to know how history was going to turn out, that all political choices would have to be continually reappraised, that the ethical subject would have to weigh the violence and evil he helped to perpetrate against the actual freedom and happiness that he was helping to create.

It was only afterward, when it became clear that his hopes were not being fulfilled in the real world, that his leap of faith froze into a form of bad faith. We can see this happening even in the last sections of *History and Class Consciousness,* where Lukács's religious and moral hopes are gradually reified into a theological system of beliefs. His concept of incarnation, orthodoxy and totality become a trinity in a secular political theology. Lukács's *credo quia absurdum est,* and his real bad faith, lay not in his 1919 hope that oppression today might help to end oppression tomorrow, but in his post-1921 doctrine that through the Party's power, oppression had ended already. He clung to this doctrine all through the Stalin era, even as it undermined and slowly poisoned his thought and his life.

There is one more big clue to Lukács's life that came to light after his death. In 1973 a Heidelberg bank released a safe deposit box full of long-lost Lukács letters, diaries and manuscripts.[9] This material uncovered the story of his first love. Late in 1907, Lukács and Irma Seidler, a young Hungarian Jewish painter, met and fell in love. She wanted marriage and a normal life with him. He seems to have genuinely loved her from the first but, like many men before and since, feared commitment. "What I wish to accomplish," he wrote her, "only an unattached man can accomplish." For three years, even as he idealized and mythicized her ("Irma is Life," etc.), he fought her off. In the spring of 1911, she killed herself. Lukács was devastated and racked with guilt. "I could have saved her if I'd taken her hand. ... I have lost my right to life." It would be foolish to reduce Lukács's (or anybody's) ideology to psychology. Still, this heart-breaking affair, and Lukács's self-lacerating judgment on his role in it, may help to clarify some of the mysteries of his thought and action in years to come. It gives us an idea why he felt so guilty – guilty, as he repeatedly said, of murder – and why he had such a deep need for confession, repentance, mortification, atonement. It gives a personal urgency and emotional depth to the idea, advanced in *Theory of the Novel* in 1915, that modern humanity's basic problem is "the torment of a creature condemned to solitude and devoured by the longing for community." And it suggests why it was Ernö Seidler, Irma's brother, who – along with Party leader and (for a little while) Prime Minister Béla Kun – recruited Lukács into the Hungarian Communist party at the end of 1918.*

---

*What a great Hungarian movie this sad story would have made! And there were two generations of fine Hungarian directors – Miklos Jansco, Marta Mezaros, Pal Gabor, Istvan Szabo, Karoly Makk, and others I've forgotten or never knew – who could

Lukács himself, for most of his career, treated the whole medium of cinema with learned ignorance; his throwaway dismissals through the years make him sound like one more park-bench *alte kocker* who can't accept that he's living in the twentieth century. That wouldn't be a problem if so much of his writing weren't framed as a demand for "Realism." But then, in the glorious month of May 1968, Lukács not only supported the troubles, but gave the cinema special credit for starting them: "In Hungary," he said, in an interview with the cinema magazine *Filmkultura,* "or at least in Hungarian culture, film nowadays plays the role of the *avant-garde.*"[10] This sentence isn't only about movies, or about Hungary. It is about *being there*: about an old realist who wants to make whatever imaginative leaps he must to be part of the real world around him; about an old modernist who remembers that to seize the day is to be alive; about an old man who isn't ready to go gentle into the good night. It is the reason you can't ever give up on Lukács: just when you are ready to close the books on him – as he so often yearns to close the books on himself – he makes a spurt of new life and growth.)

So where does Lukács leave us in the end? The sketches and interviews that make up *Record of a Life* offer no final epiphany, but only more layers under layers and wheels within wheels, more of Lukács's enticing and infuriating blend of blindness and insight, of bad faith and transcendent

---

really have grasped it, who knew how to situate a phenomenon like communism and an emotion like love in the same frame, and knew there was a rich variety of possible ways for them to play out. Alas, *Irma and Gyorgy* will never be made. It is too late now: the memory is gone. Eastern Europe in the 1990s has lost its tragic sense of communist life, lost it as inexorably as Western Europe once lost the art of medieval stained glass.

inspiration. He says, with an apparently straight face, "I am perhaps not a very contemporary man. I have never felt frustration or any kind of complex in my life. I know what these mean, of course, from the literature of the twentieth century and from having read Freud. But I have not experienced them myself." Yet even as he says this, he recognizes, fugitively, how much of his life's energy has gone into repudiating his thoughts and burying his feelings. When he says, "It has cost me nothing," he reveals to us how much it really has cost.

Lukács is still intermittently swallowed up by the totalities he created for himself in the 1920s. When asked what he said to himself during the monstrous excesses of Stalinism, he replies that "the worst form of socialism was better to live in than the best form of capitalism." And yet, just a few pages before and after, he shows a bitter clarity about the so-called socialism he has served for so long. When the Warsaw Pact armies invaded Prague in 1968, he told István Eörsi, "I suppose that the whole experiment that began in 1917 has now failed, and has to be tried again at some other time and place." Lukács comes to believe, in his last years, that only a "complete rupture" with Stalinism will enable the communist movement to reclaim its creative powers; but he sees no "objective forces" that might fulfill this hope. In the end he condemns all communist regimes for betraying the original promise of communist revolutions, "genuine socialist democracy … democracy of everyday life." He sees capitalist and communist powers at home in a détente of domination, oppressing both their own and foreign people. He hopes – not in his lifetime, he knows, but someday – for a convergence of freedom. "Both great systems in crisis. Authentic Marxism the only solution." These were virtually the last words he wrote before he died.

Georg Lukács is one of the real tragic heroes of the twentieth century.

Tragic in the price he had to pay – indeed, the price he fought to pay. Heroic in the demands he made on modern art, on modern politics, on the whole of modern life – demands he affirmed to his life's end. It seems uncanny that he was here, in our midst, only yesterday. He seems too big for these times, times when people in both capitalist and socialist countries are demanding so little: big cars, villas in the country, trips abroad, pension plans. These are updated models of the things Lukács grew up with and learned to see through. Maybe after more of the people who haven't grown up with these things have had a crack at them they, too, will learn to see through the many forms of comfortable reification that pass for life. Maybe we will live to see the day when the people who don't want to be commodities in a market, even luxury commodities, and the people who don't want to be items in a plan, even top-priority items, will discover each other, and struggle together for what Lukács called "democracy of everyday life."

Notes

1. *History and Class Consciousness*, trans. Rodney Livingstone (Cambridge, Mass.: MIT Press, 1968).

2. See Morris Watnick, "Georg Lukacs: An Intellectual Biography," *Soviet Survey*, January–March, April–June, and July–September 1958, and January–March 1959.

3. "The Ideology of Modernism," in *The Meaning of Contemporary Realism*, trans. John and Necke Mander (London: Merlin, 1962), 17–47. The essays before and after "Modernism" are blows in the same culture war, and just as bad.

4. See Judith Marcus [Tar], *Georg Lukács and Thomas Mann: A Study in the Sociology of Literature* (Massachusetts, 1987), on Lukács and Naphta, and Lukács and Mann.

5. *Theory of the Novel*, trans. Anna Bostock (Cambridge, Mass.: MIT Press, 1971).

6. Said by Lukács's friend Anna Lesznai. Quoted in Michael Löwy, *Georg Lukács: From Romanticism to Bolshevism*, trans. Patrick Camiller (London: Verso, 1979), 128.

7. "Bolshevism as a Moral Problem," trans. and introduced by Judith Marcus Tar, *Social Research* 44.3 (Autumn 1977), 416–24. This was written in Hungarian in December 1918 for the the journal of the "Galileo Circle," a group of radical intellectuals at the University of Budapest. Editor Karl Polanyi had asked Lukács for a contribution. "Tactics and Ethics" was written a couple of weeks later, directly after his conversion. It is reprinted in Lukács, *Political Writings, 1919–1929*, trans. Michael McColgan, ed. Rodney Livingstone (London: New Left Books, 1972).

8. Although it is indeed Razumikhin, in *Crime and Punishment*, who gives this formulation – to lie one's way through to the truth – it is not his own lies and truths he is talking about, but Raskolnikov's; and he offers the formulation as a caricature, hoping (in vain) that Raskolnikov will disavow it. Razumikhin is a delightfuly un-Dostoevskian character, poor and radical like Raskolnikov – he has been kicked out of the university for punching a policeman – but sane, emotionally sunny and unproblematical in all the ways Raskolnikov is not. (When Raskolnikov is senternced to Siberia, Razumikhin gets to marry Raskolnikov's sister, and readers are happy to throw rice.) But Raskolnikov is the one with whom Lukács identifies, and the prime model for his various betrayals and regenerations, from youth to old age.

9. See *Georg Lukács: Selected Correspondence, 1902–1920*. Lukács's tragic romance is one of the foci of this fine volume (the others are Lukács's intimacy with Max Weber, Georg Simmel, and other great thinkers old enough to be his father). After Seidler's suicide, Lukács published a heartrending dialogue, "On Poverty of Spirit." It has been translated by Jane and John Sanders, and reprinted in *Philosophical Forum* 3 (1971–72), 360–83, with an introduction by Agnes Heller. Cf. her longer essay in Heller, ed., "Gyorgy Lukács and Irma Seidler," in *Lukács Reappraised* (New York: Columbia University Press, 1983), 27–62.

10. This interview was reported in the *New York Times*, whose Central and Eastern European correspondents discovered Lukács's importance in 1956. It is discussed in detail in J. Hoberman, *The Red Atlantis: Communist Culture in the Absence of Communism* (Philadelphia: Temple University Press, 1998), 48–51, 276–8. Hoberman writes elegiacally of the Kadar era, the age of "frigidaire socialism," when, he says, "Hungarian pop offered a way to criticise Hungarian socialism," and "the worker's state incubated its own revolutionary opposition." In Hoberman's fine essays on Polish, Hungarian and Czech cinema yesterday and today, Eastern European culture converges surprisingly with North American in a shared nostalgia for radicalism born of abundance.

10

Isaac Babel: Waiting for the Barbarians

I continued on my way imploring fate to grant me the simplest
of proficiencies – the ability to kill my fellow man. ...

We are the vanguard, but of what?
– ISAAC BABEL, GALICIA, 1920

"Where are the barbarians of the twentieth century?" Friederich
Nietzsche wrote, longingly, a bit more than a century ago.[1] He was writing near the end of a hundred years of peace in Europe, and he was
convinced that peace had made Europeans sick. With their highly developed Christian conscience (even for agnostics and atheists) and their
acute sense of guilt, modern men and women had crippled themselves:
They were "broken" like their horses, "fixed" like their cats, of no more
consequence than their domestic pets. But just across the frontier,

Review of Isaac Babel, *1920 Diary,* ed. Carol J. Avins (New Haven: Yale University
Press, 1995). This essay first appeared in the *Nation,* June 26, 1995.

Nietzsche imagined, there were prides of wild beasts, untamed, ferocious, but *fully alive*. He also imagined a "fully alive" pre-Christian pride
of men whom he called "blond beasts": men who could sweep the borders and margins of their homelands and come rolling home "from orgies of murder, arson, rape, torture, jubilant and at peace with themselves."[2] Maybe the time was ripe for post-Christian men to
"re-barbarize" themselves and their world, to somehow be born again as
beasts. "Where are the barbarians?" 1914 was near; Europe wouldn't have
long to wait.

At such a rich historical moment, Nietzsche thought, there was a great
new mission for intellectuals: to "live dangerously."[3] They should spring
from their studies and build their houses under volcanoes; they should
live through every day as if it were their last. In a rebarbarized world, the
dangers in living dangerously would be intensely physical, but inward
and psychic as well. "He who fights with monsters should be careful lest
he thereby become a monster. If you look too long into the abyss, the
abyss will look back into you."[4] Long after their abysses ate them up
(Nietzsche's mind snapped in 1889), their lives and works would stand as
monuments to how far a human being could go.

I haven't been able to find out whether Isaac Babel (1894–1940) read
Nietzsche;[5] but it may be that he didn't have to – Freud once said something like this about himself – because there was so much of Nietzsche
already saturating the air in turn-of-the-century culture. In any case, Babel abundantly fulfilled Nietzsche's prophecies and hopes: He lived more
dangerously, made himself at home under more volcanoes, looked
deeper into more abysses, than any intellectual of the century.

It's interesting that he did this as a citizen and lifelong supporter of the
USSR. "Lifelong" is just the sort of gallows humor that Babel, murdered

by the NKVD in 1940, would have liked. As horrible as life in the USSR could be, and Babel got as close to the horror as anybody, it had a spiritual depth that its enemies never knew.

Babel came up as a protégé of Maxim Gorky, who told him he couldn't develop as a writer until he knew more of life. The date of this advice was 1916, a fine time for a young man to learn about life in death and death in life. Babel volunteered and fought in assorted campaigns with the Russian Army, and then, after 1917, with the Red Army. He fought to defend Petrograd under siege. He joined an expedition to the countryside to extort grain for starving cities. He joined the Cheka, the first incarnation of the Soviet secret police. (How long did he last? What did he do? We still don't know. Even with millions of files opened, it's still a secret police!)

Writing for soldiers' papers, Babel gradually convinced people he might have talent as a war correspondent. The breakthrough event in his life occurred in 1920, at the height of the Civil War: he was assigned to cover the First Cavalry, the one band of Cossacks that supported the Reds, in their campaign against the Polish Army. (Poland had support from British and American armies, along with artillery and air power.) The Cossacks, a privileged estate under the czars, whose borders they guarded, were world-famous for their anti-Semitic frenzies. In 1905, as a boy in Odessa, Babel had lived through one of their pogroms, and was lucky to stay alive. Did this assignment come down from above (maybe some bureaucratic joker thought his experience in 1905 made him a Cossack expert), or, as some people say, did he perversely seek it out? It's something else we'll never know. But his superiors (party? press? police?) clearly felt he was in danger, because they prepared papers for him that dropped his Jewishness along with his name, and converted him to a

Russian Orthodox man named Lyutov, "ferocious." (All this is explained
in Carol Avins's excellent introduction to the *Diary*.) So he went forth, a
spy in the enemy camp – only his supposed enemies were also supposed
to be his comrades.

Babel's year with the Cossacks generated a remarkable series of stories, published individually through the 1920s and then as a book, *Red
Cavalry*, in 1926. *Red Cavalry* is a *Bildungsroman*, one of the most powerful
and persistent forms in modern literature. It thrives not only in written
fiction and drama but in movies, TV series, rock and roll. (Bruce Spring-
steen is a genius of the *Bildungsroman*.) One of its central themes is that
in order to become himself, the hero must learn not only to face but
somehow to internalize his anti-self. Both Babel's self and his anti-self
turn on an axis of violence. He sees violence/nonviolence as a crucial
issue for any modern man trying to answer the question "Who am I?" to
create what Erik Erikson calls an ego-identity.

Babel's self and anti-self evoke Nietzsche, or E. M. Forster, or D. H.
Lawrence. The self is a learned, rational, critical intellectual, tending
toward melancholy, "a man with spectacles on your nose and autumn in
your heart." The anti-self is a man of action, rarely literate, but inno-
cently "physical," "animal," "primitive," unreflectively cruel and glamor-
ously sexual. Here, for instance, in the story "My First Goose," we meet
the Cossack general whom Babel calls "captivating Savitsky":

Savitsky, Commander of the VI Division, rose when he saw me, and I
wondered at the beauty of his giant's body. He rose, the purple of his
riding breeches and the crimson little tilted cap and the decorations stuck
on his chest, cleaving the hut as a standard cleaves the sky. A smell of
scent and the sickly sweet freshness of soap emanated from him. His long
legs were like girls sheathed to the neck in shining riding-boots. He

smiled at me, struck his riding-whip on the table, and ...

"Where are the barbarians?" asked Nietzsche. Babel could have given him some good addresses.

Cynthia Ozick, in the May 8, 1995, *New Republic,* puts Babel up against the wall. He should have known all that she knows about the USSR. He should have known that all collective attempts to create a better life are fated to turn monstrous. (Including Zionism?) He should have been as smart as her family, and emigrated to America. (I've often thought this myself. He would have made a terrific Hollywood screenwriter of *films noirs,* and a terrific victim of the anti-communist blacklist. He would have given cryptic and provocative answers to the FBI, just as he did to the NKVD; he would have done time, but at least he would have survived. People would have pointed him out in the L. A. Farmer's Market or on Central Park West; he would have walked up and down Broadway with I. B. Singer, translated him into Russian. They could have become characters in each other's stories. ... Wouldn't it have been a wonderful life? Be still, my heart, be still.) Ozick's lack of generosity is surprising because Babel's romance of violence and *shtarkers,* "tough guys," is identical with that of her hero, Babel's fellow Odessan, Vladimir Jabotinsky.

In *Red Cavalry,* the overwhelming question for Babel's narrator is whether he can become a barbarian. The typical plot goes like this: the hero is dissed by the Cossacks for being the person he is; in order to be accepted, he must do something vicious, preferably to a woman; he does something (it isn't rape); he has passed the test, and the men do accept him—for the time being. He is thrilled and happy to be with them – almost. Thus, in "My First Goose,"

We slept, all six of us, beneath a wooden roof that let in the stars, warming one another, our legs intermingled. I dreamed; and in my dreams saw women. But my heart, stained with bloodshed, grated and brimmed over.

In the story "After the Battle," he fails. He has been in the thick of the fighting, and exposed himself to heavy fire, but it turns out he hasn't loaded his own gun. A Cossack bawls him out and beats him up, and he "implores fate to grant me the simplest of proficiencies, the ability to kill my fellow man." But we suspect Babel's heroes will keep flunking the Cossack initiation; in this Mafia, they will never get "made."

What inner force holds them back? Maybe the intellectual power and honesty that made them special in the first place. Alongside Babel's rhapsodic celebration of the anti-self, *Red Cavalry* features a powerful assertion of the self. It turned out that the man "with spectacles on your nose and autumn in your heart" could write about combat and the battlefront in a way that was remarkably compelling: clear, terse, penetrating, stripped down, emptied of all the grand sentimental words – *homeland, civilization, courage, sacrifice, hallowed,* etc., etc. – that have been used forever to justify killing and getting killed. Paul Fussell, in *The Great War and Modern Memory,* argues that, ironically, the horrors of World War I drove people to create more honest ways of seeing war. Ernest Hemingway, who set a standard for honest war writing, thought Babel did it even better than he did.

At the climax of many a *Bildungsroman,* the hero, who has expanded and deepened himself (or herself) through love, grows disenchanted, and learns to see through the one he loves. In *Red Cavalry,* the self cuts in on the anti-self: Babel's smart military analyst interrupts his reverent groupie, and shows that the Cossacks may look glamorous, but in the real conditions of twentieth-century war they are inept, they can't fight.

Against an army that has artillery and airplanes for support, the Cossacks' M.O., the gallant charge with horses and swords in open country, is a recipe for disaster. In the battle of Czesniki (the battle in "After the Battle"), in Galicia in September 1920, the disaster finally happens. Just like Pickett's charge at Gettysburg, wave after wave of men on horseback rush up a hill into an emplacement of machine guns and get blown away. Inside an hour, the magnificent Red Cavalry disintegrates. Now everybody starts screaming at everybody else. This is where Lyutov gets beaten up for refusing to shoot, and silently prays for the power to kill. (Whom would he like to kill, the Poles or the man who hit him?) But Babel's writing is always driven by wheels within wheels of irony. He has shown us that even if the hero could shoot to kill, and even if he did kill, it would be for nothing, because the barbaric ignorance and arrogance of the Cossack leaders have doomed their barbarian army from the start and imperiled the civilized civilians whose lives they were supposed to protect.

The peril of civilians, the vulnerable people caught in the Russian Civil War's crossfire, turns out to be a central theme in Babel's *1920 Diary*. Before I read this book, I imagined it would be a rehearsal (with outtakes) for *Red Cavalry*, and in many ways it is. There is the same pathos of the sensitive intellectual in the midst of an army he despises, trying to protect people he instinctively loves, but powerless to help these people unless he is accepted as a comrade in arms by the army. There is a similar dialectic of enchantment and disenchantment: initial polarization between *shtetl* Jews who appear withered and dying and Cossacks who seem to be overflowing with life; the same sense of revelation when the Red Cavalry disintegrates and Babel comes to see that the Cossacks themselves may be *schlemiels*, and the Jews may be stronger and more resourceful than he initially thought.

What's new and startling here is, first, the directness, the turbulence, the sloppiness, the repetitiveness, the unmediated, anguished, implosive tone of the writer's voice. It's amazing to hear Babel without composure, without smoothness of surface, without apparent irony. It makes us appreciate anew the intricacy and craftsmanship and constructivist complexity in *Red Cavalry* and the *Odessa Stories*. At the same time, it makes us wonder if maybe they aren't a little *too* brilliantly constructed. To get the perfect Rothkoesque symmetry and luminosity of Babel's great stories, maybe he left too much out, paid too high an emotional price? (Maybe he did, but it would have been perverse to expect Rothko to paint like Pollock, say, or Picasso; artists create as best they can, and art consumers like us should be damned grateful for all we get to eat.)

The second surprise in this *Diary* is the depth and complexity of Jewish life in it: the Jewishness of the *shtetls* that Babel's cavalry passes through; the more assimilated Jewishness of Odessa, where Babel was a child; and Babel's own personal adult post-Revolution Jewishness, which is very intense but volatile and uncertain in its meaning, and which, in his mid-twenties (he was twenty-six in 1920), he seems to be making up as he goes along. "What a mighty and marvelous life of a nation existed here," he says in wonderment as he explores the ancient synagogues and markets of Komarow. He sees that he is more deeply Jewish than he thought.

The Soviet–Polish campaign of 1920 cut directly through the heart of Galicia, the densest and culturally richest settlement of Jews in Europe. The names of the towns Babel passed through – Zhitomir, Brody, Dubno, Chernobyl, Demidovka, Kovel – are rich with resonance in Jewish history. (Hemingway said that in war writing, the names of towns and dates were the only honest things you could say.) Editor Carol Avins has provided excellent maps, photographs and demographic data. The four years of the Russian Civil War set off dreadful massacres, with dozens of Jewish towns totally destroyed, and something like 100,000 Jews killed. Historians (even the professional anti-communists of the Hoover Institution, who have done a standard casebook on the Civil War) agree that nearly all the mass murder, arson, rape and torture of Jews was done by the Whites – the Polish Army, Ukrainian peasant bands, and the Cossack majority fighting for the Czar. Still, the Cossack minority did some, and Babel was close to the knives. He was forced to play the role of a sensitive *goy*, fighting to protect his people from his comrades, knowing that any minute they could turn on him:

> The little girl: aren't you a Jew? Uchenik sits watching me eat, the little girl on his lap, trembling. "She's frightened – cellars, shooting, then your side [the Red Army]." I tell them everything will be all right, explain what the Revolution means, I talk on and on. "Things look bad for us, they mean to rob us, don't go to bed."

Think of Queen Esther under fire, without the happy ending.

One dramatic incident that most upsets Babel happens on July 24, 1920, in the small Jewish town of Demidovka. Lyutov is billeted with a Jewish family, along with Prishchepa, a dashing young Cossack, a deserter from the Whites who has committed at least one mass murder (see "Prishchepa's Revenge" in *Red Cavalry*). Today is the Sabbath, tomorrow the fast day of Tisha b'Av, anniversary of the destruction of the first Temple. Prishchepa decides he wants fried potatoes, and orders the family to dig and cook them. The head of the household, a woman dentist, "pale with pride and a sense of her own dignity, declares that no one is going to dig potatoes because it is a holiday." But "Prishchepa, restrained by me for quite a while, finally breaks out – fucking Yids, whole arsenal of abuse," and a clear threat that he will kill them all. Terrified, "hating us and me," they go and dig. A little later, "We eat like oxen." (In Jewish idiom, *ox* always signifies a beast with no soul.) Lyutov is ashamed, yet enjoys it: "I tell them fairy tales about Bolshevism – the blossoming, the express trains, Moscow's textile mills, universities, free meals ... and I captivate all these tormented people." Does he feel like "captivating Savitsky"? A little later that night, an old woman sobs, and her son begins to sing, from the Book of Lamentations, about the aftermath of the Temple's destruction:

> The terrible words of the prophet – they eat dung, their maidens are ravished, their menfolk killed, Israel subjugated, words of wrath and sorrow. The lamp smokes, the old woman wails, the young man sings melodiously. ... Demidovka, night, Cossacks, just as it was when the Temple was destroyed.

"Just as it was ..." Is progress nothing but a dream? Later still, Prishchepa makes a sexual advance to one of the young women in the house. This time the aggressor is charming and mellow, but everyone knows his shadow:

> She blushes prettily. Prishchepa is easy to talk to, she blossoms and behaves coquettishly, what can they be talking about. ... he wants to go to bed, to pass the time, she is in agonies, who understands her soul better than I?

It is Babel's genius to show us, from this girl's perspective, the dashing young murderer's charm.

The overall perspective of the *Diary* is pretty bleak. Sometimes Babel sees the situation in dialectically tragic terms: "We're striving for light, but we have no lighting"; "people everywhere trying to rebuild, but they have no building materials, no cement." At other times, the note is one of total betrayal and despair: "I ask a Red Army man for bread, he says, 'I don't have anything to do with Jews.' I'm an outsider, I don't belong, I'm all alone"; again, "This isn't a Marxist revolution, it's a Cossack rebellion"; again, "how is it different from the times of [seventeenth-century pogrom-maker] Bogdan Khmelnitsky?"; again, "Grief for the future of the Revolution .... We are the vanguard, but of what?" Again,

> Why can't I get over my sadness? Because I'm far from home, because we are destroyers, because we move like a whirlwind, like a stream of lava, hated by everyone, life shatters, I am at a huge, never-ending service for the dead.

It's hard to imagine how the author of this *Diary* could have stayed in the USSR. Indeed, it's even hard to imagine how he could have got out of bed in the morning. But sometime in the early 1920s, we know Babel made his peace, or at least made a truce. It was then, too, that he developed his signature style of poetic prose, the terse luminosity that would astonish the world in *Red Cavalry*. This idiosyncratic but visionary work is probably the best book ever written about the Russian Revolution.

The book's most inspired characters are two Jews, the elderly "Gedali" and the youthful but mortally wounded "Rabbi's Son." In barely a couple of pages, they mark the spiritual hopes of the Bolshevik Revolution and the spiritual poverty of what that Revolution soon became. Here is Gedali, keeper of Zhitomir's old curiosity shop:

> Where is the joy-giving Revolution? ... I want an International of good people. ... I would like every soul to be listed and given first-category rations. ... There, soul, please eat and enjoy life's pleasures.

The Prishchepas of today have long since left Communism behind, and they are happily "ethnic cleansing." Gedali, guardian of Babel's vision, reminds us why there had to be a Russian Revolution – not just another coup d'état – and why that revolution was something to be proud of, at least at first, but also why it couldn't last.

So, to come back to where we began, where are the barbarians of the twentieth century? They're everywhere. We can turn on CNN and see a pile of dead bodies from a different part of the world every night. Some are from places we've never heard of – be honest, how many of us had ever heard of Kigali? – others are menacingly familiar and close to home. If we stay tuned, we get to see the killer militias, too, and – heralded by Elvis Costello's "Oliver's Army" and Leon Golub's "Mercenaries and Interrogations" – what a wonderfully multicultural band they are. Most are young men, and they look like they have seen many pictures of young men who look like them, so they know how to pose – cigarettes are as vital a prop as rifles. (Other props: high mountains, parched prairies, burnt towns.) There are usually old men behind them, but patriarchs aren't so eager to get in front of cameras. Now, because the world really is changing, there are also women in the cast – sometimes with a baby on one shoulder, a cartridge belt on the other – even in movements where the repression of women is one of the militia's basic aims. (Cf. Frantz Fanon's classic essay on the women of the Algerian FLN, fighting heroically for their own repression – or so he said.) And children! It isn't only in "Doonesbury" that young Raoul Dukes are growing up too fast. You can see the twelve-year-olds in the militia team photos, flashing their hardware, telling the world it's never too early to learn to kill. (You may recognize kids like these from the streets of your own hometown.) Democracy may be in trouble today, but the democratization of violence lives and thrives on trouble. In the 1920s they said, with Ford Madox Ford, "No More Parades." At the end of the twentieth century, the parade looks bigger, more ecumenical and more triumphal than ever.

Isaac Babel lived and died at the start of this long wave. In his youth he had a great romance with the idea of violence. For a little while, his romance of violence converged with a romance of revolution. Both possibilities thrilled him because they seemed to offer a chance to leap "beyond good and evil" and become "fully alive." He staked his life on them in the thick of a real megalethal civil war – and then he recoiled with disgust and dread. What's the verdict? Babel tried but failed to become a barbarian; he succeeded, maybe against his will, in being a *mensch*. His writing brings to life both the daring and the dread, the failure and the success. We need to know both when the next band of captivating Savitskys comes over the rise.

Notes

1. *The Will to Power* (1885–88), ed. Walter Kaufmann, trans. Walter Kaufmann and R. J. Hollingdale (New York: Vintage, 1978), Section 868.

2. *The Geneaology of Morals* (1887), trans. Francis Golffing (New York: Anchor, 1956). "Blond Beasts" are in Part I, Section II.

3. *The Gay Science* (1882), Section 283, "Preparatory Men." In *The Portable Nietzsche,* ed. and trans. Walter Kaufmann (New York: Viking, 1954), 97–8.

4. *Beyond Good and Evil* (1886), trans. with an introduction by Marianne Cowan (New York: Gateway, 1967), Section 146.

5. He isn't mentioned in Beatrice Glatzer Rosenthal's impressive study, *Nietzsche in Russia* (Princeton, N.J.: Princeton University Press, 1986). On the other hand, he was part of the Gorky circle, which plays an important part in Rosenthal's story.

11

Meyer Schapiro: The Presence of the Subject

When I wrote this piece at the very end of 1995, at the request of *New Politics* magazine, Meyer was still alive. He died March 5, 1996, while the piece was in press. At first I thought it might make sense to change the present tenses to past; but I decided to keep them present, alive, in memory of his overflowing life.

I fell in love with Meyer Schapiro the first time I saw him. As I write this, more than thirty years later, I am just about the age now – middle fifties – that he was then. I think it's important to reconstruct the feel of it – the shock, the rush – to give him the homage he deserves. My friends at Columbia were saying, You have to see this guy, he's a living legend. I was cynical about living legends, but at last I went, and jammed against the

---

This essay first appeared in *New Politics*, Winter 1996.

wall in an overheated, overcrowded room. Inside five minutes I was knocked out. He talked about Gauguin and Van Gogh – and Zola and Shakespeare and Augustine and Engels and William James and Tolstoy and Picasso and non-Euclidean geometry; as he spoke, he projected an amazing flood of images, modern and medieval, paintings and newspaper photographs and blueprints and cartoons, representational and abstract, high and low, works thousands of years old and works that he said weren't finished yet. He made dazzling jumpcuts into the past, into radically different cultures, into visions of the future.

His talk reached a dramatic climax a couple of minutes before the bell, and finished exactly when it rang. But it sounded like he could go on forever. I sighed: Did he have to stop? The friend who had brought me and some of the people around us said they were "regulars," they had been going to his lectures for years, and they still felt the pull, the flood, the intensity, the desire. DON'T STOP! It was like sex, or music, or a few other peak experiences: he had shown us the richness of being. And every one of us seemed to feel he had done it for ourself alone. "So what did he say?" my girlfriend asked that night. I felt I could spend my whole life trying to explain, and never reach the end.

I didn't get to know Meyer right away. For one thing, I was dazzled by his brilliance: could I offer a coda to Beethoven? For another, I was already in love with Columbia's other larger-than-life figure, Lionel Trilling. Trilling had a very different presence and human touch: he appeared genteel (although shabbily genteel), where Meyer was proudly plebeian; Meyer was open and expansive in a lecture room, while Lionel was uneasy, brooding, melancholy, full of Beckettesque hesitation about communication (it was in seminars, in small groups, in dialogue, that he opened up and soared); where Meyer bathed us in art that made us see the joy and beauty of modern life, Lionel forced us to read modern literature in ways that made us wonder whether we could live at all.

When I was twenty, there seemed a great gulf between those titans; I felt I couldn't love both. As I got older, it became obvious how much of a world they shared. Both were children of the century – Meyer was born in 1904, Lionel in 1905 – products of Jewish immigrant culture and the New York public school system, brilliant upstarts in a university that still belonged to Anglo-Saxon gentlemen, granted tenure and recognition only grudgingly, when it turned out that lots of people in the rest of the world knew their worth. Both were *intellectuals engagés,* close to the Communist Party in their youth, liberal democrats in their mature years (in Meyer's case, through much of the 1930s and 1940s a militant left-wing socialist, later a liberal social democrat, a founding editor of *Dissent*), dialectical in sensibility, oriented toward history and social development, always focused on the politics of culture. Both built their careers around the exploration of modernism. They asserted the dignity of modern art and literature, and fought for recognition of its permanent value; they showed how this art and literature could help us – and also force us – to see into the heart of modern life. That life, they both believed, was animated by contradictory drives, both around and within us, and was at once a thrill and a horror. The writers and artists they loved most were radical critics of their culture, yet expressed its deepest values. In their feeling for cultural contradictions, Schapiro and Trilling both gave a new subtlety and depth to intellectual Marxism. Along with a few other children of the century – Walter Benjamin, Hannah Arendt, Theodor Adorno, Herbert Marcuse, Harold Rosenberg, Paul Goodman – they were just the sort of "freethinking Jews" that T. S. Eliot warned his readers against: they expressed "the modern spirit" better than anyone, but were menaces to "the idea of a Christian society."

Listening to Meyer, it seemed that all he said was, as Goethe said, "part of a great confession." All those who had ever heard him looked forward to seeing the great work in print, the work that would tell the whole story of mankind through art. Yet it never seemed to appear. His writings were spread out, fragmentary, hard to get hold of. (I remember the thrill when I finally tracked down the 1937 *Marxist Quarterly,* which contained one of his most exciting pieces, "Nature of Abstract Art.") He was rumored to hold back his best work, including some of what we had heard in lecture form, on the grounds that it wasn't as full, as complete, as exhaustive as it conceivably could be. This reticence created an aura of mystery around him. Why couldn't he accept imperfection and let go, like the rest of us mortals?

It was a thrill to see that, in 1978, he finally did let go, and brought out a splendid collection, *Modern Art: 19th and 20th Centuries, Selected Papers,* published by George Braziller. More volumes were said to be coming soon. *Modern Art,* whose contents span five decades, contains the 1937 "Nature of Abstract Art" essay, a *tour de force* that situated abstract art amid the conflicts of modern history, and highlighted the critical, combative impulse that drives it: in leaving nature and society out, or distorting them drastically, the abstract painter "disqualifies them from art"; this essay explained, a decade in advance, why abstract expressionism would have to happen, and happen here. The book includes two shorter, more recent pieces on abstract painting; his brilliant 1941 essay, "Courbet and Popular Imagery": fascinating studies of Van Gogh, Seurat, Mondrian and Gorky; and my all-time favorite, published in 1956, "The Armory Show: The Introduction of Modern Art in America." Like Schapiro's lectures at their best, these essays were dense but intensely dramatic: he captured the subjectivity and inner life of modern artists, the totality of historical forces around them, the rivers that ran through them, the spiritual twists and leaps they experienced, the breakthroughs they finally achieved.

In the late 1950s, when the best of Schapiro's "modern" essays were written, the idea of modernism was important in aesthetics. But the only concerns for a modernist painter were supposed to be the purely formal attributes of painting: the nature of the canvas and the nature of the paint. Those boundaries were proclaimed with dogmatic ferocity by Clement Greenberg and his followers, border guards along a cultural Berlin Wall. For a modern artist to transgress formalist boundaries – to explore his or her own feelings or fantasies, or the modern world itself – was condemned as a betrayal of the artist's calling, a devolution of art's high dignity to "illustration," to "entertainment," to *kitsch*. This critical vocabulary was imprisoning art, constricting its imaginative power, narrowing it into a still point in a turning world. In the suffocating 1950s, Schapiro helped create breathing space, not (so far as I know) by entering into polemics with Greenberg, but by telling better stories. He situated modern art in the midst of the volatile, explosive atmosphere of *fin de siècle* European social life.

Actually, Schapiro presented several closely related but distinct visions of modern art and the society it came from:

1. Modern art is a liberator of human feeling from social and cultural repressions, a breakthrough to the self's deepest unconscious sources, and an ongoing force for transparency, gaiety and joy in modern life:

It affirmed the value of the feelings as essential human forces unwisely neglected or suppressed by a utilitarian or hypocritically puritanic society. ... This corrective simplicity and intensity seemed to revive a primitive layer of self, like the child's or the savage's ... [and] gave a new vitality to art. The painters admitted to their canvases, with much wonder, gaiety and courage, uncensored fantasies and associations of thought akin to the world of dreams; they joined hands with the moralists, philosophers and medical psychologists [I asked him, "Freud?" He said, "Yes, he was all three"] who were exploring hidden regions and resources of human nature. ... The artists' search for a more intense expression corresponded to new values of forthrightness, simplicity and openness, to a joyous vitality in everyday life.

2. Modern art generates intense pressure, in audiences as well as in artists, for metamorphosis and self-development. The endless succession of modern periods and styles makes people obsessed with history: they "seek history-making effort through continual self-transformation." They come to feel they must overcome tomorrow everything they are today.

> ... The modern movement has provoked a perpetual uneasiness from its followers. It is necessary ... to keep up with history. The world-shaking art of the revolutionary period has become a norm; one expects a revolution every decade. This strenuous ideal breeds in the artist a straining for modernity and a concern with the historical position of his work; it often prevents him from maturing slowly and from seeking depth and fullness as much as freshness and impact.

3. Modern art, in both production and consumption, is intensely private and individualized:

Formerly tied to institutions and fixed times and places, to religion, cere-
mony, state, school, palace, fair, festivity, the arts are now increasingly
localized in private life and subject to individual choice; they are recrea-
tions and tastes entirely detached from collective occasions. ... [Every
work is] offered to the spectator as one among many.

This opens up new possibilities for original creation:

This character of culture as a sphere of personal choices open to the
individual who is conscious of his freedom ... affects the creation of new
art, stimulating inventive minds to a fresh searching of their experience,
and of the resources of art which enter into the sensory delight of the
spectator and touch his heart.

But it also constricts the scope of imaginative life and cuts artists off from
other people and from society as a whole:

Artists today who would welcome the chance to paint works of broad
human content for a large audience, works comparable in scope to those
of antiquity and the Middle Ages, find no sustained opportunities; they
have no alternative but to cultivate in their art the only or surest realms of
freedom – the interior.

4. On the other hand, this very loneliness gives modern artists the power
to see through their culture, a culture based on class and lies. In his 1957
lecture "Recent Abstract Painting," Schapiro celebrates modern art in an
existential Marxist way, as a model of authenticity in a world built on bad
faith:

Paintings and sculptures, let us observe, are the last hand-made objects within our culture. Almost everything else is produced industrially, in mass and through a high division of labor. Few people are fortunate enough to make something that represents themselves, that issues entirely from their hands and mind, and to which they can affix their names …

What is most important is that the practical activity by which we live is not satisfying: we cannot give it full loyalty, and its rewards do not compensate for the frustrations and emptiness that arise from the lack of spontaneity and personal identifications in work: the individual is deformed by it, only rarely does it permit him to grow.

… All these qualities of painting may be regarded as a means of affirming the individual in opposition to the contrary qualities of the ordinary experience of working and doing.

In his focus on work, identity and growth, Schapiro sounds a lot like the young Karl Marx – whose "Alienated Labor" and other early essays had just appeared in popular editions, with sensational impact – and like the young writers of the emerging New Left. This critical vision does not exactly contradict the earlier ones, but the tone color is harsher, the indictment of contemporary life is bitterer and angrier. Schapiro's earlier vision of modern art as a source of "joyous vitality in everyday life" seems to fade away. He believes, more ardently than ever, that we need modernism to make us authentic, but he may have given up hope that it can make us happy.

A new collection of Schapiro's papers has just appeared, entitled *Theory and Philosophy of Art: Style, Artist and Society* (Braziller, 1994). Alas, this book lacks the focus and dramatic power of *Modern Art*. It is surprising, and disappointing, that it fails to reprint Schapiro's great 1936 lecture,

"The Social Basis of Art," one of the all-time classic statements of Marxism. (I sought an explanation on the phone from Braziller; the best I could get was assurance that it was planned for yet another future volume; nobody would say more.) Still, it includes several splendid essays, some well-known, others obscure till now. The most striking pieces are a classic 1962 essay, "Style"; a meditation on Perfection and Completeness in art; a dispute with Freud's study of Leonardo; an argument with Martin Heidegger about Van Gogh; and, at the book's end, a passionate indictment of Bernard Berenson. Now, it is always a thrill to feel Schapiro's mind at work; but people who have grown up on his work may feel something missing here. In his lectures, in the best pieces in *Modern Art*, and in his work on the Romanesque, his intellectual powers are like a sorcerer's: he spreads a whole world before us, with what seems like a magical fluency, so that we feel instantly at home there. We miss those magical expansive gestures here. These essays seem to be pointed strangely inward; they often read like parables, and we have to interpret. The luminosity is still there, but it is hidden, as if in eclipse, in a subtextual underworld; we have to work harder to make contact with the magic, to get the golden tripods back from the night.

Schapiro's argument with Heidegger, "The Still Life as a Personal Object" (1968, 1994), is about a Van Gogh painting of an old, worn-out pair of shoes. This painting plays a central heuristic role in Heidegger's celebrated 1935 essay, "The Origin of the Work of Art." Van Gogh's painting, Heidegger argues, conveys one of the primal truths of life, "the equipmental being of equipment." The boots in this painting, the philosopher says, belong to a peasant, and moreover, he thinks, to a peasant woman. This premise generates an evocative picture of peasant life: "In the stiffly solid heaviness of her shoes," Heidegger says, there is the accumulated tenacity of her slow trudge through the far-spreading and ever-uniform furrows of the field, swept by a raw wind. Under the soles there slides the loneliness of the field-path. ... This equipment is pervaded by uncomplaining anxiety about the certainty of bread. ... The equipment belongs to the earth, and it is protected in the world.

Schapiro asks Heidegger what seems like an innocent art-historical question: Which Van Gogh painting of boots are you talking about? It turns out he wrote Heidegger about this in 1965, and that Heidegger's reply was vague. Schapiro thinks he knows which painting it must have been (it is reproduced), but he also thinks Heidegger could have developed his peasant rhapsody without looking at the painting at all. But if he had tried to look at Van Gogh's representation of boots, Schapiro says, it would have been hard *not* to see that Van Gogh represented boots in two sharply different ways: when they belonged to peasants, he painted them clear, smooth and unworn, as an unproblematic element in still-life; when he painted them old, wrinkled and worn-out, as Heidegger describes, they were always *his own*.

Heidegger ignores what those shoes meant to the painter Van Gogh himself. [They] are seen as if endowed with feelings and revery about himself. In isolating his old, worn shoes on a canvas, he turns them to the spectator, he makes of them a piece from a self-portrait. ... a memorable piece of his own life, a sacred relic.

Reading Van Gogh's letters and diaries, and other people's accounts of conversation with him, Schapiro finds "the idea of the shoe as a symbol of his life-long practice of walking, and an ideal of life as a pilgrimage." So the truth about the shoes turns out to be a truth about "the artist's presence in his work." Schapiro has become a sort of ontological detective, returning the boots to their real owner.

What is the subtext of this detective story? It may be about modernism and post-modernism. Schapiro has been explicating and defending modernism for – it's incredible! – more than seventy years. When he began, the consensus of art historians and museums in the USA and Western Europe was that the life of art had ended long ago. The Stalinist USSR and Nazi Germany both stigmatized modern art as "degenerate," though both regimes tried to enlist it in selective ways. Against them all, Schapiro (and some others, though not so many) fought for modern art as the twentieth century's most authentic way of being alive. He knew he would win, knew sooner or later people would be forced to recognize modern art's overwhelming brilliance, amazing variety and ongoing power.

He won – for about two minutes. Then, soon after 1968, the post-modern worldview was stridently proclaimed. It launched vicious attacks on everything and everyone associated with modernism or modernity as a whole. One of the pervasive post-modern themes is what the French writers Michel Foucault and Roland Barthes called "the death of the subject." The modern self, subject of declarations of rights, talking cures and abstract art, was revealed as a bankrupt fraud; the individual was simply a sum of codes, an embodiment of rhetorical and cultural conventions, and these codes and conventions turned out to be the only subjects worth studying. Everybody connected with modernism was dissed and dumped. Now, in condemning their predecessors to the dustbin of history, the post-moderns were no different from any of the other innumerable modern avant-gardes. Decertifying one's predecessors from history is one of the ways a movement certifies itself, and cultural life goes on. Schapiro has known this for at least half a century (it was one of the themes of "Nature of Abstract Art"). But many other intellectuals who should also have known it, whose education should have given them some perspective and sense of historical irony, instead went rushing to catch the cultural Concorde.

Now, as it happens, the philosopher most venerated as the patron saint of post-modernism is the (happily de-nazified) Martin Heidegger. How did this happen? It will puzzle readers who grew up reading *Being and Time* as a great modernist book, one whose spiritual desperation evokes Van Gogh and Rilke, Pound and Eliot. Maybe the only explanation is that that was then and this is now. In any case, it was Heidegger who folded Van Gogh's boots into markers of pure conventionality, "the equipmental being of equipment." Schapiro wants to make it clear not only that the modern subject is alive, but that he's *there*, at the core of the work of art. Like many classic detective stories, this short essay starts small. But it expands fast, and by the time it ends, it has grown into a ringing affirmation of modernism: an art where "the artist's presence in his art" is a primary source of truth and power.

This is not only an issue in art: Schapiro has helped us see how modern art is part of a whole world culture where "the individual, his freedom, his inner world, his dedication, become primary." In 1956 ("The Armory Show") he wrote that, thanks in part to modern art, individual self-fulfillment had become a "collective value ... a matter of common striving." It was clear there that Schapiro affirmed that striving and that value. (His Marxism has always been in the humanist tradition that strives, in the words of the *Communist Manifesto,* to create a world where "the free development of each is the basis for the free development of all.") Yet only a year later, in "Recent Abstract Painting," his vision was far darker and more pessimistic. Did he still think people were striving together for authenticity in 1968, or in 1994? He doesn't say; but there is a melancholy undertow running through the Heidegger essay which suggests deep doubts. And once we notice his doubts, we can see an intensely personal dimension in the argument about "the artist's presence in his work": Schapiro is insisting on *his own* presence, claiming space for *his* subjectivity, and for his lifelong pilgrimage, reminding us only last year – 1994, the essay's last date – that, though his shoes may be worn, he's still here.

"On Perfection, Coherence, and Unity of Form and Content" (1966) takes some big steps not only in aesthetics, but in ethics and politics as well. It refutes the idea that a work of art – a poem, a painting, a film – should be "a well wrought urn," self-sufficient, perfect, complete. This was aesthetic dogma when I was growing up: the New Critics (Cleanth Brooks, Allen Tate, Robert Penn Warren and their friends) plugged it in literature, Erwin Panofsky and his followers in the visual arts. Schapiro argues that these "perfect" qualities "are more likely in small works than in large. The greatest artists – Homer, Shakespeare, Michelangelo, Tolstoy – present us with works that are full of problematic features." He mentions the incongruities of scale in the Chartres cathedral, in the Sistine ceiling, in *Anna Karenina*: "in the greatest works of all, incompleteness and inconsistency are evidences of the living process of the most serious and daring art."

Schapiro compares the experience of a work of art as a whole to a mystic's experience of oneness with God: both experiences may lead to ecstasy, but both leave a great deal out. "We do not see all of a work when we see it as a whole." Instead of wholeness, he says, we should aspire to *fullness*; instead of flashes of ecstasy, we should aim for a sensibility that he calls "critical seeing":

Critical seeing, aware of the incompleteness of perception, is explorative. It takes into account others' seeing, it is a collective and cooperative seeing and welcome comparison of different perceptions and judgments.

Critical seeing does not exclude ecstasy – it "knows moments of sudden revelation" – but it situates those moments within a larger totality, as part of the psychic "fullness" that seems to form his aesthetic ideal.

Once more, Schapiro's subtext is even more striking than his text. It should be clear from this diction that he is not only telling us what to do at the Museum; he is telling us *how to live*. It is fascinating to see that, as much as John Ruskin or William Morris or Walter Pater or Oscar Wilde or any other *hasid* of the aesthetic movement, he believes our responses to art should be the model for the way we live. But his "critical seeing" is aesthetically richer than theirs, and morally more complex. First of all, he wants the world of art to be "collective and cooperative," not just the monopoly of a few smart guys at one another's throats, but truly public, as art in modern times has rarely managed to be. Next, he wants a critical discourse "extending for generations." Now this has conservative and traditionalist reverberations that might at first surprise us. But Schapiro's art world must be an open society, ever receptive to "new points of view"; it must include the excluded, and must be aware that excluded groups have the capacity to renew art with "revelation." He wants art to be a channel for empathy, a parable of pluralism, a way for people (and peoples) to see each others' ways of seeing, so they can cooperate collectively, constitute a public, and strive together for a fuller future.

This is asking a lot from art, and why not? And yet, Schapiro knows better than virtually anybody how militant, combative, contentious, sectarian, tormented, extremist, perverse, how fruitfully narrow and intolerant modern art has always been. Knowledge of art can teach us knowledge and acceptance of others, can open us to empathy and pluralism, if, like Schapiro himself, we have seen so much art, and seen a long history in which so many artists and art movements evolve, and a world in which so many artists and art movements coexist with each other. But very few artists themselves have this largeness of vision and understanding. They are much more likely to strive for what Schapiro calls wholeness than for fullness, for ecstasy rather than empathy; they don't want the totality of vision, but rather the narrow revelatory *zap*! And if that's what they need to create what they can, in all its splendor and all its limitation, we can be pretty sure Schapiro wouldn't want it any other way. But there is a great gulf between the fullness of life and expression that Schapiro has always fought for, and the peace and healing and mutual acceptance and sense of community that he has often yearned for.

I'm sad that Meyer Schapiro has been relatively quiet for the last thirty years. The public that loves him, and maybe even more, the public that's never had a chance to know him, hasn't been able to hear his voice. I'd have loved to hear him on Pop Art, on affirmative action, on Frank Gehry, on "Broken Obelisk," on "Tilted Arc," on the breakup of the USSR, on the homeless people on the streets, on Cindy Sherman, on Chinese cinema, on ethnic cleansing, on art and victimization – he, who knows Christian art so well, knows it goes back a long way – on so much of what we've had to live with and still haven't been able to figure out how, on how art can still help us be human. And yet, and yet: Look! there he is on his book's cover, ninety-one years old, his smile radiant enough to light up Grand Central. Open the book and there's that amazing flow, just as it was thirty years ago. Get into the flow, don't stop! We probably don't deserve him, but he's still here; like Van Gogh's shoes, he's worn but not worn out. The least we can do in his honor is to focus and concentrate our own minds, to grasp how the world holds together, to see how beautiful it can be, to feel how exciting, to work to keep the flow going on.

12

Walter Benjamin: Angel in the City

Walter Benjamin is said to have been a shy and awkward man, yet there was something about him that made people want to take his picture. One of the nicest things about Momme Brodersen's lavishly illustrated biography is that, more than half a century after Benjamin's death, American readers can finally get a good look at his face. His mop of floating hair; his glasses – framed, heavy-lidded, soulful eyes, looking down or aimed into the middle distance (looking not into the camera, but beyond the camera, or maybe *through* the camera); the hand that forms a V under his chin and gives his face a point; the dangling cigarette that seems to be there not so much to be smoked as to be crushed out – it all makes us feel that we are in the presence of the most serious man who ever lived.

Some of the most radiant visions of Benjamin emerged late in his life,

Review of Momme Brodersen, *Walter Benjamin: A Biography* (London: Verso, 1996); and *Walter Benjamin: Selected Writings, Volume I: 1913–1926*, edited by Marcus Bullock and Michael W. Jennings (Cambridge, Mass.: Harvard University Press, 1996); and Jay Parini, *Benjamin's Crossing* (New York: Henry Holt, 1996).

in his beloved Paris at the end of the thirties, the age of Renoir's *Grand Illusion,* after the Popular Front broke down, before (but not long before) the Nazis came. In 1937 Gisèle Freund photographed Benjamin at work in the Bibliothèque Nationale. She is one of European culture's *grandes dames* today, but then she was a fellow German-Jewish refugee, but twenty years younger than Benjamin and living even more precariously. In one shot Benjamin searches through a bookshelf, in another he is writing at a table. As usual, his gaze occludes the camera, though clearly he knows it is there. These library shots are visions of a man wholly absorbed in his work and at one with himself. His aura of total concentration can make the rest of us feel like bumbling fools. Or it can remind us why God gave us these big brains and taught us to read and write.

What was he working on that day? Probably his immense *Arcades* manuscript, the exploration of nineteenth-century Paris that enveloped his life all through the thirties. (When he crossed the Pyrenees on foot in 1940 to escape from France, he carried it with him and wouldn't let go. Lisa Fittko, his guide, later said she felt the manuscript was worth more to him than his life.) But it might have been one of his great late essays in that distinctively modern genre, Theology Without God. Here is a sample from "Theses on the Philosophy of History":

> A Klee painting named "Angelus Novus" shows an angel looking as though he is about to move away from something he is fixedly contemplating. His eyes are staring, his mouth is open, his wings are spread. This is how one pictures the angel of history. His *face* is turned toward the past. Where we perceive a chain of events, he sees one single catastrophe which keeps piling wreckage upon wreckage and hurls it in front of his feet The angel would like to stay, awaken the dead, and make whole what has been smashed. But a storm is blowing from Paradise; it has got caught

in his wings with such violence that the angel can no longer close them. This storm irresistibly propels him into the future to which his back is turned, while the pile of debris before him grows skyward. This storm is what we call progress.

Benjamin's very modern angel is prey to every anxiety and inner contradiction that haunts our history. And yet, here in the library, he is as perfectly at home in the modern world as any of us is ever going to be.

Maybe even too much at home for his own good. For years, his friends urged him to get out of Europe. Theodor Adorno, probably his closest friend, made a last-ditch trip to Paris in 1938 to get him out. But he insisted he would hang in there, "like one who keeps afloat on a shipwreck by climbing to the top of a mast that is already crumbling. But from there he has a chance to give a signal leading to his rescue." As poetry this is stunning. But as reality – signal to whom? rescue by whom? – it's insane. After Hitler started the war, Brodersen tells us, "twice at the turn of 1939/40 he met up with his ex-wife Dora, but he did not yield to her entreaties to leave Paris [as she did with their son Stefan] and bring himself into safety. Instead, he had his reader's card at the Bibliothèque Nationale renewed so that he could proceed with his work."

He couldn't work long. Brodersen and Jay Parini tell this grim and absurd story well. After he was arrested by the helpful French police and interned in a camp for enemy aliens – he edited the camp paper! – Benjamin saw he had to go. But the gates were closing fast. (This is what *Casablanca* is all about.) He headed for Marseilles, where he met Arthur Koestler. Koestler said later that they talked about drugs and suicide. Some conversation that must have been! ("Like carpenters they want to know *what tools* / They never ask *why build*" – Anne Sexton on her meeting with Sylvia Plath.) Thanks to the diplomacy of Max Horkheimer,

Benjamin had the amazing good luck to get an entry visa to the United States. But he couldn't use it without first escaping from France, where Nazi armies were closing in. In a small group of refugees, he made a heroic trek across the Pyrenees to Spain. Hobbled by a heart condition, he had to stop constantly for breath. At last he and his group got across. But they were stopped that night in the village of Portbou, where the local authorities refused their papers and threatened to send them back the next day to France and the Gestapo. The other refugees decided to wait and see: Maybe the local police could be cajoled or bribed. Benjamin didn't wait. A longtime serious drug user, he was carrying plenty of morphine. Sometime that night, he took an overdose, and within a few hours he died. Ironically, right after his death the police changed their minds, and all the other refugees in his group got through alive. Half a century later, in 1994, with Spain a democracy once more, the townspeople of Portbou erected a striking but chilling stone monument in his memory, designed by the Israeli sculptor Dani Kavan, a stark staircase leading down to cliffs perched above the sea. The Australian filmmaker Richard Hughes has made a documentary that brings this tragic landscape beautifully to life.

This is one of the classic heart-rending stories of the twentieth century. It's important, especially for people who admire Benjamin and venerate his memory, to notice his participation in the story: he was a victim of the most vicious regime in history, but he beat it to the punch. Maybe we should say he made a pre-emptive strike on himself. Underrated for most of his life, he hit the charts with his death. The monument in Portbou is engraved with a single sentence from one of his last works, the essay "On the Concept of History": "It is more arduous to honour the memory of the nameless than that of the renowned. Historical construction is devoted to the memory of the nameless." Brodersen offers a gloss: "It is hard not to ask whether Benjamin's death was 'preventable,' 'unnecessary,' though these are unanswerable, pointless questions. [So many] others were dying, unnecessarily, anonymously, on other borders; millions would die with no border in sight."

I'm sure both Benjamin and Brodersen are right, yet both sound a little complacent. Humphrey Bogart at the end of *Casablanca* nobly effaces himself and his happiness, but he knows and we know the camera is on him; he's the star. Benjamin, insulted and injured for much of his life, found a way to be a star in death. His essay, his monument, his biographer, and I trying to write about them, are all in some basic way off-key. It may be impossible to talk about the murders and the victims of Nazism without some false notes. But, in a Benjaminian twist, it would be even falser not to talk about them at all.

Benjamin's death overshadows his life; it's a hard act to follow. But we need to fight to bring him back to life because he had so much to say. One problem is that so many very different people who loved him – Brecht, Adorno, Gershom Scholem, Hannah Arendt – all wrote moving testaments that deep down he was really just like them. Since the 1970s, Benjamin has been the focus of a Sylvia Plath–like deathcult that consecrates suicide as the most authentic response to modern life. The cult has magnified everything eccentric, perverse and menacing in his sensibility – and there's plenty! Happily, the authors and editors of these books see him and love him for his attachment to life.

Brodersen has done impressive research and excavates a great deal of fascinating material. His book is indispensable for unraveling Benjamin's life and work. Alas, he tends not to know what to do with what he digs up. For instance, when Brodersen discusses Walter's father, Emil, he takes at face value the son's Oedipal vilification of the old man as a stupid, conventional German philistine. Then he mentions the fact that Emil had lived for many years in Paris and made his money in the art auction business. He also mentions that Walter grew up with French governesses. He treats these facts as throwaway lines. Here he is guided by Benjamin himself, who treats them as throwaways in his 1932 memoir, "A Berlin Chronicle." But if we think about them even a little, they suggest that the son had not moved so far from his father as he usually liked to think. In Benjamin's essay, "Paris, Capital of the Nineteenth Century," there is an epigraph that suggests a kind of *hommage*. He quotes Karl Gutzkow, radical poet and friend of the young Marx: "My good father had been in Paris." Benjamin's good father not only had been in Paris, but kept Paris alive in his household in Berlin. As a result, Benjamin was effortlessly fluent in French language and culture. This fluency nourished some of his best work, but it made him at once envied and suspect in the German cultural world where he spent most of his life. Since Heine, there has probably never been another German so thoroughly *at home* in French culture. This effortless (and unconscious) ease comes through vividly in his essays on Baudelaire, on Napoleon III and Haussmann, on Proust, on Surrealism. To use one of his own keywords, Benjamin's writing on Paris has an *aura* that's wholly missing in his writing about his hometown, Berlin. In his Parisian writings, even when he gets things all wrong, he is intuitively close to his material in ways that you and I can never hope to be, even if we get things right. I always wondered where he learned this intimacy. It's fascinating to see that it arose from his life as a child, from his earliest human relationships and deepest sources of feeling.

For at least two centuries, since the French Enlightenment, way before the Revolution, Paris has been Germany's ancestral Other. Germans have always seen Paris as a primal source of two things they feel they lack: Sex and Style. So much of German identity politics – what is creative and fruitful in German thought, and what is delusional and dangerous – grows out of a collective embittered sense of the German subject as a soulful klutz who lives just next door to a sexy and stylish musketeer. Of course, these are stereotypes, but when people believe in them, they shape their lives; and when millions of people fight monstrous wars in their name, they shake the world. Imagine a Benjamin who saw himself as a homegrown klutz, but was seen by others as an un-German musketeer. He could never figure out why he couldn't fit into German *Kultur,* to which he felt so loyal. But all the while he was hated not only as a Jew who knew their culture better than they did, but also as a musketeer who could fit in so well and was so easily at home in the City of Light.

Brodersen shows how much of Benjamin's spirit and energy went into the pre–World War I German youth movement, in which hundreds of thousands of teenage boys (in the big cities there were girls as well) went into the countryside, in highly organized groups, to commune with nature, hike in the mountains, sleep in hay-lofts, bathe in streams, play guitars, sing folk songs and celebrate a "simple life" they considered "authentic" – so radically different from the business, professional and military careers their parents had raised them for. In some ways "Young Germany" evokes the sixties counterculture; in others, it sounds like a prep school for fascism. Benjamin knew that, as a Jew, he would always be an outsider there. But he held on, encouraged by his friendship and intimacy with Gustav Wyneken, a follower of Nietzsche and the movement's charismatic guru. (From what we know of Wyneken's life and his way of living, there is a chance that this friendship shaded into some sort of erotic love. But Brodersen is no help on this: his writing, never vivid, grows especially opaque where human emotions come into play.) Benjamin worked on several movement papers, and was often reproved by his editors for "going too far"; alas, we aren't told what "too far" meant. When World War I began, Wyneken urged the boys on to patriotic gore – keeping himself and the movement in the good graces of the state, but losing many of his most devoted *hasidim,* including Benjamin. But Benjamin never lost the dream of a "free youth" that could renew the world.

Benjamin's own little world, the Berlin Free Students' Union, must have been a weird scene. We are told by Brodersen how, a week into the war, one of Benjamin's dearest friends, the young poet Fritz Heinle, and his fiancé, Rika Seligson, turned on the gas in the Union kitchen and killed themselves. Benjamin would mourn this boy all his life, yet also – an ominous leitmotif – would admire his friend's act. Did this boy and girl think their self-destruction would turn people against the war? (Think of the suicides of Buddhist monks in Vietnam.) Is there any evidence that anybody cared, or even noticed? If Brodersen finds evidence, he doesn't say. The next phase is even more upsetting, because it takes place entirely in the orbit of German youth culture; this time the General Staff can't be blamed. Benjamin's whole crowd seems to have leaned on Heinle's younger brother, Wolf, and Rika's younger sister, Traute, to follow their siblings over the cliff. The girl killed herself in 1915; the boy stayed alive until 1923. What should we make of these murderous fusions of the personal and the political?[1] Teenage suicide has a universal fascination in modern youth culture. (And a universal horror for modern parents.) It has had a special luster in Germany, because Goethe's 1776 suicide story, *The Sorrows of Young Werther,* is one of the places where German culture is born and makes the world recognize its vitality. Erik Erikson has written very sensitively about youthful suicide. He believed

that a suicide attempt may even turn out to be part of healthy development – if only the kid survives! The saddest part of the Heinle story is
that our hero and his friends don't seem to have been in touch with
anybody who thought it would be a good thing for them to live.

Brodersen's chapters on Benjamin in the Weimar Republic are full of
interesting material, but they seem to tell the same old story again and
again. Benjamin is encouraged to work in a university department, but
then the one professor who understands him abruptly retires, and the
new one can't stand him. He becomes an editor of a national magazine,
only to see it go out of business before he can start. He makes what looks
like a lucrative book deal, but the publisher goes bankrupt while his book
is in press. Oy! Is this an I. B. Singer story called "Benjamin Shlimazl" or a
cantata on the Stations of the Cross?

Benjamin's troubles were real. ("Even paranoids have enemies," Del-
more Schwartz liked to say.) He was disliked by some because he was a
Jew, a cosmopolitan and, though apparently never a card-carrying Communist, always a fellow-traveler of Revolution. He was disliked by others
– starting with the Communist Party – because he thrived on irony, paradox and dialectical play, and nobody could predict, much less control,
what he was going to think or say. But he earned this trouble because of
the man and the writer he was proud to be.

Much of the material Brodersen has gathered can be read much less
gloomily than he reads it. It's impressive that, even in daunting circumstances, Benjamin kept on writing. (Nor was he ever forgotten: publishers
kept calling and he was always making deals, though the deals were
always falling through.) It's fascinating that so many of Weimar's great
writers – Hesse, von Hofmannsthal, Rilke, Brecht, Thomas and Heinrich
Mann – even when they couldn't stand each other, thought the world of

him. And not only was he one of the first serious writers in any language to grasp the possibilities of radio – no surprise to readers of "The Work of Art in the Age of Mechanical Reproduction" (1936) – but he actually made more than a hundred broadcasts, and built a devoted audience, turned off only by the Nazis in 1933. (Do scripts, tapes or transcripts exist? It would be great to hear or see them.)

Brodersen chronicles Benjamin's many abortive attempts to get his father to subsidize his academic career. But he misses the central irony of this situation. Emil Benjamin, by forcing his son to make his living as a journalist, threw him onto the streets, and into the midst of a speeded-up metropolitan, mass-media-saturated, ultramodern environment. His triumph was that he turned out to be far more at home there than he could ever have been in the Gothic, anti-Semitic, closed world of German universities.[2] Remember, in that claustrophobic cellar, Benjamin's teacher Georg Simmel, one of the great minds of the century, was frozen as an adjunct till he was fifty-six – *fifty-six?* – and not even years of pressure from Max Weber helped him get a real job. In that world, students and professors alike supported the Nazis years before the general public did. How could Benjamin have thought that these people would see him as any more than K. trying to break into their Castle? The real question, which Brodersen does not bring up, is why Benjamin ever wanted to get in there in the first place. When we can explain that, we may be close to the origins of his tragic drama.

Brodersen gets us up close to the parade of fascinating women who passed through Benjamin's life: his wife, Dora Kellner, thriller writer and feminist editor; his lover, communist dramaturge Asja Lacis; psychoanalyst and sexologist Charlotte Wolff; Julia Cohn, Dora's closest friend, who did a splendid bust of Benjamin; Toet Blaupot ten Cate, a young Dutch painter with whom he fell in love on Ibiza; Sasha Stone, who designed his books; Hannah Arendt; Gisèle Freund; and many more. All through his life, there was always at least one very special woman around. They are the stars of Brodersen's great store of illustrations. But he doesn't want to talk about them. He digs up luminous images, but sometimes seems to want to bury them again. Who is that girl with the hair in her eyes? How close did she and Benjamin get? What did she mean to him? Brodersen's own policy seems to be, Don't ask, don't tell. His women are sisters from another planet. It's too bad, because women helped Benjamin feel at home on this one.

A poet in his youth, Benjamin began in gladness. This is the ambience of the first of three volumes of his *Selected Writings*. The editors must have debated whether to organize the set chronologically or thematically; they made the right choice. Time progression helps us see how his mind developed in passages from Berlin to Paris, from youth to middle age, from gentility to marginality, from Weimar's springtime to Hitler's. (My own feeling is that his best stuff came last, when things were worst.)

A glance at the table of contents of *Selected Writings* – he writes on language, time, colors, children's books, love, violence, messianism – shows us at once Benjamin's provocativeness and his infinite variety. The two longest pieces, both from the early twenties and neither translated till now, are his doctoral thesis, "The Concept of Criticism in German Romanticism," and his long essay on Goethe's late novel, *Elective Affinities*.

His thesis on romanticism, emphasizing the Schlegels and Novalis, develops an idea of "universal progressive poetry." Benjamin explodes the reactionary canon of German culture that is pulling like an undertow against democracy. He is trying to capture the army of right-wing culture heroes for the French – and, implicitly, the German – Revolution. His

Goethe essay shows how the great man at the height of his fame was really of the devil's party; how much he hated the straight German world that had made him a national monument. It is an exemplary piece of lit crit, brilliantly analyzing the book's layered images, leitmotifs, symbols and subtexts. It is also a pioneering study in the sociology of culture, analyzing Goethe's "image" and his tangled relationship with his audience. Studies of art's reception and its audiences have become commonplace today, but what makes Benjamin's cultural sociology so strong is that, unlike contempopary writers, he knows the books by heart and in depth. Finally, it is an in-your-face, eat-your-heart-out gesture to the German universities, showing them all they lost when they passed him by. (But considering what they were, they were probably relieved.) Benjamin's reverent feeling for tradition gives weight to his radical readings of tradition. Both essays could be an inspiration to people doing cultural studies today. Could be, but probably won't be, because readers of these essays have to work really hard before they can get into their flow.

Jay Parini's novel *Benjamin's Crossing* offers something that all the biographies lack: a clear vision of what the man might actually have been like. Parini makes us see and feel his sweetness and nobility; his mood swings and volatility, which could make him a commanding presence one moment and a pile of broken glass the next; his quick changes from empathy and generosity to narcissism and back; his sexiness (look at those pictures), which tends to get airbrushed out of the commentary, maybe because critics don't think it's noble enough. I have two problems with *Benjamin's Crossing*. First, while it's a great idea to tell the story in different voices, Parini allows Gershom Scholem and his Jewish mystical agenda to increasingly muscle out the other voices, without letting us know why. Second, while Parini concentrates entirely on the end of Benjamin's life, he goes surprisingly blank about his death. The book seems to be moving toward a climactic set-piece where Parini will try to get inside the hero's mind on his last night, as he tosses in his bed and waits for the morphine to kill him. But it doesn't happen. He's tormented, he's tired, then suddenly he's a verb in the past tense. Why Parini takes us so close to Benjamin's edge, and then cuts away at the last moment, I wish I knew. Is he actually writing a post-modern interactive novel, in which the readers, presumably for the good of our moral character, are forced to compose Benjamin's last crossing ourselves?

Any reader who has bonded with Parini's or Brodersen's hero is bound to be overwhelmed by anguished questions of the kind survivors always ask. What drove him over the edge? Why should a man who had faced the Gestapo be daunted by some crummy village cops? Was he really daunted, or was it all a charade? Was he determined to die in his beloved Europe and never board the ship to the promised land? Did he look forward to joining his dear Fritz? That night, if someone had knocked on his door, or put their arms around him, might they have saved him? Would he have been glad? ("He laughed because he wasn't dead" – Maurice Sendak, *Pierre.*) As he lay in bed, would he have had any regrets? Would he have felt complete? For survivors, questions like these are unavoidable, unbearable and unanswerable.

God knows what Adorno must have felt. Think of him reading Benjamin's last letter, where he says suicide is inevitable, trying to piece it together with his next-to-last letter, where Benjamin looks forward to walking with him in Central Park. (Bernard Malamud may have put those pieces together in his chilling early story, "The German Refugee.") In his epigram, "No Poetry After Auschwitz," Adorno punished us all; what torments did he keep back specially for himself, in his thirty years as a survivor? Benjamin must have been very determined not to be a survivor.

There is a profound problem with much of the literature on Benjamin, and on Central European culture as a whole. The young men and women who came of age in that culture – from the Age of Goethe way up to the 1930s – grew up on German romanticism, with its cosmic nostalgia, its soulful, heavy-laden yearning for dark forests, its willful isolation from the modern world, its suicide pacts and *Liebestod*. This is Brodersen's culture; his heart leaps up when he hears those tragic chords. For Parini, it is the heart of Benjamin's story. I would never deny that it is *part* of Benjamin's story. But in the culture of Central Europe's Jews, from Mahler to Freud to Kafka to Benjamin himself to Lubitsch, Ophuls, Sternberg, Stroheim, Billy Wilder, romantic doom always coexists with a comic and ironic spirit, cosmopolitan and urbane, seeking light on the modern city's boulevards and in its arcades and music halls and cafes, and in its displays of fashion and advertising and its endless proliferation of new media. Benjamin thrived on the contradiction between the doom in his soul and his joy on the streets. Remember Gene Kelly in *An American in Paris*? As the young Kelly flew over the boulevards with his body, so the middle-aged Benjamin, with equal flair and finesse, whirled and soared with his mind. He did it in the brilliant 1935 essay (which he never stopped revising) "Paris, Capital of the Nineteenth Century" and in essays on Naples, Marseilles, Moscow and Berlin. He did it in "The Work of Art in the Age of Mechanical Reproduction," where he unveiled what he called a "dialectical optics" that show how movies and psychoanalysis are part of the same historical long wave, and where he proclaimed that now, at the crest of this wave, "the distinction between reader and author is about to lose its basic character. ... At any moment, the reader is ready to turn into a writer." He was dancing that day in 1937 when Gisèle Freund took his picture in the Bibliothèque, and all through the *Arcades* manuscript that he carried till he died. (At last a complete text has come out in German, and Harvard will publish an English translation soon.) Even as the Nazis and his own sense of doom pulled him down toward death, he showed his readers how to dance in the streets and stake their claim to the modern world. It was too late for him to dance in Central Park, but it isn't too late for us to remember him by dancing.

All these books grasp Benjamin and help bring him back. But now that we have him, we should revere him not for his death but for his overflowing life. File him under Eros, not Thanatos: Auden's "Eros, builder of cities." Enjoy his largeness of vision, his imaginative fertility, his openness to the future, his grasp of the comedy that was part of the tragedy of modern times. Be glad. The Angel of History is back on the streets again.

Notes

1. One way in which it is worth comparing Benjamin with Lukács is as survivors of youthful suicides. Both felt shattered when those dearest to them died. But Lukács does not seem to have felt there was anything good about his First Love's suicide, for which he always blamed himself. For Benjamin, his best friend's suicide seems always to have had a fatal allure; like a morbid boulevard neon sign that blinked on and off but never went out, his vision of Fritz Heinle may never have stopped beckoning to him from "the other side."

2. Before 1945, academic careers required these subsidies, and nobody became a professor whose family wasn't both rich and indulgent. The G.I. Bill and the exigencies of the Cold War changed the pattern for a while and opened university careers to talents from the lower orders. Here the Cold War unquestionably worked as a democratizing force. President Clinton is probably its most illustrious beneficiary. I am one myself, along with thousands of others. But with the contraction of the welfare state and the end of the Cold War, it may be that the window has closed again, with academic life returning to the genteel tradition that dominates most of its history.

13

Unchained Melody

The best story I've ever heard about *The Communist Manifesto* came from Hans Morgenthau, the great theorist of international relations who died in 1980. It was the early seventies at CUNY, and he was reminiscing about his childhood in Bavaria before World War I. Morgenthau's father, a doctor in a working-class neighborhood of Coburg, often took his son along on house calls. Many of his patients were dying of TB; a doctor could do nothing to save their lives, but might help them die with dignity. When his father asked about last requests, many workers said they wanted to have the *Manifesto* buried with them when they died. They implored the doctor to see that the priest didn't sneak in and plant the Bible on them instead.

This spring, the *Manifesto* is 150 years old. In that century and a half, along with the Bible, it has become the most widely read book in the

Review of Karl Marx and Frederick Engels, *The Communist Manifesto: A Modern Edition*. With an introduction by Eric Hobsbawm (London: Verso, 1998). This essay first appeared in the *Nation*, May 11, 1998.

world.[1] Eric Hobsbawm, in his splendid introduction to the handsome
new Verso edition, gives a brief history of the book's reception. It can be
summed up fast: Whenever there's trouble, anywhere in the world, the
book becomes an item; when things quiet down, the book drops out of
sight; when there's trouble again, the people who forgot remember.
When fascist-type regimes seize power, it's always on the short list of
books to burn. When people dream of resistance – even if they're not
Communists, even if they distrust Communists – it provides music for
their dreams. Get the beat of the beginning and the end. First line: "A
spectre is haunting Europe – the spectre of Communism." Last lines:
"The proletarians have nothing to lose but their chains. They have a
world to win: "WORKERS OF ALL COUNTRIES, UNITE!"[2] In Rick's bar in *Casablanca,* you may or may not love France, but when the band breaks into
"La Marseillaise," you've got to stand up and sing.

Yet literate people today, even people with left politics, are amazingly
ignorant of what's actually in the book. For years, I've asked people what
they think it consists of. The most popular answers are that it's (1) a
utopian handbook on how to run a society with no money or property,
or else (2) a Machiavellian handbook on how to create a Communist state
and keep it in power. Moreover, people who were Communists didn't
seem to know the book any better than people who were not. (At first I
thought this might be another case of "American exceptionalism"; but
when I found the same ignorance in Bologna, where I talked about the
Manifesto to a mostly Communist group in the mid-1980s, I saw something big was up. Could it be that Communist education was Talmudic,
based on a study of commentaries, with an underlying suspicion of sacred primary texts? Maybe Communist parties saw the *Manifesto* as a kind
of adult movie, which is the way Orthodox Jews see the Bible: it's some-

thing for students to be exposed to only after years of education, and only for those with security clearance.)[2]

Now that security is gone. In just a few years, so many statues and magnifications of Marx have vanished from public squares, so many streets and parks named for him are going under other names today. What does it all mean?

For some people, like our Sunday morning princes of the air, the implosion of the USSR simply confirmed what they had believed all along, and released them from having to show respect. One of my old bosses at CCNY said it concisely: he said I couldn't teach a course in Marxism because "1989 proves that courses in Marxism are obsolete." But there are other ways to read history. What happened to Marx after 1917 was a disaster. A thinker needs beatification like a hole in the head! So we should welcome his crash from the pedestal as a fortunate fall. Maybe we can learn what Marx has to teach if we confront him at ground level, the level on which we ourselves are trying to stand.

So what does he offer? First – and startling when you're not prepared for it – praise for capitalism so extravagant, it skirts the edge of awe. Very early in the *Manifesto,* he describes the processes of material construction that it perpetrates, and the emotions that go with them, especially the sense of being caught up in something magical and uncanny:

> The bourgeoisie has created ... more massive and more colossal productive forces than have all preceding generations together. Subjection of nature's forces to man, machinery, application of chemistry to industry and agriculture, steam navigation, railways. ... clearing of whole continents for cultivation, canalization of rivers, whole populations conjured out of the ground – what earlier century had even a presentiment that such productive powers slumbered in the lap of social labour?

Or a page before, on an innate dynamism that is spiritual as well as material:

> The bourgeoisie cannot exist without constantly revolutionizing the instruments of production, and thereby the relations of production, and with them the whole relations of society. ... Constant revolutionizing of production, uninterrupted disturbance of all social conditions, everlasting uncertainty and agitation distinguish the bourgeois epoch from all earlier ones. All fixed, fast-frozen relations, with their train of ancient and venerable prejudices and opinions, are swept away, all new-formed ones become antiquated before they can ossify. All that is solid melts into air, all that is holy is profaned, and man at last is forced to face with sober senses, his real conditions of life, and his relations with his kind.

Part I, "Bourgeois and Proletarians," contains many passages like these, asserted in major chords with great dramatic flair. Somehow, many readers seem to miss them. But Marx's contemporaries didn't miss them, and some of his fellow radicals, like Proudhon and Bakunin, saw his appreciation of capitalism as a betrayal of its victims. This charge is still heard today, and deserves serious response. Marx hates capitalism, but he also thinks it has brought immense real benefits, spiritual as well as material, and he wants the benefits spread around and enjoyed by everybody rather than monopolized by a small ruling class. This is very different from the totalitarian rage that typifies radicals who want to blow it all away. Sometimes, as with Proudhon, it is just modern times they hate: they dream of a golden-age peasant village where everyone was happily in his place (or in her place behind him). For other radicals, from the author of the Book of Revelation to the Unabomber, it goes over the edge into something like rage against reality, against human life itself. Apocalyptic rage offers immediate, sensational cheap thrills. Marx's perspective is far more complex and nuanced, and hard to sustain if you're not grown up. (On the other hand, if you *are* grown up, and attuned to a world full of complexity and ambiguity, you may find that Marx fits you better than you thought.)

Marx is not the first communist to admire capitalism for its creativity; that attitude can be found in some of the great utopian socialists of the generation before him, like Saint-Simon and Robert Owen. But Marx is the first to invent a prose style that can bring that perilous creativity to life. His style in the *Manifesto* is a kind of expressionist lyricism. Every paragraph breaks over us like a wave that leaves us shaking from the impact and wet with thought. This prose evokes breathless momentum, plunging ahead without guides or maps, breaking all boundaries, precariously piling and layering of things, ideas and experiences. Catalogues play a large role in Marx's style – as they do for his contemporaries Dickens and Whitman – but part of the *Manifesto*'s enchantment comes from our feeling that the lists are never exhausted, the catalogue is open to the present and the future, we are invited to pile on things, ideas and experiences of our own, to pile ourselves on if we can. But the items in the pile often seem to clash, and it sounds like the whole vast aggregation could crash. From paragraph to paragraph, Marx makes readers feel that we are riding the fastest and grandest nineteenth-century train through the roughest and most perilous nineteenth-century terrain, and though we have splendid light, we are pressing ahead where there is no track.

A feature of modern capitalism that Marx most admires is its global horizon and its cosmopolitan texture. Many people today talk about the global economy as if it had only recently come into being. The *Manifesto* should help us see the extent to which it has been there all along:

The need of a constantly expanding market chases the bourgeoisie over the whole surface of the globe. It must nestle everywhere, settle everywhere, establish connections everywhere.

The bourgeoisie has through its exploitation of the world market given a cosmopolitan character to production and consumption in every country. ... All old-established national industries have been destroyed or are being daily destroyed. They are dislodged by new industries, whose introduction becomes a life and death question for all civilized nations, by industries that no longer process indigenous raw material, but raw material drawn from the remotest zones; industries whose products are consumed, not only at home, but in every quarter of the globe. ...

The cheap prices of its commodities are heavy artillery with which [the bourgeoisie] batters down all Chinese walls, with which it forces the barbarians' intensely obstinate hatred of foreigners to capitulate. It compels all nations, on pain of extinction, to adopt the bourgeois mode of production; it compels them to introduce what is called civilization into their midst, i.e. to become bourgeois themselves. In one word, it creates a world after its own image.

This global spread offers a spectacular display of history's ironies. These bourgeois are banal in their ambitions, yet their unremitting quest for profit forces on them the same insatiable drive-structure and infinite horizon as that of any of the great romantic heroes – as Don Giovanni, as Childe Harold, as Goethe's Faust. They may think of only one thing, but their narrow focus opens up the broadest integrations; their shallow outlook wreaks the most profound transformations; their peaceful economic activity devastates every human society like a bomb, from the most primitive tribes to the mighty USSR. Marx was appalled at the human costs of capitalist development, but he always believed that the world horizon it created was a great achievement on which socialism must build. Remember. the grand appeal to unite with which the *Manifesto* ends is addressed to "WORKERS OF ALL COUNTRIES."

One of the crucial events of modern times has been the unfolding of the first-ever world culture. Marx was writing at an historical moment when mass media were just developing, and he called it "world litera-ture."[3] I think it is legitimate at the end of our century to update the idea into "world culture." The *Manifesto* shows how this culture will evolve spontaneously from the world market:

> In place of the old wants, satisfied by the production of the country, we find new wants, requiring for their satisfaction products of distant lands and climes. In place of the old local and national seclusion and self-suffi-ciency, we have intercourse in every direction, universal interdependence of nations. And as in material, so also in intellectual [or spiritual – *geistige* can be translated either way] production. The intellectual [spiritual] crea-tions of individual nations become common property ... and from the numerous national and local literatures, there arises a world literature.

This vision of world culture brings together several complex ideas. First, the expansion of human needs: the increasingly cosmopolitan world market at once shapes and expands everybody's desires. Marx doesn't elaborate on this in detail; but he wants us to imagine what it might mean in food, clothes, religion, music, love and in our most intimate fantasies as well as our public presentations. Next, the idea of culture as "common property" in the world market: anything created by anyone anywhere is open and available to everyone everywhere. Entrepreneurs publish books, produce plays and concerts, display visual art and, in our century, create hardware and software for movies, radio, TV and computers in order to make money. Nevertheless, in this as in other ways, history slips through the owners' fingers, so that poor people get to possess culture – an idea, a poetic image, a musical sound, Plato, Shakespeare, a Negro spiritual (Marx loved them) – even if they can't own it. Culture stuffs people's heads full of ideas. As a form of "common property," modern culture helps us to imagine how people all around the world could share all the world's resources someday.

This is a vision of culture rarely discussed, but it is one of the most expansive and hopeful things Marx ever wrote. In our century, the development of movies, television and video, and computers has created a global visual language that brings the idea of world culture closer to home than ever, and the world beat comes through in the best of our music and books. That's the good news. The bad news is how sour and bitter most left writing on culture has become. Sometimes it sounds as if culture were just one more Department of Exploitation and Oppression, containing nothing luminous or valuable in itself. At other times, it sounds as if people's minds were empty vessels with nothing inside except what Capital put there. Read, or try to read, a few articles on "hegemonic/counterhegemonic discourse." The way these guys write, it's as if the world has passed them by.

But if capitalism is a triumph in so many ways, exactly what's wrong with it? What makes it worth spending your life in opposition? In the twentieth-century, Marxist movements around the world have concentrated on the argument, made most elaborately in *Capital,* that workers in bourgeois society had been or were being pauperized. Now, there have been times and places where it was absurd to deny that claim; in other times and places (like the United States and Western Europe in he fifties and sixties, when I was young), it was pretty tenuous, and Marxist economists went through strange dialectical gyrations to make the numbers come out. But the problem with that discussion was that it converted questions of human experience into questions of numbers: it led Marxism to think and talk exactly like capitalism! The *Manifesto* occasionally makes some version of this claim. But it offers what strikes me as a much more trenchant indictment, one that holds up even at the top of the business cycle, when the bourgeoisie and its apologists are drowning in complacency.

That indictment is Marx's vision of what modern bourgeois society forces people to be: They have to freeze their feelings for each other to adapt to a cold-blooded world. In the course of "pitilessly tear[ing] asunder the motley feudal ties," bourgeois society "has left remaining no other nexus between man and man than naked self-interest, than callous 'cash payment.'" It has "drowned every form of sentimental value in the icy water of egotistical calculation." It has "resolved personal worth into exchange-value." It has collapsed every historical tradition and norm of freedom "into that single, unconscionable freedom – free trade." The worst thing about capitalism is that it forces people to become brutal in order to survive.

For 150 years, we have seen a huge literature that dramatizes the brutality of the bourgeoisie, a class where those who are most comfortable with brutality are most likely to succeed. But the same social forces are pressing on the members of that immense group that Marx calls "the modern working class." This class has been afflicted with a case of mistaken identity. Many readers have always thought that "working class" meant only men in boots – in factories, in industry, in blue collars, with calloused hands, lean and hungry. These readers then note the changing nature of the work force over the past half-century or so – increasingly educated, white-collar, working in human services (rather than growing food or making things), in or near the middle class – and they infer the Death of the Subject, and conclude that the working class is disappearing and all hopes for it are doomed. Marx did not think the working class was shrinking: in all industrial countries it already was, or was in the process of becoming, "the immense majority," and its swelling numbers would enable it to "win the battle of democracy." The basis for his political arithmetic was a concept that was both simple and highly inclusive:

> The modern working class developed, … a class of labourers, who live only so long as they find work, and who find work only so long as their labour increases capital. These labourers, who must sell themselves piece-meal, are a commodity, like every other article of commerce, and are constantly exposed to all the vicissitudes of competition, to all the fluctuations of the market.

The crucial factor is not working in a factory, or working with your hands, or being poor. All these things can change with fluctuating supply and demand and technology and politics. The crucial reality is the need to sell your labor to capital in order to live, the need to carve up your personality for sale – to look at yourself in the mirror and think, "What have I got that I can sell?" – and an unending dread and anxiety that even if you're OK today, you won't find anyone who wants to buy what you have or what you are tomorrow, that the changing market will declare you (as it has already declared so many) worthless, that you will find yourself physically as well as metaphysically homeless and out in the cold. Arthur Miller's *Death of a Salesman*, a twentieth-century master-piece, brings to life the consuming dread that may be the condition of most members of the working class in modern times. The whole existentialist tradition dramatizes this situation with great depth and beauty, yet its visions tend to be weirdly unembodied. Its visionaries could learn from the *Manifesto,* which gives modern anguish an address.

One reason for Marx's long-range faith in the working class is that lots of the people in this class don't know it. Many are the people who fill up the huge office buildings in all our downtowns. They wear elegant suits and return to nice houses, because there is a great demand for their labor right now, and they are doing well. They may identify happily with the owners of capital, and have no idea how contingent and fleeting their benefits are. They may not discover who they really are, and where they belong, until they are laid off or fired – or deskilled, or outsourced, or downsized. (It is fascinating how many of these crushing words are quite new.) And other workers, lacking diplomas, not dressed so nicely, working in cubicles, not offices, may not get the fact that many of the people who boss them around are really in their class, and share their vulnerability. How can this reality be put across to people who don't get it, or can't bear it? This is what organizing and organizers are for.

One group whose working-class identity was crucial for Marx was his own group: intellectuals.

> The bourgeoisie has stripped of its halo every occupation hitherto honored and looked up to in reverent awe. It has transconverted the physician, the lawyer, the priest, the poet, the man of science, into its paid wage labourers.

Marx is not saying that in bourgeois society these activities lose their human meaning or value. If anything, they are more meaningful and valuable than ever before. But the only way people can get the freedom to make discoveries, or save lives, or poetically light up the world, is by working for capital – for drug companies, HMOs, movie studios, media conglomerates, boards of education, politicians, etc., etc. – and using their creative skills to help capital accumulate more capital. This means that intellectuals are subject not only to the stresses that afflict all modern workers but to a dread zone all their own. The more they care about their work and want it to mean something, the more they will find themselves in conflict with the keepers of the spreadsheets; the more they walk the line, the more they are likely to fall. This chronic pressure may give them a special insight into the need for workers to unite. But will united workers treat intellectual and artistic freedom with any more respect than capital treats it? It's an open question; sometime in the twenty-first century, workers will "win the battle of democracy" and get real power somewhere, and then we'll start to see.

Marx sees the modern working class as an immense worldwide community waiting to happen. Such large possibilities give the story of organizing a permanent gravity and grandeur. The process of creating unions is not just an item in interest-group politics but a vital part of what Lessing called "the education of the human race." And it is not just educational but existential: the process of people, individually and collectively, discovering who they are. As they learn who they are, they will come to see that they need one another in order to be themselves. They will see, because workers are smart: bourgeois society has forced them to be, in order to survive its constant upheavals. Marx knows they will get it by and by. (Alongside his fury as an agitator, the *Manifesto*'s author also projects a brooding, reflective, long patience.) Solidarity is not sacrifice of yourself but the self's fulfillment. Learning to give yourself to other workers, who may look and sound very different from you but are like you in depth, delivers the self from dread and gives a man or woman an address in the world.

This is a vital part of the moral vision that underlies the *Manifesto*. But there is another moral dimension, asserted in a different key but humanly just as urgent. At one of the book's many climactic moments, Marx says that the Revolution will end classes and class struggles, and this will make it possible to enjoy "an association, in which the free development of each is the condition for the free development of all." Here Marx imagines communism as a way to make people happy. The first aspect of this happiness is "development" – that is, an experience that doesn't simply repeat itself, but that goes through some sort of change and growth. This form of happiness is distinctively modern, informed by the incessantly developing bourgeois economy.

But bourgeois society, although it enables people to develop, forces them to develop in accord with market demands: what can sell gets developed; what can't sell gets repressed, or never comes to life at all. Against the market model of forced and twisted development, Marx fights for *"free* development," development that the self can control.

In a time when crass cruelty calls itself liberalism (we're kicking you and your kids off welfare for your own good), it is important to see how much ground Marx shares with the smartest and noblest liberal of all, his contemporary John Stuart Mill. Like Marx, Mill came to see the self's "free development" as a fundamental human value; like Marx, he believed that modernization made it possible for everybody. But as he grew older, he became convinced that the capitalist form of modernization – featuring cutthroat competition, class domination, social conformity and cruelty – blocked its best potentialities. The world's greatest liberal proclaimed himself a socialist in his old age.

Ironically, the ground that socialism and liberalism share might be a big problem for both of them. What if Mister Kurtz isn't dead after all? In other words, what if authentically "free development" brings out horrific depths in human nature? Dostoevsky, Nietzsche and Freud all forced us to face the horrors, and warned us of their permanence. In response, both Marx and Mill might say that until we have overcome social domination and degradation, there is simply no way to tell whether the horrors are inherent in human nature or whether we could create benign conditions under which they would wither away. The process of getting to that point – a point where Raskolnikovs won't rot on Avenue D, and where Svidrigailovs won't possess thousands of bodies and souls – should be enough to give us all steady work. And if we do reach that point, and we come to see that our inner bad guys will never go away, our steady work will have given us experience, and taught us how to cooperate for our mutual self-defense.[4]

The 1990s began with the mass destruction of Marx effigies. It was the "post-modern" age: we weren't supposed to need big ideas. As the nineties end, we find ourselves in a dynamic global society ever more unified by downsizing, deskilling and dread – just like the old man said. All of a sudden, the iconic looks more convincing than the ironic; that classic bearded presence, the atheist as biblical prophet, is back just in time for the millennium. At the dawn of the twentieth century, there were workers who were ready to die with the *Communist Manifesto*. At the dawn of the twenty-first, there may be even more who are ready to live with it.

Notes

1. Both books are published in multi-million-copy "official" editions. In both cases, people who want to advance are expected to know how to quote "The Book," whichever book has canonical status. The act of *reading* doesn't much come in here.

2. When this piece first appeared in the *Nation,* its copyeditors insisted on printing this as "Working *men,*" at a stroke cutting Marx's audience and his potential revolutionary class in half. Their basis for doing so was that this was how Samuel Moore's 1888 translation put it. Marx's successors once more, ironically, cripple the workers' movement by imagining it far too small.

3. In the 1840s, this expression was still quite new. Marx may derive it from Goethe, who used it in the early 1830s in *Conversations with Eckermann.*

4. When revolutions engulfed half of Europe after World War I, Freud didn't think those revolutions nullified the truths of psychoanalysis, and didn't think the truths of psychoanalysis would destroy the revolutions; but he hoped, he briefly let himself hope, that now psychoanalysis would be open to everyone, regardless of their class, as a normal part of public health. According to Isaac Deutscher, Trotsky in the mid-1920s began to think about psychotherapy as a revolutionary right: Shouldn't Soviet citizens be entitled to a kind of self-knowledge that can protect them from themselves? (Reading this gives the Soviet tragedy yet another turn of the screw: If only someone could have protected *him!*)

Index